HISTORY OF EDUCATION IN IOWA
Volume II

HISTORY OF EDUCATION
IN IOWA

BY
CLARENCE RAY AURNER

VOLUME II

PUBLISHED AT IOWA CITY IOWA IN 1914 BY
THE STATE HISTORICAL SOCIETY OF IOWA

AUTHOR'S PREFACE

THE chapters in this volume treat mainly of those activities and organizations which are the outgrowth of experience. The educational plant having been equipped with the machinery, it seems to have required an increasing number of agencies to develop and direct it. Hence supervision in due time found its place; the institute took on a new form; and the mutual interest of a common occupation led to the formation of associations which subsequently were organized into special groups. Moreover, the means of communication and the public expression of principles involved in the process of instruction induced a variety of effort in educational journalism; while the increasing output of books suitable for self-education encouraged the establishment of school libraries. Finally, the decline of old practices in which the home provided for exercise in domestic duties and an apprenticeship in industrial pursuits has thrust upon the public educational system a new function in the shape of shop, kitchen, sewing-room, and experimental plot.

CLARENCE RAY AURNER

THE STATE HISTORICAL SOCIETY OF IOWA
    IOWA CITY IOWA

CONTENTS

PART III

TEACHERS INSTITUTES

PART IV

TEACHERS ASSOCIATIONS

PART V

MISCELLANEOUS ACTIVITIES

PART VI

PROPOSED LEGISLATION

PART I
SCHOOL SUPERVISION

I

SUPERVISION IN THE TERRITORY OF IOWA
1838–1846

THE more specialized forms of school supervision are of recent adoption in Iowa. Indeed, some of the more important phases of supervision have yet to become a part of the educational system of this State. Although the county is by law the lowest area of school supervision, it is significant that in the beginning the township was the ultimate unit — for which there was provided a "township inspector" of schools. Thus it would seem that the ideal presented by Superintendent Henry Sabin in 1897 had its beginning in the first attempt at establishing a local school organization, in which the rural community was to have its share of attention from one who was skilled in shaping and directing elementary instruction.

Had this original plan of supervision been faithfully pursued, out of it might have come the realization of what Superintendent Sabin proposed in 1897. In the educational history of the State changes occurred so rapidly and the introduction of the practical demanded so much ability and special equipment, that it became evident that the method of supervision which existed in 1897 could not permanently endure. It was then pointed out that the educational supervisor must possess a scholarship that was broad "without being shallow", for the days of the "examiner" and "clerk" were past. The educational supervisor must be able to discern, to think, to construct, to originate, to accomplish, and to influence a community. Thus, in 1897 the supervision of the rural school was designated by Henry Sabin as a new field wherein the supervisor must have not only general preparation on the book side of the problem, but he must also understand the actual application of theory to constructive work. Furthermore, a personal acquaintance with community needs should be the preliminary to a successful ministering to its wants.

From the simple duties of a "township inspector" in 1840 to the highly specialized field of supervision as proposed in 1897 by the far-sighted Henry Sabin, there is a vast difference, not only in the conception of the problem but also in the actual opportunities and possibilities offered by the developments of nearly sixty years. Consider, for example, the meaning of the terms "visit" and "supervise" as applied to the functions of township inspectors or district trustees during the Territorial period and the more recent interpretation and application of the same language, and it becomes at once clear and evident that to trace the changes which are thus suggested necessitates a careful study of local and State authorities who have recognized, in part, the needs as they have arisen.

One may pass over that early legislation wherein township inspectors appear as supervisors of education under laws which were applicable to Iowa, and proceed to a consideration of the first statute of the Territory relative to schools which provided that "it shall be the duty of the trustees to superintend the schools within their respective districts; to examine and employ teachers, to lease all lands belonging to the district", and to make an annual report to the county commissioners.[1]   Such legislation probably met the necessities of the occasion.   At the same time it appears that there were more ambitious projects in the minds of those who were familiar with the laws of other States, for a year later not only was the township made a unit for supervision but there was also provided an authoritative head, known as "Superintendent of Public Instruction", for the whole Territory.   The local officers (that is, the township inspectors) were directed to visit, twice each year, all the schools within their jurisdiction, and "to inquire into the condition, examine the scholars, and give such advice to both teachers and scholars as they shall deem proper."[2]

From 1840 to 1847 the laws of the Territory of Iowa provided for three township inspectors; but in the latter year the number was reduced to one.   He retained the supervisory power, however, and the statute required him to visit each school in his district (township) "at least once each year" and to give such advice to "directors, teachers and pupils" as might appear proper.   The change from three such township supervisors of schools to one was probably due to the fact that one man could easily perform all the necessary duties connected with the office. Moreover, upon the creation of the office of county school fund commissioner there appeared to be no necessity for retaining longer the office of inspector, inasmuch as the county became the unit in authority for district organization. Then, too, the supervisory duties of the inspector seem to have been valued too little when each district was an authority unto itself.[3] With the passing of the township inspector, who had been authorized to examine and certificate the teachers employed, and to revoke licenses for cause, there remained the district board — the only group which had any authority to direct or supervise. Thus, the brief period during which a form of township supervision was provided for closed in 1849 without provision for the transference of functions to any other officers.

Returning to the office of Superintendent of Public Instruction as referred to in the law of January 16, 1840, it appears that the township clerk, who was ex officio the clerk of the township board of school inspectors, was to receive all communications "directed to him by the superintendent of public instruction". As a matter of fact, however, no Superintendent of Public Instruction was provided for until a year later, when the Governor of the Territory was directed to appoint such an official for a term of three years. The principal function then assigned to the Superintendent of Public Instruction appears to have been the care and disposition of the school fund. Nowhere does the law provide for any duty connected with instruction or other phases of school organization beyond that of reporting the condition of the primary schools. It is clear that the purpose of the law of 1841 in establishing the office of Superintendent of Public Instruction was not primarily to provide a head for a school system, but rather a financial agent for the management of school lands and funds.[4] The title of "Superintendent of Public Instruction" did not therefore properly express the purpose and function of the office.

Dr. William Reynolds, a recent arrival in the Territory, was appointed by Governor Lucas to the position of Superintendent of Public Instruction — after, it is said, the office had been refused by Mr. T. S. Parvin, the Governor's private secretary. Although the Superintendent was appointed for three years, he was legislated out of office within a year.[5] In the meantime, however, he had made some effort to carry out the provisions of the act under which he was appointed and by which he was governed. He declared that "one of the most striking features" of the law was the provision "making it the duty of the Superintendent to use every exertion to effect an immediate organization of the primary school system". With this object in view Dr. Reynolds prepared to visit the several counties of the Territory where by lecturing he hoped to arouse action relative to the interests of the schools. But after consultation with Governor Lucas it was conceded that this plan was not adapted to the conditions then prevailing in the Territory — there being at that time no general organization of townships and no school inspectors. Nor were there school districts established in sufficient number to warrant much traveling about. Moreover, since the people were not sufficiently acquainted with the school law better results could be obtained by giving communities the "necessary instruction" as to organization, and by the general dissemination of information which circumstances might demand or render expedient. The wishes of the several communities might thus be understood, and with a knowledge of their needs a better plan of procedure might be matured.

Governor Chambers, who succeeded Lucas in 1841, also approved the plan thus projected; and so Dr. Reynolds remained at the seat of government instead of making a journey over the Territory to lecture on the public school system that was to be. In due time he issued a circular to the county clerks — who constituted the immediate local connection between his office and the school districts — requesting the reports which the law contemplated. As one would expect, where there was little or no general organization there were few returns, although enough to make this document — the only Territorial school report — of great value.

In December, 1841, Dr. Reynolds submitted his observations and report as the law required. The document contained information which had been obtained largely through his own personal efforts, rather than through the formal reports of county officers. His optimistic views are suggested in the following extract:

The interest taken in schools and the school law [of 1840], almost universally, and the fact that the interest is daily increasing, cannot fail to be highly gratifying to every person who is anxiously looking forward to the time when we shall have a good 'system of public instruction', and the funds to enable us to carry it into effect.

The Superintendent reported great difficulty in distributing the school law as well as in its interpretation to the people. While no complaint was presented against the law as such, there was a general feeling that its provisions were "hard to be understood". It was therefore recommended that the law be distributed in circular form, accompanied with explanations. Again, Dr. Reynolds urged the necessity of the Superintendent of Public Instruction giving his entire time to the office so that he might render effective assistance in constructing a school system on strong foundations. The right of the child to a free school, the enlisting of popular support through a full publication of plans, and provision for the care of the school lands as soon as they came under State control were emphasized as of special importance in this first report.[6]

When the question of retaining the office of Superintendent of Public Instruction and of approving the recommendation made by him came before the Territorial legislature, the committee to whom the matter was referred were unanimously agreed on the policy of continuing the office and of encouraging the influence of the Superintendent throughout the Territory. They referred particularly to the beneficial results that might accrue from the information relative to systems of organization being collected at that time by the Superintendent from the several States. Nevertheless, the Legislative Assembly disagreed with the committee; and so, on February 17, 1842, the office was abolished.[7]

Thus, it appears that the attempt to establish a central authority for the projected educational system of Iowa met with small favor in the days of the Territory. There was manifested a feeling that such matters must wait until the State had become an independent Commonwealth. That the fundamental law of the new State would contain some provision for such an official head was to be anticipated. Indeed, previous action in the Territorial legislature would almost warrant such a conclusion.

II

STATE SUPERVISION: A PERIOD OF REORGANIZATION
1846–1858

WITH the adoption of a Constitution and the admission of Iowa into the Union in 1846 the office of Superintendent of Public Instruction was reëstablished — not by legislation but by the provisions of the fundamental law. The people were now authorized to elect the head of the school system for a term of three years; while the definition of his powers and duties was left to the General Assembly. And so, in the general act of 1847 amending the school law of 1840 it was provided that at the next township election a Superintendent should be chosen whose duties should include the maintenance of an office at the seat of government, the preservation of all documents and reports which should be received at his office from the counties of the State "each year separately", and the keeping of these materials "in readiness to be exhibited to any committee of either House of the General Assembly of this State, or to the Governor".

By the same act the Superintendent was charged with the care and distribution of the school funds coming into his hands, as well as with the general

11

oversight of all schools established under the provisions of the law. It was a statutory requirement, also, that he proceed as early as practicable to "put into operation, and cause it to be uniform in all its operations" the contemplated school system; to visit every county at least once during his official term; to confer freely with township inspectors and render such service as seemed necessary; and finally "to deliver a public lecture to the teachers and people of each township on the subject of education, if deemed practicable, and to do generally such business as may be necessary for the promotion of public instruction." This was surely a liberal amount of labor with considerable latitude for its execution; but little authority was given the Superintendent to secure compliance with what he might consider desirable for the schools.

The law of 1847, moreover, empowered the Superintendent to appoint a deputy or clerk; but he must compensate his appointee out of his own salary — which was $1200 — and be accountable for all of his official acts. From the time that this law became effective, the reports which the General Assembly required have been submitted at each session, although more or less incomplete for some of the earlier years. The law required specifically that these reports should include a statement of the whole amount of the school fund at interest and the proceeds of the same, of the amount appropriated for schools and the sources from which it was derived, of the number of organized districts, of the persons of

school age, of the schools taught and of scholars
therein, and of the teachers employed, with their
average pay. The Superintendent was not, however,
confined to these items. He could present any matters which in his opinion were essential to educational advancement; while the General Assembly
might order him to submit data on any subject.[8]

At the spring elections in 1847 it appears that
Mr. James Harlan was elected as the first State
Superintendent of Public Instruction. In this connection one can not enter into the political phases of
the contest, nor discuss fully all the subsequent
events which led up to the decision of the Supreme
Court that the election of April, 1847, was not legally
consummated. Indeed these facts, which may be
gained from authoritative sources, have little or no
direct relation to the development of the office itself.
It is well known, however, that Mr. Harlan entered
upon the office with a view to performing its duties
as defined in the law of 1847. Moreover, he published an open letter to local officers in which he
declared his belief in the validity of their election.

There were, however, many difficulties in the way
of observing all the provisions of the law of 1847,
since in many instances no precedent was at hand to
guide the Superintendent. This was notably true in
the matter of the selection of school lands. Finally,
he was disturbed in his office by a summons from the
court to "show by what authority he was holding the
office of Superintendent." The case being carried to
the Supreme Court, the election of 1847 was declared

void, thus making all action under it questionable.[9] Under these circumstances effective administration was made difficult — although it was declared that the school system made substantial advances during the short period of Harlan's administration as Superintendent.

In response to a resolution of the House of Representatives, Superintendent Harlan submitted a report in which the details of his official acts were set forth in accordance with the items designated in the law. This report was received and printed; but it does not appear among the documents as do other reports subsequently issued. The General Assembly legalized the acts of the Superintendent and made an appropriation for his annual salary, although the matter of the election had not at that time been passed upon by the courts. Indeed, the legislature by its action anticipated a new election in April, 1848.

It was at this point that Thomas H. Benton, Jr., first appeared as a candidate for the office of Superintendent in opposition to James Harlan. Notwithstanding the political significance of the election and events connected therewith, it is only necessary in this connection to note that James Harlan was succeeded by Thomas H. Benton, Jr., in the spring of 1848.[10] Thereafter for the greater part of the time, until about 1862, Mr. Benton was a conspicuous figure in the educational work of this State, first as Superintendent of Public Instruction and later as Secretary of the State Board of Education.

The decision of the Supreme Court in reference

to the contested election was a prime reason for the extra session of the General Assembly in 1848, inasmuch as remedial legislation was imperative if the transactions during 1847–1848 were not to become a source of litigation. Moreover, the claims of the common schools, as shown by the report of Superintendent Harlan, demanded immediate and careful attention.

On May 23, 1848, the duties of the Superintendent of Public Instruction were assumed by Thomas H. Benton, Jr. His first act as Superintendent was to send his credentials to the registers of the land offices in Iowa and to the general land office at Washington so that his authority would be unquestioned; for, under the provisions of the law of 1847, whereby the selection and sale of school lands devolved upon the Superintendent, he had become more and more of a financial agent having control of school funds. Another important duty confronting him at the very beginning was the interpretation of the school law, since it was asserted that districts had not organized because of ''doubt and uncertainty''. As in the case of Dr. Reynolds in 1841, the new Superintendent concluded that more could be accomplished by correspondence and instructions with references to the provisions of the law than by lecturing in the townships.

The ''incipient stage of our School system'' was offered as an excuse for the incomplete data of school fund commissioners in the first published report of Superintendent Benton. While the local officers were

commended for their efforts to comply with the law
and with the instructions from the Superintendent,
there were difficulties which must be overcome in the
formation of districts owing to settlements being
made on the border lines of counties and townships.
There being no legal definition of the qualifications
of teachers, this subject was covered by the recommendation of the Superintendent who would endeav-
or also to accomplish better results by grouping
pupils according to advancement.

To bring about the results desired Mr. Benton
recommended that an amount be collected from those
receiving advanced instruction sufficient to provide
for the compensation which would be necessary
above that received from the school fund apportionment. Although in his opinion primary instruction
must always stand first, it was nevertheless desirable
that higher branches be introduced into the common
schools. It would, of course, be prudent to determine
at the very beginning the extent of such instruction
and first of all to consider the available means. With
such conservative plans for starting right, he recommended that the larger towns and villages be granted
authority to establish a system of public instruction
under the direction of the regular constituted town
authorities. Moreover, in such cases they might be
permitted also to levy a tax which should supplement
the annual apportionment of interest from the school
fund, to the end that a higher order of instruction
might be established than could possibly be provided
in thinly settled communities. Thus, at his first op-

portunity Superintendent Benton declared for higher schools and a property tax for public education.

Neither did the Superintendent fail to comment on the wages of teachers — a subject which has had consideration in every report from that day to this. The actual facts relative to compensation were submitted from the incomplete returns from thirty-two counties. But the important point in this connection is the fact that an increase was recommended.

The situation with regard to text-books was such that legislation was desired in order that uniformity, either through selection by the General Assembly or by the Superintendent, might be secured. Incidentally Webster's dictionary was recommended for each of the school libraries — then authorized by law. It was ascertained, also, that while the colored population were taxed they were not provided with separate schools; and so, among the observations and recommendations of the Superintendent was one relative to instruction for colored pupils. Finally, it was suggested that all school laws be repealed and that a new measure be substituted which should not only retain the general outlines of the laws then in force but should also define specifically and minutely the functions of all school officials; for in this respect, it seems, the former acts were defective.[11]

Following the suggestion of the Superintendent the General Assembly passed a law governing common schools, which was approved January 15, 1849, and by which all former acts on the subject were repealed. The office of Superintendent of Public In-

3

struction was retained, but with some new functions. The Superintendent was required to "examine and recommend" a uniform series of text-books for the district schools, to provide suitably printed forms for reports, and to issue instructions relative to the organization and government of schools. Courses of study might also be recommended from his office; and he was empowered to make such rules and regulations as might be necessary to carry the new law into effect. Although his salary still remained at $1200 (which was more than was given the Governor at that time) he was by this act allowed his necessary contingent expenses.[12]

By another statute, enacted at the same session, the Superintendent was directed to visit the several counties and "examine the books and accounts of the Fund Commissioners" in order to adjust the accounts then becoming a matter of vital interest to the State. The work of Superintendent Benton in carrying out the provisions of this statute has already been described, and attention has been called to his prophetic declarations as to what would result if conditions were not changed.[13]

With the evident purpose of informing school officers and citizens of what the school law contemplated, a circular including the Constitution of Iowa and all statutes relating to education was issued from the office of the Superintendent. Certain sections of the laws were explained for the benefit of those whose duty it was to execute them; at the same time an effort was made "to create in the public mind a due appreciation of a well regulated system of public instruction.'' It was foreseen that there would be certain difficulties in the formation of districts and in the construction of school houses, and he therefore counseled "compromise and concession" that litigation might be avoided. Schools, it was affirmed in this circular, were not established for the few, neither for rich nor poor, but for all, and all were to be held responsible for the success of the legislation thus far enacted. The national government had been liberal, and now the State was under obligation to maintain and preserve its gifts in a manner befitting the Commonwealth.

Particular attention was called to "system" in the matter of public records. Few districts were careful in this respect. Nor were the available records altogether intelligible. But this, it was concluded, was due to negligence rather than to incompetence. Further observation on the school law recently enacted pointed to the fact that no law could be perfect, although it might be sufficient for the current needs. Reference was made to the school law of New York, which had been in force since 1812 but which had been amended at nearly every session of the legislature — showing that time and patience were essential to the perfecting of a school system.

Accompanying this message of information and instruction were numerous blank forms for all grades of officials and school employees, suggesting the exact method which the Superintendent would use in preserving the history of each day or each transaction. It was in this way that the school fund commissioners were informed of the necessary books which they should keep in reference to sales of land and loans of funds as well as in reference to a complete record of contracts and mortgages. Although this was a form of supervision that did not result in producing the desired clearness in accounts, the duty of the Superintendent was performed in making these recommendations. Moreover, these were the records that he was later to examine for the purpose of adjusting the permanent fund accounts according to the law by which he was governed.

Included in these instructions were some practical designs for buildings — a plain and rather mean collection, indeed, when compared to the buildings of 1914. The furniture designed for these houses was an improvement on that of the first schools — when benches were without backs and shelves along the log wall answered for desks — but it needed careful selection, as may be implied in the warning of the Superintendent that the desk should be accommodated to the pupil. To illustrate his point he quoted the following:

I have visited many schools in which the majority of the scholars reverse the ordinary practice of *standing up* and *sitting down*. They literally *sit up* and *stand down,* their heads being higher while *sitting* than when *standing*.

In the opinion of Superintendent Benton good and presentable buildings were the first important improvement then demanded; and in describing the situation he pointed out the difference in the cost of other public buildings as compared to those for the schools. It was frequently the case that in villages and in country neighborhoods churches cost fifty to eighty times as much as school houses. To illustrate this point he used the following description of the capital of the State in 1849:

In Iowa City, our seat of government, we have seven fine brick and stone churches, erected at an aggregate cost of about $25,000; a court house, jail, Mechanic's Institute and various hotels at $17,000, and the State Capitol at about $140,000. Thus we have the round sum of $182,000.00 invested in *public edifices*, and *not one dollar* in a school house! And yet I am almost daily asked why we have such poor schools? Why such poor discipline? And why so little interest and improvement among the children? Let the answer be, that we have, deducting the amount for hotels, $170,000 invested for the *restraint and reformation of wicked men, and not one dollar,* for the *proper education* of children!

He was satisfied that if school buildings were constructed with as much taste as churches, it would be of great advantage to the community and would exert a wholesome influence on the morals of the youth housed therein, since the environment was an important factor in such training. Attention was called also to that provision of the law which required a committee from the district board to visit the schools monthly to aid the teachers in establishing and enforcing rules and regulations for their government, and to assist in promoting the welfare of the schools in every particular. Thus, through the Superintendent of Public Instruction the local officer was reminded of his duty under the statute.[14]

By the law of 1849 the Superintendent was required to examine and recommend to the several school districts a uniform series of text-books; and accordingly, Mr. Benton published such an approved list in his circular. While a special chapter has been devoted to text-books it may be of interest to add something relative to the miscellaneous list of the books and apparatus recommended. Webster's quarto dictionary is mentioned, along with the important fact that every teacher in the cities of New York and Brooklyn had been provided with a copy of this valuable work. Although Iowa could in no way expect such complete equipment, it was considered desirable that a copy of this dictionary should be placed in each district library. Likewise certain apparatus was suggested — such as terrestrial globes, Holbrook's apparatus for common schools, and charts and maps. Finally, a list of books and journals for teachers was recommended.[15]

In connection with the legislation for the three normal schools in 1849, the Superintendent was authorized not only to designate the district boundaries within which each of these was to be located but also to appoint boards of trustees for the same. Furthermore, by an act which sought to prevent the waste occurring in the school fund, he was burdened with the task of approving the amount allowed school fund commissioners for services and expenses — a duty already performed by three county officers. For a similar reason, when the saline lands were sold his office was charged with the disposal of $5000 of the proceeds for the benefit of the college of physicians and surgeons at Keokuk, which sum was to be paid over at the discretion of the Superintendent, that is, in such amounts as he might determine.[16] Such duties as these were hardly in accord with the proper functions of an office established primarily for the organization of a school system; but in 1850 it seemed destined to perform any sort of work which might be assigned to it.

During the year 1850 Superintendent Benton traveled extensively through the State, lecturing wherever it was practicable. Although he declared himself as not satisfied with the existing local conditions, yet he saw progress in the organization of districts in every section of the Commonwealth which he had visited. The provisions of the new school law (1849) were being observed, and the people generally were more and more desirous of understanding its requirements — although in the newer counties the settlements were so isolated that results could not be as satisfactory as in the older communities. It was to aid in familiarizing the district authorities with the provisions of the law that the Superintendent had issued the circular of information.

It was during his journey over the State in 1850 that the Superintendent made observations relative to the more complete organizations of districts and the construction of permanent buildings. Moreover, he was favorably impressed with what had been accomplished along these lines in the State. For example, Muscatine seemed to lead in the erection of permanent school buildings, having provided for two structures which together cost $5500; Burlington also had designed a brick building of five rooms to be constructed at an outlay of $4000; Dubuque was providing for two buildings, both to cost $1300; and Fort Madison was making provision for similar accommodations. These improvements were suggestive of what would be desirable as districts were able to adopt measures that would render such buildings possible.[17]

That the office of State Superintendent was burdened with a multitude of details not rightfully belonging to it is clear from the opinion expressed by the incumbent in 1850. He seriously doubted the policy "of making the Superintendent of Public Instruction a financial officer", since the "educational duties that necessarily devolve upon him are, in this enlightened age, more than sufficient to occupy his entire time." But it required some years more of experience with the combination of financial and educational functions before necessity forced a separation.[18]

In the third and last regular report of Superintendent Benton there were certain important recommendations relative to the admission of non-resident pupils to the district schools as well as to provisions which would permit the larger towns to extend their school year. It was possible under the law for a district board to prevent absolutely the attendance of a non-resident pupil, notwithstanding the fact that his tuition was advanced. Furthermore, it was observed that laws adapted to rural districts were not suitable in all particulars to the more compact settlements. It would be an advantage if these communities were empowered to raise means additional to the public money received, and it was pointed out that it was "upon this principle that the schools of the Atlantic Cities have attained their present [1852] high degree of perfection". This plan, furthermore, was not limited to towns, since it was adaptable to any district. As an aid to carrying out these provisions the Superintendent suggested the enactment of a law authorizing a rate bill — a form of statute which had been adopted in nearly all the States which had made "progress in popular education."[19]

These were the concluding recommendations made by the second State Superintendent of Public Instruction upon the completion of two terms of three years each. His administration was marked by an industrious effort to effect an organization of the schools under the law of 1849 and to secure a change in the management of the school fund. As he was later to become the executive officer of the State Board of Education the six years already served were of great advantage to him in an understanding of the conditions in the State.

Mr. James D. Eads succeeded to the office of Superintendent as a result of the spring election of 1854. His administration has been covered in the chapters on funds and therefore needs but brief attention in this place. Indeed, his term of three years was made so conspicuous by the events on the financial side that the strictly educational matters are somewhat limited, both as to data recorded and as to the genuineness of what is set forth. There are references, however, to certain facts of progress of which the Superintendent alone has left an account.

It was during this period that the first instance of a superintendent or supervisory principal of a city school was directly cited. In his journey over the State the observations of Mr. Eads included a reference to the schools of Keokuk, which was declared to be in advance of other cities in its buildings, having invested nearly $10,000 therein, while the superintendent of its schools was allowed the liberal sum of $800 annually. Following the example of his predecessor he commended the towns of Burlington, Muscatine, Davenport, Lyons, Anamosa, Cedar Falls, Marion, Colesburg, Rochester, Tipton, Denmark, Primrose, West Point, Centerville and Oskaloosa for having provided new buildings, which he asserted would "stand as lasting monuments of the liberality of those engaged in so glorious an enterprise".

It was in this connection that reference was made to the union graded schools, a "large number" of which had been visited in the towns of the State. Great satisfaction was expressed with these organizations for promoting the work of public schools, since they promised opportunities heretofore unknown in the Commonwealth. They were adapted, however, only to centers of population with ''a large number of scholars within a convenient distance of some central point.'' Although there was an economic advantage in such schools, the important gain, in the opinion of the Superintendent, was in the opportunity which they afforded for improvement in methods of instruction and in classification. There was, furthermore, a prospect of steady advancement from grade to grade until the pupil could graduate from the highest department with a thoroughly practical education. In such a systematic plan, there was also an adaptation of instruction to the pupils of a single department, while at the same time they were stimulated to make the progress which would permit them to pass to a higher grade. Then, finally, it was said that under the supervision of a competent principal, and in the care of such teachers as would be obtainable, with an environment which was considered extraordinary, the pupil would take great pleasure in attending the sessions. Such were the observations relative to the graded schools soon after their first appearance about 1854.

Among the direct recommendations of Mr. Eads those concerning teachers seem most important, because without these ''the most indispensable of all educational auxiliaries'' would be wanting. He especially recommended the employment more generally of women teachers in the common schools —especially for the work among younger scholars. There was also a suggestion that all agencies in the operation of the schools be urged to aid in securing uniformity in text-books; and the perpetual topic of teachers' wages received its usual attention.[20]

Notwithstanding a stormy administration resulting from his management or mismanagement of the school funds, Superintendent James D. Eads continued in office for the full term of three years, when he was succeeded by Mr. Maturin L. Fisher in June, 1857.

The financial duties of the new Superintendent were such as to require a large part of his attention. Indeed, this was the transition period when the separation of the educational from the financial functions of the office was accomplished. In Mr. Fisher —who made the two reports just preceding the new law of 1858—the State had an officer who knew what was essential. His recommendations were fundamental, setting forth the needs of constructive legislation and declaring that the primary purpose should be the instruction of the whole people in the elementary branches in free schools—free in a sense not then recognized in the laws of this State.

To operate these free schools it was necessary that the State provide for the preparation of teachers. Superintendent Fisher therefore advised the establishment of two grades of institutions: first, the common school in which all the youth of the State should be taught, free of charge, "orthography, reading, writing, arithmetic, geography, English grammar and the elements of constitutional and administrative law"; and second, the "high or secondary schools for the instruction, free of charge, of teachers for the common schools, in the art and theory of teaching, and also, in all the branches of knowledge requisite for a liberal education".

Reference was made by Mr. Fisher to the normal schools recently established in several States, but it was the Superintendent's opinion that there was "no necessity for such distinct schools for the education of teachers." High schools for teachers should be provided in all the populous and wealthy counties; and when these schools had fully complied with certain imposed conditions fixed by law they should be entitled to aid from the State treasury. And the State University, which was already in operation, would complete the desired system by which instructors would be prepared for all grades of work. Thus the opportunity for a liberal education at moderate cost would be offered to any who might desire to accept it. To be sure these suggestions were, to a large extent, in the report of the Mann Commission, yet their repetition by Superintendent Fisher gave them added force and emphasis.

The recommendations relative to the creation of the office of county superintendent are the same as those of the Mann commission; but it is possible that supervisory duties which later devolved upon that officer were first recommended by Superintendent Eads who suggested the enlargement of the powers of the school fund commissioner so as to include such functions. It is not so important, however, as to when this plan originated as the fact that it was proposed as a remedy for many evils. The powers of the county superintendent (which have never been as fully conferred as enumerated in 1857) should, according to the view of Mr. Eads, include the establishment of school districts throughout the county and the determination of their boundaries. Subordinate to him a committee should be elected in each township, which should have supervision of all the schools therein. They should provide suitable teachers for all the schools of the township, visit the same once each month, see that scholars were prompt and constant in attendance, and report annually to the county superintendent the general conditions of the schools under their jurisdiction.[21] These provisions, if enacted into law, would have restored in part the functions of the former township inspectors.

Although elected by the people, Superintendent Fisher was legislated out of office by the State Board of Education after he had occupied the position from June, 1857, to December 24, 1858. His report, submitted in 1858, indicated an earnest effort to carry out the provisions of the law of March 12th of that year — notwithstanding the uncertainties existing as to the authority of the statute. Much of what was submitted in his report had direct reference to the work of county superintendents and will therefore be considered in a subsequent chapter. In the opinion of a minority of the State Board of Education the Superintendent of Public Instruction should have been retained in office, since the term did not expire until 1860 and the right of the people to elect should not be denied. It was pointed out by Mr. T. B.

Perry, a member of the Board, that one of the first principles of government would be violated in declaring this office abolished, and further that it was feasible to maintain both the office of Superintendent of Public Instruction and the Secretary of the Board at the same time with no increased outlay. Nevertheless, a resolution embodying this view of the situation was lost by a vote of four to seven. With the act of the State Board of Education, defining the functions of its Secretary, the Superintendent of Public Instruction was relieved of his duties in reference to the schools of the State.[22] Under the provisions of the Constitution and the school laws of 1858 the office was taken over by the State Board of Education.

III

STATE SUPERVISION: A PERIOD OF LIMITATIONS
1858–1872

HAD the office of Superintendent of Public Instruction been continued under the provisions of the law of 1858, the regular triennial election would have occurred in April, 1860; but the act of 1858 authorized also the abolition of the office ''at any time'' by the Board of Education and the transference of all of its duties to the secretary of the board.[23] Accordingly, on December 24, 1858, the Board of Education, near the end of its first session, proceeded to elect a Secretary when Mr. Thomas H. Benton, Jr., was chosen in preference to Mr. M. L. Fisher by a vote of nine to three. The Secretary *pro tem,* Mr. Josiah T. Tubby, was authorized to act until Mr. Benton qualified; so that it was not until January 14, 1859, that the latter assumed the duties of an office which, in general, were the same as those with which he had been familiar from 1848 to 1854.

While a Secretary was elected at each regular session of the State Board of Education it appears that Mr. Benton was the only person who held the position by successive regular elections. It became necessary, however, for him to appoint a substitute on account of absence during the war, and upon his resignation the place was filled by appointment. It was the function of the Secretary, in addition to the duties which had devolved upon the Superintendent of Public Instruction, "to keep an accurate journal" of the proceedings of the Board. This journal, moreover, is the source of general information relative to school legislation for the period from December 6, 1858, to the close of the year 1861.

The publication and distribution of the acts of the State Board of Education was among the first duties assigned the Secretary by the legislation of the Board; while the general supervision of all the county superintendents and of all the common schools was a function transferred from the office of the Superintendent of Public Instruction as provided in the law of the General Assembly of March 12, 1858. With the purpose of establishing a close connection between the secretary and the several counties he was required to meet the county superintendents of the several judicial districts in convention; whereas the Superintendent of Public Instruction had been required to meet these officers in a State convention. The Secretary was obligated to visit schools only as time and his numerous required duties might permit; but the text-books and books for libraries must be recommended by him, and the usual blank forms for teachers certificates and reports should be distributed to the several counties from his office.

The usual biennial reports, too, must be submitted by him not only to the General Assembly as hereto-

4

fore, but also to the State Board of Education. Moreover, these reports might include general recommendations in reference to the school system. That is to say, the Secretary appears to have had an opportunity to impress upon the authorities certain views, which would be probably more effective when presented to a body of eleven members than when submitted as formerly to the large number composing the General Assembly. The teachers institute, which was provided for in the general school act of March, 1858, was a feature of the law of the Board of Education, and for this meeting the Secretary was required to make all necessary arrangements as to time, place, and lectures whenever such a demand was made in accordance with law.[24]

The first act of Secretary Benton upon assuming his new duties was the printing and the distribution of the laws and the journal of the Board of Education as required — "ten thousand copies of the former and five hundred of the latter" being prepared for the public benefit. Nearly all of these were distributed within the year 1859. During the same year the Secretary had complied with the law in visiting all of the eleven judicial districts and in holding conventions of county superintendents therein. In this proceeding, while the letter of the law had been fulfilled, the results were not entirely satisfactory as will be shown later when the office of county superintendent is considered in detail.

Secretary Benton was obliged in his first report to defend the new school law, inasmuch as there were many objections lodged against it not only because of the changes required in organization but also because of the direct charge that it was more expensive, too complicated, and certain officers were unnecessary. Under such circumstances it was fortunate that his experience was available, for the critical period of inaugurating the new provisions was at hand. Being in a position to command a hearing, he secured from not less than forty county superintendents some views relative to actual results, and these he submitted as conclusive. Reference has already been made to these facts and they need be mentioned here only as indicative of the labors of the Secretary of the Board of Education at the very beginning of his service. At the time this defense was made the Secretary declared, however, that he was "wedded to no particular system of education" but wished rather "to secure that which is the most efficient, and costs the least."

Mr. Josiah T. Tubby, who had been chosen as the Secretary *pro tem* of the Board of Education, and who had been authorized to act in this capacity after the election of Mr. Benton until the latter had qualified, was thus really for a time the direct successor of Mr. Fisher and in charge of the executive duties of this office. When Secretary Benton assumed his duties Mr. Tubby became his clerk, and it was in this relation that his services in interpreting the new law were said to have been most satisfactory to the numerous correspondents who made inquiry during the absence of the chief officer. All difficult problems were submitted for "mutual consultation", and thus both the clerk and the Secretary were instrumental in answering the perplexing questions relative to the new act which came up from many quarters of the State. Strictly, then, if justice is done, Mr. Tubby must be listed with the Secretary and Acting Secretaries of the Board of Education, all of whom were in the order of succession to the office of Superintendent of Public Instruction.

By a provision of "Act No. 8" of the Board of Education, which was in fact the reënactment of the law of March 12, 1858, an extraordinary power was conferred upon the Secretary, namely, an ordinance power by which he was authorized to supplement the acts of the Board should any defect due to "oversight" be discovered therein when they were not in session. All such remedial rules or regulations were to have "the force of law" until the matter could be adjusted by the Board. The Secretary was required, however, to render in all such instances a full report of these acts and the reasons therefor.

It appears that, notwithstanding frequent requests, the Secretary refused to exercise this power to any extent lest, as he said, he "might transcend it". In this connection an important case arose which would have come under the authorization of the Board if it had been held to be a matter of "oversight". A village in the western part of the State (in 1859) had grown up on the boundary line of two counties; and under the old law (previous to 1858) the village, along with some contiguous terri-

tory from each of the two counties, was constituted
a school district. As such it levied a tax and built
a substantial school house. Under the new law, however, no district could extend beyond county lines;
and thus nearly half the people of the district were
thrown into a new jurisdiction and taxed for a new
building which was located two miles distant and at
the same time were deprived of the benefits of the
new house for which they had been taxed and which
was but a few rods away. This being manifestly a
defect in the law, not due to "oversight", the Secretary declined to use the authority which seemed to be
applicable. Questions of this nature were answered
by special correspondence, while the less important
queries were anticipated in circulars of which at
least three had been issued.[25] It is apparent, therefore, that the Secretary endeavored to carry out the
provisions of the law in all respects as well as to
perform the special duties imposed upon him by the
body whose executive officer he was.

Secretary Benton's second report was made to
the Board of Education at their final session in 1861.
There were many important recommendations in
this document, as well as a summary of the work
during the biennial period. Following the session of
the Board in December, 1859, the Secretary had
published the school law and the amendments thereto
made by the General Assembly and had distributed
these through the county judges and county superintendents to the counties of the State. It was
declared that the legislative changes made in 1859

had given rise to a "great variety of intricate questions", which led to an extensive correspondence in
order that these points might be explained.   That
ambiguity might be removed and the law made more
definite, the Secretary suggested more than twenty-
five amendments — thus showing the need of practical experience with a statute before it could be
made adaptable to all conditions.   Moreover, it was
at this time that a State Board of Examiners was
first recommended to a legislative body in this
Commonwealth.   Although the idea was not original
with the Secretary — other States having established similar boards — it was at least indicative of
the progressive spirit which dominated the officer
who was required to inform the law-making powers
of what was being done elsewhere.

During another biennial period the Secretary had
traveled about the State in meeting the county superintendents of the judicial districts; but at the end of
the second series of conventions he concluded that
the plan was not a success, for even though all the
superintendents in an entire district could be assembled at one time there would not be constituted
a body which could rouse any great interest.   He
favored, therefore, a meeting similar to the one held
at Iowa City in 1858, when a large number of these
officers were brought into one meeting at the capital
for at least a week.   Although he preferred an annual meeting, on account of the expense, he deemed
such frequent assemblies as possibly inexpedient at
the time.   And then — prophetically — he expressed

the hope that "in the course of time it will become a permanent, annual convocation of the best educational talent of the State."

In view of the present authority given to the county superintendents and the practical fulfillment of the utterance as to a "convocation", it is of interest to note the only obstacle which Secretary Benton presented to his plan as thus described. Some scheme, he said, must be first devised to meet the necessary expenses. Moreover, he was certain that "it would not be proper to require each County to pay the expenses of its own Superintendent; for then the burden would fall most heavily upon the more remote counties, which are least able to bear it." And so, he suggested the payment, finally, of the whole expense from the State treasury; but for the time being such payment could be made from the interest on the permanent school fund, and to this end the State Auditor should withhold from the apportionment a sum of not less than $2000. It does not appear, however, that this suggestion was ever acted upon, or that such a proposition was ever again made.[26]

The final report from the Secretary of the Board of Education consists in fact of three separate documents, than which no educational papers contain more interesting data. They represent the conclusions of Mr. Benton, then an officer in the regular army, of Mr. H. A. Wiltse, who had been appointed to act in his stead, and of former Lieutenant Governor Oran Faville, who had been appointed to relieve Mr. Wiltse. The latter performed the duties of Secretary of the Board of Education only from November, 1862, until April, 1863; but at the request of both the regularly appointed and the acting secretary he submitted a portion of the biennial summary. While certain parts of these three State papers must be included in other chapters it is essential that their general conclusions be stated in this connection.

As already noted the State Board of Education held its last session in 1861; and while the Secretary continued to perform the duties imposed upon his office, he had no further obligations relative to a journal of proceedings nor to legislation by the Board. And so his attention in 1862, he said, was given, first of all, to the publication of the amended school law of 1862 (enacted by the General Assembly) and its distribution throughout the State. It was observed that this statute was received generally with favor, and that it seemed to have removed "many of the objections and quibbles that previously attended its administration." It was in this connection that Secretary Benton pointed to the fact that while this statute (amending the school law of 1858) was by no means perfect, its provisions must, "regardless of the changes that may be made by different legislative bodies, constitute the basis of our school system for all time to come."

Moreover, Secretary Benton's contentions relative to the conflict that would prevail if the authority of the Board of Education and the General Assembly was to be continued for five years, as provided by the

Constitution, were supported by both of the other incumbents of the office — it being quite uniformly agreed that the General Assembly should exercise its right and abolish the existing Board. Secretary Benton would not recommend any general legislative changes in educational laws at the coming session (in 1864), believing that the law as then in force was sufficient — at least until the war was over. If, however, a new law should at some time be enacted he would recommend that "much be entrusted to the executive head of the system"— a suggestion which he felt free to make since he had filed his resignation with Governor Kirkwood.[27]

That portion of the report submitted by Mr. Wiltse, dwelt largely upon the defects in the law and the organization as provided by the Constitution. But he went farther than any former authority, and possibly than any since, in recommending a real State board of education with powers and prerogatives adequate to the establishment of a system similar to some in the older States, which authority he considered vital if the plan of a board was to be successful. Furthermore, information relative to actual conditions in the State was a matter of such importance that means should be available by which to obtain it and at the same time compel its submission by those who could be held responsible. Indeed, he would require a detailed account of the affairs of each district, and in the minor divisions having a specified population the facts should be printed for the public benefit.[28]

The third member of this group of Secretaries, Mr. Faville, submitted, in December, 1863, the eleventh regular report of the "Department", which included the two sections cited above. Since his services had extended over the latter part of the biennial period, he included valuable material relative to graded schools and a course of study which his immediate predecessor (Mr. Wiltse) had recommended. Moreover, he made it appear that a time might soon arrive when a compulsory attendance law would be desirable; and he illustrated the conditions of the schools by actual figures to show its possible necessity. He dwelt further upon the State Board of Education, the graded schools, text-books, laws, institutes, the school fund, and the county superintendent. Furthermore, he made frequent reference to the Civil War then being waged and to its influence upon the educational forces of the State which, he declared, had modified to some extent the usual urgent requests for changes or modifications in the machinery of the school system.[29]

With the retirement of Thomas H. Benton, Jr., a vacancy was created in the office of Secretary of the Board of Education to which Governor Kirkwood appointed Oran Faville, then Acting Secretary. Upon the abolition of the Board in 1864, Mr. Faville was elected by the General Assembly to the re-created office of Superintendent of Public Instruction to serve until January 1, 1866 — it being provided that the people at the general election in 1865 and "every two years thereafter" again should have the right of selecting this officer. Mr. Faville was reëlected in 1865 and served until March, 1867, when owing to ill health he resigned.[30]

During the superintendency of Oran Faville but one biennial report was made, that of 1864–1865 which included information along the lines specified by law as well as some general comments upon the period. The "well prepared teacher" was among the principal subjects upon which he wrote; and he emphasized again the importance of the office of county superintendent. Reference was made also to the graded schools; and although the high school had not yet become common in the State it was regarded by the new Superintendent as the "crowning glory of our system of free schools." Its advantages were illustrated by the recently adopted course of the Burlington independent district. In his opinion the growing influence of school journals and teachers associations was an item of considerable interest. Nowhere, however, was there any recommendation leading to fundamental changes in the laws. Indeed, it was concluded that, if one could judge from the data forwarded by county superintendents, the people desired no change.[31]

To the vacancy which occurred upon the resignation of Mr. Faville, Governor Stone appointed Mr. D. Franklin Wells, who on March 9, 1867, began the duties of his new office. Trained at the Albany, New York, Normal School, employed for some years in the public schools of Muscatine, he was called to the Normal Department of the State University of Iowa in 1856, and for ten years or more directed that branch of the University instruction, establishing a model school in connection therewith. Owing, however, to a change in organization, he was free to accept the office of Superintendent of Public Instruction just at the time the vacancy occurred.

From March 9, 1867, until November 24, 1868 — the time of his death — Mr. Wells was the executive head of the school system. As such he issued the required report in 1867, the period covered being from October 5, 1865, to October 4, 1867. His habit of thoroughness is clearly shown in this document, wherein he touched upon the subjects of funds, districts, the training of teachers and their certification, an educational board of examiners that would meet the needs of the State, and the county superintendent and his duties as well as his rights. Again, reference was made to the State Teachers' Association which had then been in existence for thirteen years, to township graded schools, to text-books and their uniformity, and finally to the current interest in the adoption of the metric system of weights and measures. But, as in the report of two years before, no radical change in the laws relative to education was in any way suggested. No report up to this time had set forth in such precise and definite terms the idea of a single State normal school; and no authority, it might be said, of greater weight on this subject could be quoted at that time.[32]

Upon the death of Mr. Wells, Mr. Abram S. Kissell was appointed by Governor Merrill to the vacancy. Although appointed on December 10, 1868, Mr. Kissell did not enter upon his duties until January 28, 1869. The biennial report due in 1869 must, therefore, have been submitted within less than a year after his appointment to the office — that is to say, it covered the period from October 6, 1867, to October 4, 1869, as the law then specified. In this, as in the former documents covering the operations of the office, the material submitted is indicative of the current thought of the leaders and the needs of the educational system of the Commonwealth. In addition to the common and customary recommendations, new features, such as drawing, music, voice culture, evening schools, lyceums, and libraries are given some attention; while supervision — district, county, and State — is treated at length. Perhaps district supervision had not before this received adequate presentation; for it is noteworthy that each occupant of the office of Superintendent of Public Instruction had contributed his experience in a special field as an important part of his recommendations. In this instance Mr. Kissell was but emphasizing that which he had worked out to some extent in a practical way.[33]

During the period between the time of Mr. Kissell's appointment and his actual entrance upon the duties of the office Mr. Lewis I. Coulter served as the Acting Superintendent. Of this fact the reports offer no information. Indeed, it appears that the only public document bearing Mr. Coulter's name is a decision made on January 27, 1869 — the day preceding that on which the appointee qualified. Nothing further seems to be recorded relative to the service of this temporary officer, and it is only through this one source that connection is made between the close of the administration of Mr. Wells and the beginning of that of Mr. Kissell. Since the laws of 1868, amending Section 642 of the *Revision of 1860,* provided for the appointment of a deputy superintendent of public instruction, it is concluded that Mr. Coulter held such position and that the functions pertaining to the office devolved upon him.[34]

Near the close of the session of 1868 the General Assembly had passed an act increasing to some extent the duties which were assigned to the Superintendent of Public Instruction. Instead of meeting county superintendents in judicial districts the State Superintendent was authorized to hold conventions at convenient points. He was required also to attend and lecture at county institutes, and to render a written opinion in all cases where inquiry was made touching the interpretation of the law. Finally, at the close of each session of the General Assembly, he must revise and codify all school laws previous to issuing a new edition thereof. It was this statute, furthermore, which repealed the right of the Superintendent ''to select or direct what kind of books'' should be used in the public schools.[35]

Personal contact as an element in creating educational enthusiasm was tested, to some extent, by Superintendent Kissell during his final term in a "tour of inspection" into different parts of the State. On this tour he traveled over 14,000 miles in eighteen months and delivered some seventy lectures. At the same time Massachusetts was inaugurating a system for the accomplishment of the same purpose, employing six men to do the work which devolved upon one in Iowa. It is not remarkable, therefore, that Governor Merrill in his message of 1870 should recommend the appointment, by the proper State officials, of six assistant superintendents for the same number of defined districts within the State.[36] It seems clear that he had observed the benefits of a personal canvass of each locality and had concluded that more specific supervision ought to be undertaken by the State department.

On January 1, 1872, Superintendent Abram S. Kissell submitted his final report to the General Assembly. It may be said that up to that time none had been more carefully prepared, and probably no other holds a more authoritative place not only as to facts and practices but also as to the presentation of theory. Reference has often been made to the exhaustive study of the Normal school as an institution which he included in this document. He summarized likewise the advantages of the district township system; gave fifteen pages to the subject of moral and religious education; pointed out the needs of the institute and the support that should be granted to the county superintendency; and declared that the time was opportune for the enactment of a compulsory attendance law. The theoretical was espe-

cially prominent in his treatment of the use of
text-books, the kindergarten system, and intuitional
and objective teaching; while emphasis on the pro-
duction of actual results in secondary instruction,
with a proposed course of study for high schools,
indicated a broad view of public service through the
school system of the State.[37]   In other chapters the
substance of these discussions may be incorporated
— but in the briefest form since they constitute in
themselves a small volume.

The period from 1858 to 1872 as thus summarized
is marked by many changes in the supervising
authority in the State. If one includes, as it appears
one should, the Secretaries of the Board of Education, there were elected or appointed at least five
Superintendents of Public Instruction, one Secretary *pro tem,* and one deputy (who exercised the authority of the Superintendent) during the fourteen
years; while the succeeding six Superintendents
covered a period of not less than twenty-six years.
It was a time of uncertainty in many respects and of
trial and proof in others, so that what was rightfully
termed supervision was not fully exercised. Much
was suggested, but there was little that could be
commanded. Throughout there seems to have been
a feeling that no system had yet been established
— a conclusion which subsequent events justify.
Nevertheless, the men, the personalities connected
with the office of Superintendent of Public Instruction, were of the highest type.

IV

STATE SUPERVISION: A PERIOD OF RESOLUTION
1872–1912

In January, 1872, Mr. Alonzo Abernethy assumed the duties of Superintendent of Public Instruction. During the session of the General Assembly that year the most radical school legislation since 1858 provided for the restoration of the independent district. Thus a new factor entered into the management and supervision of the school system. It was observed by Mr. Abernethy in his first biennial report, that the school system as originally established contemplated a ''three-fold plan of superintendence'' — State, county, and district. But in a State of such proportions as Iowa the influence that could be exerted by a single officer over the whole was exceedingly limited. It was evident, moreover, that the provisions of the law relative to local or district supervision — that is, by directors — were not complied with to any extent, and so the plan could not result in great advancement. The county supervision, which had been provided for some fifteen years earlier, was not yet fully established and great differences of opinion existed as to its usefulness. Thus one must conclude that the entire structure, the

5

three-fold plan, was not regarded as accomplishing
the purpose contemplated.

With this situation in view Superintendent
Abernethy gave large space to and quoted from leading authorities in support of the office of county
superintendent, since this agency appeared to be
absolutely necessary to any scheme of supervision
however elementary it might be. As then organized
the school system demanded such an officer. Indeed,
there were certain contingencies where no substitute
could be made. With the evident purpose of drawing attention to the importance of school inspection
or school visiting on the part of the county superintendent, the State Superintendent in the conventions
of county school officers made this a leading feature
of the discussions. Moreover, he even ventured to
issue an inquiry relative to the time employed in
inspection, the number of visits not only in schools
but in counsel with directors, the number of educational meetings held, and also the public addresses
given — all of which were to form a part of the
conclusions as to the effectiveness of the office of
county superintendent.

Thus there was a direct attack, it appears, upon
the problem of supervision; and at the same time it
was shown how impotent the office of State Superintendent was as to equipment of working force and in
the limited opportunity given to the Superintendent
to be away from his clerical duties. Indeed, Mr.
Abernethy declared that although the legal requirements as to attendance upon institutes, conventions,

and educational gatherings had been met so far as possible this work had been done so hurriedly that information necessarily of interest to the public and the General Assembly had to be neglected.[38]

Departing from the usual custom Superintendent Abernethy devoted his biennial report for 1874–1875 to a review of the Iowa school system from the beginning to the year 1875. Although the value of current information was unquestioned and its real worth would tend to increase as the school system developed, nevertheless for the purpose of determining needed modifications and legislative action its value was "limited by the limited range of view." Mr. Abernethy thought it desirable, therefore, to present, at intervals, a "more extended view, to enlarge the range of vision, for the purposes of comparison and reference, and to afford the opportunity to study the changes and the progress made for longer periods of time." Another reason for presenting this historical review was found in the fact that the next year would mark the centennial in the nation's history, and the occasion was opportune for such an undertaking.

This was a new angle from which to view the problems of educational supervision. But one must accept Mr. Abernethy's contribution as a real endeavor to promote the growth of education in Iowa in a most profitable way. Nothing of the kind had ever before been done for education in this State. Probably no legislator knew minutely the status of the Iowa school district, for example, or of previous school legislation, or of the progress of the graded schools, or of the compensation of teachers for the past thirty years. It was, therefore, proper for the Superintendent of Public Instruction to present — though, as he said, in no sense a history of education — a rather comprehensive view of what the State had stood for during the years since schools were first established.[39] This, moreover, was the true way of securing a perspective for the legislators who might be anxious to promote laws that had in previous years been tried, repealed, and then presented for reënactment.

Mr. Carl W. von Coelln, the successor to Alonzo Abernethy, was elected to the office of Superintendent in 1875, and through reëlection served six years as the head of the school system. With reference to the subject of supervision it appears from the three reports presented during these six years that he dwelt forcefully upon the increasing functions of the State office and the exercise of certain authority implied in the powers of general supervision. In carrying out these provisions of the law he had (in 1877) visited forty-three institutes and twelve associations, had delivered seventy or more lectures, and had traveled 8000 miles. Again, two years later he contrasted the experience of the larger cities and towns, where all or part of the time of a supervisor was employed, with the attention that could be given the rural school. It was in this survey that he recommended additional inspection through assistants to the county superintendent — that is, township inspectors who should be qualified not only to aid teachers individually but at the same time be able to judge of efficiency.

Finally, during his last term he declared that the school organization could hardly be called a system, since the main authority in providing for the actual operation of the schools was located in the board of directors of a district. While there was State and county supervision according to statute, this was largely advisory. It would be well to instruct the people in the benefits of competent inspection and supervision. In every instance the county superintendent must eventually become a factor or the office would be declared useless, while the State office must be relieved of its burdens by the assistance of a board of education.

It may be said, in passing, that this suggestion had actually been met in the appointment of an unofficial body from the State Teachers' Association which should serve as an advisory council to the Superintendent. The following representatives of different educational forces in the State constituted this advisory body: President Josiah L. Pickard of the State University; President William F. King of Cornell College; Professor Moses W. Bartlett of the State Normal School; Professor Charles E. Bessey of the State Agricultural College; Superintendent Homer H. Seerley of the Oskaloosa city schools, and Superintendent Rufus H. Frost of Cass County. Although it was recognized that such an advisory council would be of great assistance, it was asserted

that the State office was in need of a board which
would assume some of its obligations in the "actual
inspection and supervision of school work", including the institutes and "educational institutions" of
the State.[40]

The successor to Superintendent von Coelln, Mr.
John W. Akers, retained the office for an equal
period — that is, for six years (1882–1888). He also
suggested and enlarged upon the possibilities of a
system which would incorporate township inspection. His relations with the county superintendents
during his first term gave him a favorable impression
of their efforts. Moreover, at the sixteen conventions held in the eight districts into which the State
had been divided the attendance had been such that
every county was represented. There were many
important measures before the people during these
six years; but they were, for the most part, not
directly connected with the policy of the supervision
to be exercised or proposed by the Superintendent
or by others associated under his administration.
There were, however, among the public matters presented for consideration, some which required the
active participation of the State Superintendent.
For example, it was during the administration of
Mr. Akers that the New Orleans exposition offered
an opportunity for a collective exhibit illustrating
the entire school system of the State. Of this he
took advantage and gave personal attention to the
installation of the material. The official duties
which might be designated as supervisory are, how-

ever, so clearly connected with those that are executive, that one must refer to them in other chapters.[41]

After seventeen years of service as superintendent of the Clinton schools, Henry Sabin was elected Superintendent of Public Instruction; and before the office was finally surrendered to his successor he had completed eight years of service — a period longer than that of any other in the history of the office. Entering upon his duties at the beginning of the year 1888 he completed the first half of his period of service in 1892, and having been reëlected after an intervening term he began the second half in 1894. During the eight years there were issued under his direction four biennial reports each of which contains many valuable suggestions bearing directly upon the functions of his office or of subordinates occupying supervisory positions. He exercised his authority in summoning the county superintendents in convention, and each of the four reports dwelt upon the specific results which this county officer should endeavor to obtain. Indeed, there was an increasing endeavor during these years to enlighten the public relative to the underlying principles which should control in the selection of men for the office of county superintendent. In the first of the four documents it was pointed out that "close supervision is coming to be recognized universally as essential to a well-ordered school system." To that end it was recommended that the county superintendent be given more power and that his functions be more clearly defined.

In his final report, that for 1896–1897, Mr. Sabin declared that the country schools required a "supervision which in its entirety and in its wholesome effects challenges the respect and the support of everyone" who is interested in their welfare. Furthermore, such supervision should be "broad in its scholarship without being shallow." While supervision in general was characterized as "a blessing or a curse in proportion to the degree of intelligence and skill with which it is administered", it was asserted that the greatest need in rural supervision was an abundance of common sense and an ability to adapt itself to circumstances. Moreover, the character of the supervision should itself "commend the wisdom of the supervisor." The former type of supervision — that which was limited to the province of the examiner only — was no longer sufficient.

In the office for which Superintendent Sabin personally was held responsible there was a steady increase of powers and duties. For instance, the Twenty-second General Assembly made the Superintendent the ex officio president of the board of directors of the State Normal School. He was also president of the State Board of Examiners, president of the educational council of the State Teachers' Association, and a member of the board of regents of the State University. For many years the law had required him to render a written opinion upon any point in the school law, as well as to hear and decide appeals, while the paramount function of supervising the common schools was the original intention in establishing the office. Now it was clear, the Superintendent declared, that unless a way could be devised to relieve the department of "routine duties" which required so much time it could by no means meet the demands of the public. There was a direct suggestion, furthermore, that the department be made more effective through the granting of additional authority "to visit and inspect, through its appointed agents" the schools of the State, to counsel with school officers and teachers, and to more carefully supervise and direct the institutes — all of which would tend to arouse public interest and thus eventually benefit the entire educational system.

In 1896 Mr. Sabin observed that the work of the office had practically doubled within the period of eight years. Yet no additional assistance had been provided. With the multiplying duties, which evidently never would grow less, the question of how to carry the influence of the department to "every hamlet in the state" was one of growing importance. As then constituted the office had little more than advisory functions. But the Superintendent did not advise that its power to command be increased: it should rather have increased "facilities for extending and strengthening its influence as counselor and director." That is to say, a closer connection should be made possible between this office and the State at large through information obtained by means of "personal inspection" and "accredited agents".

Finally, at the close of his fourth term in 1897

Superintendent Sabin expressed his belief that any radical changes in administration would "work injury rather than benefit" to the public schools, while to "strengthen the things which remain, to build up what we have already commenced, is the most pressing duty of the hour." Then he closed his eight years of service with these words:

If I have not accomplished all that I hoped to, or all that others expected of me, I cannot be blamed, provided I have done my best. If I have been slothful and indolent, if I have permitted trusts and combines to prey upon the public, if I have not thrown my heart and soul into this great work, if I have been faithless in any degree to the trusts reposed in me by a generous people, then I deserve execrations here, and oblivion hereafter. But if I have striven with all my strength, if I have given myself unreservedly to the cause of popular education, if I have counted no labor too severe, no exertion too great, if thereby I could place the educational standard upon a higher plane, then it is not presumption in me to cherish the hope that my name may not be forgotten when the educational history of Iowa is written.[42]

The years 1892–1894 comprehend the period of service of Mr. John B. Knoepfler, a man who had been engaged in public school work in this State for more than fifteen years and who came immediately from the superintendency at Lansing into the office of State Superintendent of Public Instruction. While his single report covered many important subjects with which supervision was concerned, the agencies directly involved, namely, his own office and the county superintendents, are the factors pertinent to the discussion in this connection. His observations led him to the same conclusions as those of his predecessors, namely, that the limited time which the Superintendent had for actual contact with the graded and rural schools offered no opportunity for effective action therein. Moreover, the demands of the office were such that the Superintendent was deprived of the privilege which should be accorded to one charged with supervision — that is, a personal acquaintance with the difficulties which he must meet. That any serious attention should be given to the thought of abolishing the office of county superintendent was considered as impossible. Moreover, the pointed recommendation was made that not less but more supervision was desirable, and so a competent person should be appointed to supervise a group of not more than forty schools in the rural districts. To Mr. Knoepfler there appeared to be but one solution of the problem, namely, the election of a number of assistants to the county superintendent.[43]

Mr. Richard C. Barrett, for many years county superintendent of Mitchell County, succeeded Henry Sabin in 1898, and was thereafter for six years the Superintendent of Public Instruction. While he presented the educational needs of the State and advocated the most progressive movements then before the public, the problems of supervision as such are but briefly discussed in his three reports. What was said, however, was definite, and if acted upon would have removed some obscure passages in the laws governing his office. For example, it was his obser-

vation that the provision of law by which the State
Superintendent had supervision of all county superintendents and the common schools of the State was
meaningless since it conveyed no definite authority.
It was therefore proposed that the matter be clearly
set forth in the statutes under ten distinct classes of
functions, and that the necessary agencies for ex-
ecuting the same be provided.

From his experience Mr. Barrett was able to
speak with more than ordinary authority on matters
relative to the county superintendency; and so,
special interest attaches to the fact that on the occasion of his first report in 1899 he pointed out the
great waste that constantly occurred in this county
office. In general, while the county superintendency
was a factor in the educational system that could in
no wise be dispensed with, the results obtained from
the office were but a fraction of what might be realized. He would provide that the valuable asset in
the experience of the incumbents of this office should
be continued in other supervisory positions of similar character which would become possible under a
mode of selection involving but a slight change. But
the details of this plan are not pertinent in this connection. Here it will be sufficient to note that permanency in the office was held to be the effective
principle for conserving the energy therein; and
while courses of study might be prepared and submitted from his office they would not contribute to
the economic use of time without close supervision.[44]
Thus briefly may be summarized the direct recom-

mendations relative to supervision which were made during the six years of Superintendent Barrett's service.

Mr. Barrett was succeeded in 1904 by Mr. John F. Riggs who, through the constitutional change to biennial elections, served seven years and submitted four reports covering a period of large responsibility in the office. The new issues which were presented and acted upon increased largely the duties devolving upon the Superintendent, while the statutory revisions required more than the usual watchfulness to avoid friction in changing from established customs. The department recognized the work of the county superintendent as "distinctly supervisory", and it was therefore recommended that he be relieved as much as possible from clerical duties. His work was legitimately in the field rather than within the four walls of an office, and so the functions which he should perform in school inspection were duly specified. The whole purpose in supervision, it was declared, ought to be the unifying of the forces engaged, namely, those represented in the superintendent, the board of education, and the teacher — each of whom should become fully acquainted with the responsibilities and the attitude of the others.

The legislation of 1906, furthermore, required many special communications from the State office to local authorities, so that confusion relative to the organization of boards of education, the new certificate law, the annual reports, the terms of certain officers, and the qualifications of county superintendents might be avoided. Indeed, it was an occasion which required repeated efforts in order to make the departures from former customs effective in accomplishing that for which they were enacted. At the same time much additional labor was thrown upon the office of Superintendent owing to the new plan of the certification of teachers — and this, too, without a proportionate increase in office assistance.

It is apparent that this administration was noted for its effort to present facts relative to the necessity of abandoning the small school; and to that end the accumulation of data was made a part of every report. It might be said that the material thus collected will alone serve as sufficient reason for maintaining adequate equipment in the agencies of inspection and special supervision, since the economy in organization for efficiency could be demonstrated in no better way. And further, the professionalizing of teaching was not adequately provided for prior to the last five years of this period. While the definite recommendations which might be considered as in part supervisory are many, they cannot be indicated apart from the subject with which they are concerned. At the same time supervision as an abstract problem occupied but little space in the four extended reports of Superintendent Riggs.[45]

Since the organization of the Territory of Iowa seventeen individuals have held the office of Superintendent of Public Instruction, and of these two were also Secretary of the State Board of Education. The present incumbent, Mr. A. M. Deyoe, came into

office in January, 1911; accordingly but one biennial
report has been issued by him — that for the period
ending June 30, 1912. In this report it is clearly set
forth that the State department should be so
equipped that it might lead in "educational matters,
with special reference to the improvement of the
elementary and secondary schools in the state." It
is declared further that the office in Iowa is limited
"too much to hearing appeal cases, rendering opinions concerning disputes arising over trivial school
matters, preparing reports, answering correspondence, and a great deal of merely clerical work." A
more vigorous constructive policy was desirable,
which would be possible only through increased
authority and an adequate office force. Recent legislation, it may be said, has provided in part for the
assistance required, and at no time has the department had the prospective opportunity which now
seems near at hand. The office having been made
appointive, with largely increased powers and a
longer term of service, it appears that the desired
ends so long sought may be reached.[46]

Thus in Iowa it has required a long period of
experience, the demonstration of trials and results,
repeated illustrations of the practices of progressive
States, as well as the repetition of recommendations
in successive years, to insure any advance in the
supervision of education by the State.

V

COUNTY SUPERVISION: A PERIOD OF UNPOPULARITY

THE office of county superintendent was created by the general education act of March 12, 1858. Such an office had been recommended by the Mann commission in 1856, but its functions were not such as later provided in the statute. It appears that the existing office of school fund commissioner must have caused the Mann commission to include some of his duties relative to school lands and the apportionment of funds in the office of county superintendent. At the same time the general supervisory powers of the county superintendent as recommended were entirely new. When, however, the act of March 12, 1858, was finally approved it contained no reference to any financial function of the county superintendent for the obvious reason that the Constitution had already provided for the discharge of such obligations through other channels. Thus, fortunately, the office was not confused with that of the former fund commissioner.

By the act of 1858 the election of the county superintendent was to occur biennially in March. Thus the office was removed from the political influence of the general elections — a plan advocated many times since, but actually in force only during the period from March 12, 1858, to the time that the State Board of Education enacted new provisions in December following.[47]

There was general agreement, however, between the act of the legislature and that of the Board of Education in the definition of functions. The principal purpose of the legislation appears to have been the establishment of an authority over the certification of teachers; while the implied powers of the office would make the supervision of the instruction an element in determining the qualification of those employed in the schools. Moreover, the power to remove any teacher or to annul the license for cause was particularly specified. The superintendent was commanded to "visit personally and inspect" the schools of his county at least twice each year. He was further empowered to appoint at any time "a special committee to make such inspection" as he might require.

Another reason for the creation of the office of county superintendent was the need of some agency by which the State Superintendent could communicate with the numerous district officers throughout the State. Thus the law made it the duty of the county superintendent to "conform to the instructions and directions of the Superintendent of Public Instruction, as to all matters within his jurisdiction", and he must see that both board and teachers complied with the regulations of the State office. The same obligations were imposed by the act of the

6

State Board of Education by which their Secretary was substituted for the Superintendent of Public Instruction.

The compensation of the county superintendent appears to have been a troublesome matter from the very beginning. For instance, by the law of March 12, 1858, he was allowed a sum equal to one-half the amount paid the clerk of the district court, and in addition thereto any "further sum" that might be authorized by the county board of district presidents. But it was required that in no instance should the sum be "more than one eighth greater" than the salary of the clerk. This part of the statute remained unchanged by the Board of Education, except as to the last provision which was made to read: "But in no case shall the salary of the Superintendent be increased so as to exceed that of the said Clerk".[48]

Although, as heretofore mentioned, the law of March 12, 1858, was declared to be unconstitutional those county superintendents who were elected in April (regularly the election would have occurred in March) were confirmed in their offices by the Board of Education in December and would therefore serve until their successors had qualified — the election under the new provisions occurring in October, 1859. In the meantime the first State convention of county superintendents convened in Iowa City at the call of Mr. M. L. Fisher, Superintendent of Public Instruction, on September 22, 1858. The convention was chiefly concerned with the interpretation of the new school law, and in this respect it was an assembly previously unknown to the educational forces of Iowa.

During this convention a committee, appointed for the purpose, arranged all the questions arising under the new law of March 12, 1858, and submitted them to Superintendent Fisher for interpretation. Not fewer than sixty-four such queries were presented; and it is assumed that they were answered, although there is no record of the fact. At the same time a committee of county superintendents recommended a number of changes which were desirable and which should be considered by the State Board of Education at their first meeting in December, 1858. The suggestions of the committee do not appear, however, in the legislation of the Board.

While these problems relative to the application of the new act were being explained great faith was expressed in its efficiency, and the declaration that "it fully meets our approbation" and was admirably adapted to place the State in a superior position relative to educational advantages was made a part of the record of the convention.[49] According to the opinion expressed by Superintendent Fisher this convention was truly an educational council, and it was considered fortunate that the Board of Education could have the assistance of such a body in "perfecting the system of public instruction of the State."[50]

The Board of Education required their Secretary to meet county superintendents in convention in each

judicial district. Reference has already been made
to the outcome of this provision and also to the
recommendations of Secretary Benton relative to a
change in the requirement. It was learned that
during the period (1858–1859) the county superintendent was regarded in many quarters as super-
fluous and that the new system was too expensive.
But this conclusion was met by the assertion on the
part of the Secretary that the actual expense for
the entire State was less by $50,000 than under the
preceding independent district plan. Furthermore,
the amounts formerly paid to the fund commissioners showed a balance in favor of the county superintendent — an office which must be retained or some
other having similar functions established as the
head of the county organization.[51]

During their second session in 1859 the Board of
Education revised the general education law; and in
so doing the visiting authority of the county superintendent was repealed. Among the leaders who
supported the new law this was regarded as a serious
reactionary step, since the duties of the superintendent were now restricted to the examination of
teachers and the making of reports to the Secretary
of the Board and to the county judge. That is to
say, the most important and valuable function of the
county superintendent had been destroyed that there
might be saved to the State some $20,000. Another
act of the same session authorized the county superintendent to hear appeals; but the law itself was so
indefinite in its provisions that a postage stamp, it

was declared, might interfere with justice. The critics were severe in their condemnation of such legislation, especially that relative to the county superintendent.[52]

When the State Teachers' Association met in 1860 it was resolved that the Board of Education had yielded to popular prejudice excited for political effect and had, therefore, destroyed the efficiency of the office of county superintendent. Moreover, the charges which had been brought against this office were entirely unreasonable and contrary to facts not only as to the matter of expense but also as to the claims of inefficiency. It was further resolved that the entire time of the superintendent was essential to the success of the work in every county, and that he should be in communication with each teacher and school officer in order to stimulate activity in all departments. In short he should be, as the original act intended, the educational head in the county. Finally, the members of the Association mutually agreed to labor for the restoration of the functions of the county superintendent and for a stipulated salary for the office.[53]

In his report of 1861 Secretary Benton not only recognized the demand for a restoration of the authority of inspection but he also suggested a way to meet it. It appears that the financial objection could be overcome only through some plan that would avoid reference to salary; and so, it was proposed that the former compensation, based upon the salary of the clerk, should be allowed for his miscellaneous duties, while for visiting and lecturing in each subdistrict once a year a stipend of three dollars each should be paid from the county treasury. The latter claim must be supported, however, by a certificate from the subdirector that the duty had been performed as required. Another scheme which was recommended would allow a stipulated sum for the field work to be paid from the temporary fund of the county, which sum was to be withheld from the apportionment and paid over on the testimony of the subdirector. The plan last proposed seems to have been originated by Mr. Rufus Hubbard, superintendent of Lee County. It was adopted in Des Moines County by Mr. William Harper after it had been approved by the superintendents in convention in the first judicial district.[54]

By the consolidation and revision of the school laws in 1862 no change was made in the status of the county superintendent, except in his compensation which thereafter should be two dollars per day for each day actually employed. To secure this remuneration, however, he was required by law to file a sworn statement of the facts relative to his claim, while in counties of less than twenty-five subdistricts it was provided that the total amount allowed, exclusive of fees for examinations, should never exceed fifty dollars, and in others not more than two dollars for each subdistrict therein.[55] But this action would not in any degree result in the desired restoration of the supervisory function, since no individual would engage in such a temporary occupation. This fact seems to have been appreciated to some extent previous to the session of the Tenth General Assembly; for among sundry other amendments to the school law a provision was incorporated by which the county superintendent should be allowed a per diem of two dollars for all time employed in general duties, and for the visiting of schools at least once in each year the county board of supervisors should make provision at their discretion. The sworn statement was still required before the superintendent was entitled to any compensation.[56]

By a further amendment in 1866 the per diem for necessary service was established at three dollars, other requirements remaining unchanged except that one-half day should be spent in each school visited.[57] Such legislation was in harmony with the opinion expressed by a committee of the State Teachers' Association five years before, when it was declared that the Board of Education had "materially injured the cause of Education by abridging the powers and duties" of county superintendents. The restoration of the "visiting power" had, therefore, been demanded.[58] It seems clear that the united effort on the part of the leaders in the State Teachers' Association, in institutes, and in their published opinions resulted in this somewhat limited legislation in 1866. Furthermore, the Secretary of the Board of Education, in January, 1864, had suggested a form of petition to be used by the people of any community in order that the General Assembly might learn their desires in the premises.[59]

Another convention of county superintendents was held in Cedar Rapids on August 23, 1866, during the annual session of the State Teachers' Association. State Superintendent Oran Faville presided over the small gathering composed of Superintendents Amos Dean of Benton County, M. T. Harlan of Boone County, Richard J. Crouch of Clinton County, Rev. Jonathan Osmond of Johnson County, Wm. J. Ronalds of Louisa County, Rev. J. G. Beckley of Story County, S. G. Pierce of Buchanan County, P. W. Reeder of Linn County, T. L. Downs of Tama County, E. C. Rigby of Cedar County, John C. Gates of Black Hawk County, Mr. Abbott of Sac County, and Mr. Tirrill of Delaware County. Although constituting a small proportion of the total number in the State, they put on record a declaration of their purpose to unite in an effort to elevate the standard of qualifications for teachers, and resolved that they would in no instance issue certificates where applicants failed to reach the required excellence, notwithstanding the "petitions from members of sub-districts and sub-directors". It was their opinion also that county superintendents should attend the State Teachers' Association, and the "absence of seven-eighths of them from the present meeting" was "to be reprehended."[60]

Again, on April 21, 1869, another convention assembled at Des Moines in the high school room of the second ward building. Three days were occupied, morning, afternoon, and evening, in the consideration of current problems. While this was recognized as a convention of county superintendents it was composed, as a matter of fact, of about forty of these officers and as many more public school superintendents, principals, and teachers; and so, it should be designated rather as a general educational meeting. The interest which attaches to this meeting lies in its conclusions and in what occurred during the session. State Superintendent Kissell presided, and the members were welcomed to the capital city by Governor Merrill. Among the subjects considered were the following: the limits and benefits of appeals; the examination of teachers; the influence of district and city high schools; the school laws and their defects; the importance of school visits and school meetings; and the ventilation, warming, and general structure of school houses. There were illustrative lessons given by Mrs. M. A. McGonegal, the principal of the Davenport training school, on the teaching of reading, and by Miss P. W. Sudlow, principal of the Davenport grammar school, on the teaching of language. And there was a demonstration of the "method of instruction by object lessons" with a class of young girls. The session was not confined, however, to the interests of the elementary schools, since Rev. James Black, the president of the State University, addressed the convention on the relation of the public school to the University.

At the close of the session a legislative committee, consisting of one member from each congressional district and the State Superintendent, was instructed to secure amendments to the school law which would prohibit the attendance of children under six years of age, which would require directors to visit all schools once a month, which would provide that paid directors be elected for two years (one-half of their number retiring annually), and which would permit the selection of suitable school house sites. A resolution relative to normal schools declared that while abundant appropriations for the Normal Department of the State University were approved, the most pressing need of a larger supply of qualified teachers demanded the immediate establishment of at least one normal school, "separate and apart from any other educational institution".[61]

About one year later (in March, 1870) a similar convention was summoned to meet in the high school room of the East Des Moines district, when special consideration was given to a bill then before the General Assembly (S. F. 150) affecting the status of the county superintendents. The bill was finally approved by the convention after it had been amended so that the power of the Governor to appoint a county superintendent in case of a vacancy was transferred to the county board of supervisors. But the labors of the convention were in vain, for the bill was buried somewhere in the House. It appears from the minutes that a large share of the session was given up to the discussion of this bill, although the questions of uniformity in text-books, of a single normal school, and of adequate compensation for the State Superintendent were also before the meeting.

A letter from Jonathan Piper, president of the State Teachers' Association, called attention to the conflict then being waged as to the policy of "free schools and no schools" supported by the State, to the value of the institute law then in force compelling attendance, and to the recommendation by the Governor for district supervision. In view of the present proportion of men to women in the office of county superintendent it is of interest to note the ungallant attitude of some members on this occasion. Miss Julia C. Addington of Mitchell County, the first woman to occupy the office of county superintendent, was unable to reach the convention on account of severe storms. A resolution of regret, therefore, was offered, and with it a "cordial welcome to this field of labor"; whereupon five members out of twenty voted against it.[62]

While these conventions were recommending and debating certain measures, the actual inability to enforce the legal requirements of the office of county superintendent which then prevailed may be illustrated by the following incident. A township board in Allamakee County was reported by the superintendent in 1869 as having "seceded" from his jurisdiction. That is to say, the board not only paid teachers who had no license to teach, but also employed some whose certificates had been revoked because of failure to attend the county institute as required by law. Indeed, they denounced by resolution "everybody who had anything to do with institutes." As the law had been interpreted such illegal action could be prevented only by a citizen of the township — the county superintendent being without sufficient authority in the matter.[63]

It does not appear, however, that the legislation of 1870 removed these difficulties, although some additional power was bestowed upon the county superintendent and some further special functions were enumerated. For example, he was authorized to appoint appraisers for school house sites when the owner refused to make the necessary concessions, or when he could not be found; he was made ex officio a member and president of the board of trustees whenever his county adopted the statute providing for a high school therein; and he was charged further with the duty of reporting all the blind of school age to the institution established for their benefit. A similar requirement relative to the deaf and dumb was made in 1872.[64]

During this period there appears to have been a growing appreciation of the work of the county superintendent, for it was pointed out that boards of supervisors were becoming more liberal in their allowances, some of these extending, indeed, to the payment of all expenses incurred in attending conventions and the State Teachers' Association. Such liberality was declared to be indicative of an "enterprising spirit" and of the fact that school supervision was favored to such an extent that its importance would soon be felt not only in every county but also in every district.[65]

Although there were signs of improvement the

general situation was far from satisfactory. Two things —"politics" in the selection of the super-intendent and inadequate compensation — were effectually preventing the office from becoming a permanent influence in any section of the State. It was as yet "simply collateral and subsidiary to something else." It was said that the lawyer sought the office that he might use "the per diem of an occasional jaunt through the county" in enlarging his practice. Or the minister found in this way "a convenient method of supplementing the very meagre salary" which he obtained from his church work. It was clear that no solution of the matter was possible until men were granted a compensation that would warrant full time service.

To remedy the first of these evils — that is, the political — it was suggested in 1871 that the county superintendent be elected for four years by the dis-trict boards of the county at their annual meeting in March. Moreover, the selection should not be limited to the county, nor for that matter to the State, but should be made upon the same principle as that exercised in the choice of a city superintendent.

As to the second obstruction — that is, inadequate compensation — there was no remedy except a stat-ute which would establish a minimum fixed salary. Indeed, there was no reason, it was declared, for this being the "solitary exception" among county of-ficials in matters of compensation.[66] It may be said, by way of illustration, that the average compensation for county superintendents in 1872 was a little more than $550 per annum, while for 1873 it had risen to something more than $600, but from this amount the incumbent must pay his traveling expenses. There were probably forty men at that time giving some attention to supervision in towns who were paid more than the ninety-nine county superintendents. Moreover, the former had few schools as compared to the 9000 with 350,000 pupils under county superintendents. It was pointed out also that the secretaries and treasurers were paid not less than $15,000 more than all the county superintendents. The superintendent of Fayette County had $600 yearly for his entire time, while the several secretaries and treasurers received over $1180. That is to say, there was unfair discrimination between those performing clerical and those exercising supervisory functions.[67]

Thus, for fifteen years the office of county superintendent was really a temporary institution, and a disposition to abolish it was frequently manifested. One may trace this opposition to its ultimate source in the old independent district system and to the inherent unwillingness to submit to any outside interference or even oversight. About 1872 the opposition to the office of county superintendent reached its height.

VI

COUNTY SUPERVISION: OPPOSITION AND RECOGNITION

DURING the session of the Fourteenth General Assembly (1872) at least three bills affecting the county superintendent were introduced. The first of these proposed to abolish the office; but the House committee on schools, of which Mr. J. G. Newbold was chairman, recommended that "it do not pass." The same recommendation was made relative to the other two bills — one of which defined the duties and the other changed the time of election.[68] Among reasons presented for such legislation were the assertions that the office was doing no good; that it cost more than it was worth; that the persons selected for the office were of no benefit to the schools; and that the office was too often filled by "politicians and incompetents".

In order to reveal the facts and also to counteract the effect of such declarations the actual work of the county superintendent was reviewed more than once in publications — immediately following these efforts to destroy the office. If school supervision was of value in a city, if Davenport or Des Moines or other districts could pay two or three thousand dollars a year for supervision, why, it was asked, could not Scott County or Polk County pay at least half as much for the supervision of a hundred and fifty or more schools, one-fourth of which at least were taught annually by persons without any experience? Against the charge of incompetency and worthlessness there was arrayed the best of authority and abundant proof of conscientious work in the counties of the State. It was declared that as a class county superintendents were "earnest, devoted men, giving their time, their talents, their whole energies" to the raising of standards in the schools. Moreover, they were working "with poor pay, without honor, with little credit," to create a more vital interest in education by explaining difficulties, by advising, and by settling disputes. The insinuations made against such men were denounced as most unjust, since the facts would reveal the truth that "instead of odium, they deserve the highest praise."[69]

But the office of the county superintendent was to receive further criticism and definition before it could be recognized as having reached a permanent status. In 1875 the State Teachers' Association recommended, through a committee composed of Mr. Samuel J. Buck, Mr. Edwin R. Eldridge, and Mr. C. P. Rogers, that the county superintendent be appointed by a county board of education constituted from the presidents of the "school boards in the county", and that aspirants to the office be required to hold a State certificate or diploma.[70] This was indicative of the sentiment then forming and which was destined at some time to be written into the laws.

Again, in 1878 an attempt was made to reduce the compensation to $100 annually, and to repeal the provision relative to visiting schools — in fact to virtually abolish the office. It was on this occasion that Henry Sabin, then superintendent of the Clinton schools, took up the defence of the office and sought to point out reasons for its continuance and support. It was shown that during the year 1877 ninety-nine institutes, attended by nearly 12,000 teachers, had been managed by these county officers, and that 17,000 certificates had been issued in the course of which more than 22,000 persons had been examined, each of whom prepared manuscripts upon nine subjects. Moreover, during the same year 13,000 visits were made to schools, while 400 educational meetings were called in different parts of the State. It was useless, therefore, to argue that this office was a sinecure — as it was later declared to be by a Republican convention in Johnson County. That the office was expensive was clearly false, since not a single taxpayer would notice the difference if it were abolished. That incompetent men were sometimes elected was no argument against the office itself. Indeed, the actual benefits conferred upon the 6600 new teachers entering the work that year — whose only source of assistance was through this officer — was sufficient reason for his being retained in the school system.[71]

The "lake conventions" of county superintendents — State meetings which were held during the summer for several years — are worthy of special

7

notice. At one of these, held at Clear Lake in 1879, the interest was centered upon a case before the Supreme Court which would affect the authority of every superintendent. Since all were interested in the outcome it was proposed that all should contribute to the expense, and to that end pledges were secured. The case in question, *Bailey vs. Ewart,* came up to the highest court from Delaware County, where it appears a decision had been rendered against the county superintendent, Mr. R. M. Ewart. The matter involved the refusal of the superintendent to grant a certificate; whereupon mandamus proceedings were instituted to compel him to do so. The Supreme Court found for the county officer and thus materially strengthened the authority of all superintendents.[72]

Again in July, 1883, an eight day session of this same organization was held at Lake Okoboji, at which principles were adopted which served not only for their own guidance and control, but which were also of State-wide importance. It was the opinion of the superintendents that through established regulations provision should be made for permanent certificates; that supervision when efficient should protect the schools from the incompetent instructor; that the growth and progress of scientific teaching was gratifying; that the normal institute was never more needed than at the present time; that the school laws were so confusing and contradictory that an entire revision was absolutely essential; and that a township unit and only two funds instead of three were desirable provisions. And further, since the *Code of 1873* made no provision for the care of district records, it was recommended that a law requiring their deposit with the county superintendent be enacted.

Two years later (in July, 1885) another assembly convened at Lake Okoboji. The meeting, it appears, had now grown to include others than county superintendents, and the entire session of a week was devoted chiefly to the new educational movements. A committee, which had been previously appointed, consisting of superintendents J. S. Shoup, J. R. Elliot, and Jacob Wernli, reported on a course of study for ungraded schools; but definite action on this matter was postponed until a year later, and in the meantime copies of the course were to be submitted to each county superintendent.[73]

The determined effort on the part of some to abolish this office did not cease, however, with the action in 1878, for again in 1880 a bill was brought before the General Assembly to prohibit the visiting of schools by the county superintendent. It was at this time that a friend of the office inquired why a measure was not introduced to prohibit legislative committees from visiting the State institutions. Soon after the introduction of the bill a joint meeting of five hundred teachers and friends of education in southeastern Iowa condemned by unanimous vote the bills before the General Assembly which aimed at the abolition of the office or the reduction of the already wretchedly small compensation.

It was in the later eighties that a number of suggestions were made which seem to be indicative of a changing attitude toward the office of county superintendent and of supervision in general. Thus, four years as a term limit was recommended by the superintendents' section of the State Teachers' Association; city superintendent Robert G. Saunderson of Burlington advised that the incumbent should be selected by representatives of the several boards of education rather than by the people; bills were introduced in the legislature of 1890 providing for definite qualifications, equal at least to the standard of a State certificate; Dr. William T. Harris, United States Commissioner of Education, made it known that he recognized this office as the most important of all supervisory agencies, since it was concerned with the training of three-fourths of all the people; a longer term was declared to be desirable that policies might become more permanent, whether the office was filled by election or appointment; and there was a growing disposition to recognize the futility of complete supervision by one individual in a large county.

It was clearly shown by Mr. Rufus H. Frost, superintendent of Cass County, that no one could "personally supervise the workings of the schools in the most profitable way, and also attend to the duties of the office." In his county 178 teachers were employed in an area of 576 square miles. To visit each one but once a year it was necessary to drive 2300 miles. It was pointed out that in a city with the same number of teachers the authorities would not only employ a superintendent but probably an assistant also; and no one would consider such action as extravagant. It was suggested, therefore, that power be given to the boards of "two, three or four townships" to employ jointly a supervisor of schools who should be accountable to the superintendent in the county. Mr. Frost concluded with the declaration that it was no longer a question of the abolition of the county superintendent but rather a question of what should be done to increase his powers and efficiency.[74]

While Mr. Frost was preparing his recommendations there was being tried in another part of the State an actual application of his theory. The township of Fairfax in Linn County had employed Mr. C. E. Bonner as principal of the township high school and also as supervisor of the district schools in the township. The arrangement, it was said, was "working finely"; and the county superintendent, Mr. Frank J. Sessions, observed that two other townships were considering the plan. It appears that an appropriation of $100 was made for supervision; and the teacher best qualified for the work having been selected arranged his terms so that a month or more would be available for the inspection of other schools within the township. During the time he was engaged with his own school, moreover, he was required to advise teachers and directors and attend to details which the county superintendent must of necessity omit in his hurried visits. Clearly, this township assistant was serving in the capacity recommended by Superintendent Frost and no legislation had been necessary to make it an accomplished fact.[75]

After 1890 there were fewer references to the office as being unnecessary. On the other hand, there was frequent insistence upon it as "indispensable to our school system" if maintained at a standard which would prevent its falling into the hands of "inexperienced and incompetent persons." The school master's round table of eastern Iowa in 1894 requested the executive committee of the State Teachers' Association to provide a place on the annual program for a full discussion of questions bearing upon the selection and the tenure of the county superintendent. Again, it was said that the office was "better understood and appreciated each year"— so much so that party lines were often ignored, and there appeared to be no further question as to its permanency. But the problems of efficiency and the demand for higher qualifications were yet unsolved. In the opinion of Superintendent Sabin in 1895 there was some doubt as to the advisability of molesting the direct control of the office by the people through elections. The term, nevertheless, should be extended to not less than four years; at the same time, if the example of other States was indicative of tendencies, a specialist should be selected for the supervision of the rural schools.[76]

A bill providing specified qualifications for the office passed the House in 1892, but it was indefinitely postponed in the Senate. Superintendent Knoepfler had recommended three years of teaching experience as a minimum, two of which should be consecutive, and all within the five years immediately preceding the election. It was his opinion that the incumbent should come directly from the school room into this work. Nor would it be considered too extreme to require a diploma from some institution legally empowered to grant degrees. Moreover, these standards were said to be quite generally approved by the county superintendents then in office. It may be said that an amendment to the bill as proposed by the committee of the House in 1892 contained these words: "Or who has not received the diploma of a University, College, or High School, approved by the State Board of Examiners, or who has not had twenty-seven (27) months practical experience as a teacher in the public schools of Iowa."[77] This amendment was scarcely in line with the recommendations previously made, but it may have been necessary to secure the consideration of the bill.

The great waste due to frequent changes in the administration of the office of county superintendent was recognized and deprecated, yet no proposed remedy seemed to be agreeable to those who were most responsible for existing conditions. For instance, in 1894 there were forty-nine changes in the ninety-nine offices; in 1896 there were forty-one such changes; in 1898 there were over forty; and in 1900 there were forty-six. At the same time, it was pointed out that city superintendents were retained for periods ranging from six to twenty years.

There were other influences also that militated against the efficiency of the office of county superintendent. The clerical duties which might be performed by a clerk, and the methods of conducting examinations and issuing certificates which should be cared for by an examining board, were cited as cases in which a false idea of economy was responsible for waste. Under these circumstances it was not surprising that Superintendent Barrett should recommend the selection of the county superintendent by a committee appointed by the judge of the district court or board of supervisors "from among the presidents of school boards within the county"; and that examinations should be held quarterly and two persons appointed to aid in conducting the same.[78]

That there were different opinions as to what constituted efficiency or a practical effort to meet the requirements of the office is clear. A superintendent reported in 1897 that he had visited twenty schools, held no educational meeting, had no active members in the reading circle course, and drew a salary of $1250. At the same time another superintendent had visited one hundred sixty-five schools, held thirty-nine educational meetings, enrolled one hundred sixty teachers in the reading circle course, and drew a salary of $1200. That both of these reports were from men seems certain, since it was declared without qualification that "women have uniformly filled this office with a painstaking conscientious fidelity to duty which has rendered their work of great benefit to the schools under their charge."

It should be said that Iowa was the first State in which a woman was appointed or elected to the office of county superintendent. In 1869 Miss Julia C. Addington was appointed to fill a vacancy in the office in Mitchell County, and thereafter was elected for the next full term.[79] The increase in the number of women holding the office since that time is of interest. In 1870 there was but one; in 1872 there were three; in 1874 there were five; in 1876 there were ten; in 1878 there were seven; in 1880 there were five; in 1882 there were nine; in 1884 there were eleven; in 1886 there were ten; in 1888 there were eight; in 1890 there were fourteen; in 1892 there were twelve; in 1894 there were thirteen; in 1896 there were fifteen; in 1898 there were eleven; in 1900 there were fourteen; in 1902 there were seventeen; in 1904 there were eighteen; in 1907 there were twenty-nine; in 1909 there were thirty-one; in 1911 there were forty-six; and in 1913 there were fifty-nine. That is to say, at the last election, more than half of the county superintendents chosen were women.

The duties devolving upon this office were steadily increasing during these years, even when efforts were being made to abolish it or to increase the qualifications of candidates. For example, in 1874, the law required a normal institute to be held in each county, for which the superintendent must provide not only the instruction but also the financial management; in the same year he was made the responsible director of industrial exhibitions which independent or other districts might hold; in 1878 he was made the arbitrator in case boards disagreed as to the place of a pupil's attendance; in 1882 he was required to see that school boards observed the law relative to the planting of trees, and in the same year the duty of reporting all feeble-minded children to the institution prepared for their care was assigned to him; and in 1900 the provision of the law relative to county uniformity in text-books required him to care for the book supply and its distribution among the depositaries.[80]

Although the office of county superintendent was created in 1858 the compensation was a source of contention and dissatisfaction until it was finally fixed at a minimum of $1250 in 1902. Previous to this provision had been made, for a short time only, for certain allowances in attendance upon meetings called by the Superintendent of Public Instruction, while more recently a fixed maximum amount for the expenses incurred in visiting schools has been established by law. Thus, a long deferred action has provided a compensation quite different from that of former days when payment, insignificant in amount, was made according to a per diem and when a sworn statement must be submitted to the governing authority with the prospect, in many instances, of less than the full allowance.

With the establishment of a minimum compensation it was certain that the qualifications would at some time be increased. Although the requirements had been revised in 1898 and made equivalent to a two-year certificate, by the certificate law approved in 1906 they were fixed at a minimum of the three-year or a first grade certificate as defined therein. Finally, in 1913, with the change from election by the people to appointment by a convention of school officers, the qualifications of the county superintendent after September 1, 1918, shall include "a regular five year state certificate or life diploma" and not less than five years experience in teaching or supervision. At the same time the amount of compensation after September 1, 1915, was established at the minimum of $1500, with expenses for attending meetings called by the Superintendent of Public Instruction as heretofore as well as for those incurred in the performance of duties within the county — subject to the approval of the county board of supervisors.[81]

That the office of county superintendent was for so many years held as an unnecessary institution and that its duties for a long period were regarded as subordinate to every other county function may be accounted for, it appears, through the arrangement of independent districts adopted in the early organization of the schools. Furthermore, counties were of such an extent that effective results, taking the State as a whole, were practically impossible until a more friendly attitude was manifested. The old independent district idea was so firmly established that any supervision seemed like an interference with democratic prerogatives. Then, as the more or less close supervision exercised by town principals or city superintendents became more prominent, there was a continual withdrawal from the rural schools of

the best teachers who entered the graded systems;
for those who were prepared by scholarship found
ready advancement under such supervision.   Such
losses tended to increase the difficulties of the county
superintendent, while the increasing clerical duties
and the legislation affecting visitation and compensation were almost annually causing greater confusion as to his exact status.   Under the latest
provisions, however, the office has been given more
permanency, a greater degree of professional standing, and a more adequate compensation.

VII

TOWN SUPERVISION: AN ORIGINAL MOVEMENT

THE laws of Iowa nowhere provide for a town or city superintendent of schools as such; nor is there any statutory definition of the duties devolving upon such an executive whereby he may be distinguished from a supervising principal. It is therefore customary in the Iowa educational directory to list these collectively, the title being apparently a matter of small significance. There is, however, a choice of terms where the larger high schools are maintained and where such institutions have a separate organization removed from any elementary school, or where a principal of a high or of a ward school is held responsible to a superior officer for its entire control. This does not preclude the work of instruction which might be performed by a superintendent, for it can not be said in this State that a superintendent is one who gives all his time to the work of supervision. Nor is it possible to fix upon a definite district population or enrollment in seeking a classification; for the actual conditions would reveal a superintendent giving all his time to oversight in districts of much less population than in others where the supervising officer was teaching to some

93

extent. In this chapter on the supervision of town schools, therefore, no distinction is made.

By the Board of Education at their first session in December, 1858, through an act which amended the law of the General Assembly of March 12th provision was made for "graded or union schools wherever they may be necessary", and the district board was authorized to select, if occasion should require, a person who should have the "general supervision" of the schools in the district. But this refers to the township in the first instance, and it is only through another statute that it came to apply to separate town districts which should have "the same general powers" as boards in township districts. Thus, a supervising agency was authorized, the nature of which rested entirely, as at the present day, upon local regulations adopted by the governing board.[82]

As mentioned above, there were in 1872 but seven men giving all their time to public school supervision in the towns of this State. The appellation of superintendent, however, was frequently used when the three hundred others who were giving but part time were mentioned. Moreover, the two-fold official designation of "principal of high school and superintendent" was common. In 1856 Mr. D. Franklin Wells was principal of the Muscatine Schools; while the Union Schools at Tipton claimed a superintendent in Mr. C. C. Nestlerode. Davenport was the first to unite districts under a supervising principal, Mr. Abram S. Kissell, and the time soon arrived when all his time was given to supervision, and thus his title came to be distinct. At the same time Dubuque employed ward principals only — a policy which was maintained, it will be shown, until recent years, and involved the transference of some of the duties of a superintendent to the secretary of the board. It was in 1857 that Rev. J. T. Cook retired from the "supervision" of the Des Moines schools, although it is known that the school system as then constituted included a single building with a principal and four teachers.[83] In 1865 Mr. Thomas M. Irish was designated as "Principal of the High School and Superintendent of all City Schools" in Iowa City; and it was then declared that "experience has abundantly proved that the work of education is best pursued and its objects most satisfactorily attained when the supervision of the schools is placed in charge of a competent individual, who, for a compensation, is enabled to attend, not only to the general classification and grading of each school, but also to the minutiae; and for this reason the Board of the City Schools has created the office of City Superintendent." At the same time his functions included the "government and discipline" of the high school. One may note, however, a special function as superintendent, namely, the requirement that he should spend the hours from "two until four o'clock" on each Saturday afternoon in his office "for the purpose of examining pupils, conversing with parents, &c."[84]

In 1865 Mr. James E. Dow was "superintendent" at Burlington, but was chosen that year for the same work at Ottumwa — his salary being specifically mentioned as $1000. On his release from Burlington, Mr. J. A. Smith, "principal" at Mount Pleasant, succeeded him. It appears, however, that Mr. Dow accepted work in Peoria, Illinois, instead of the office at Ottumwa, and Mr. L. M. Hastings was thereafter appointed to the Iowa position. The Oskaloosa schools were then "under the superintendence" of Mr. J. McCarty whose salary had recently been "advanced to 900 dollars."

In 1867 Mr. W. O. Hiskey, who had succeeded Mr. A. S. Kissell, was called from the superintendency in Davenport to a similar position in Minneapolis. He in turn was succeeded by Mr. Wells A. Bemis, the grammar school principal who had served under him; but two years later Mr. Bemis accepted the supervision of the Rock Island schools, and was followed in Davenport by Mr. W. E. Crosby of Lima, Ohio. The same year Mr. A. W. Stuart, the superintendent at Marion and formerly principal of the Clinton high school, was employed as superintendent in East Des Moines; and Mr. Samuel B. McLane was mentioned as "supervising" the Keokuk schools.[85]

Again, an announcement issued by the board of the Muscatine schools in 1870 names Mr. Finley M. Witter as "Sup't of City Schools" and principal not only of school number one but also of the high school. In the city at that time there were four separate schools each with a principal; but it appears that the distinctive services of a supervisor were not yet recognized. The Clinton board of education in 1870

defined the superintendent's functions, which do not
differ materially from those of the present. Nevertheless, it is noted that while Mr. W. B. Howe was
the "superintendent" only one teacher was mentioned as of high school grade for a course of three
years. One may therefore conclude that the superintendent was giving part of his time to duties not
signified by his title.[86]

It was about 1868 that Mr. William W. Jamieson
became superintendent of the schools of Keokuk — a
position in which he remained for twenty-five years,
thus establishing an uncommon record in this capacity. During the same period, and possibly commencing at an earlier date, Mr. J. A. Wood was in charge
of the Clarinda schools, serving there nearly a fourth
of a century. Entering upon his work in Marshalltown in 1874 Mr. C. P. Rogers was for twenty-two
years recognized as an authority on questions relative to the management of a city school system. No
name probably will appear oftener in these pages
than his, since it was his province to lead in matters
with which these volumes are concerned. Going
from the State University of Iowa into the public
schools of Marengo in 1869, he was among the first,
if not the very first, to put into practice the individual laboratory work in science which had been
inaugurated at the University and adapted to the
public school. In 1872 he outlined "the duties of
principals" before the State Teachers' Association
at Davenport; and it was in this connection that reference was made to the seven men who were giving

8

all their time to supervision. Contemporary with these men was Mr. William Wilcox who had been employed as a superintendent or supervising principal in 1868 and who for nearly thirty years continued as a prominent figure in the State Association, finally concluding his public school work as superintendent at Atlantic.[87]

For long periods of continuous service in the capacity of a supervising principal one must turn to the independent district of Dubuque, where the names of Mr. Charles G. Kretschmer and Mr. Thomas M. Irish appear as early as 1859 and 1867 respectively. The former was the head of the Audubon school from 1859 to 1897. The latter assumed his duties in the district in 1867 and over the Prescott School in 1870 where he continues in service to this day. Mr. William J. Shoup, a master in his line, was also for many years a principal in the city of Dubuque. Professor Samuel Calvin, later the distinguished scholar and State Geologist, became a ward principal in Dubuque in 1869; and it was during these years of service that he conducted his special class in geology on each Saturday evening in the rooms of the Institute of Science and Arts.[88] As has been suggested above, previous to 1895 the city of Dubuque employed no superintendent, the ward principals being responsible directly to the board.

It was in 1868 that the office of city superintendent was created in Council Bluffs and that Mr. Allen Armstrong began his eight years of supervision in that place. Thereafter for twelve years he directed the work of the public schools of Sioux City until his death in 1888. About the same time — but beginning a little later as high school principal — Mr. Robert G. Saunderson was at the head of the Burlington schools. He, too, served his city and its schools for nearly twenty years.[89] For twelve years during this period Mr. Homer H. Seerley was superintendent at Oskaloosa, and from there was called to the presidency of the State Normal School at Cedar Falls. These were uncommon terms of service in a State which had not at the outset developed a system providing for a city superintendent. It may be said also that each of the three last mentioned superintendents has been president of the State Teachers' Association — the first in 1874, the second in 1880, and the third in 1884.

One of the most conspicuous periods of service which began about the same time as those just mentioned was that of Mr. Albion W. Stuart at Ottumwa, who, as stated above, entered upon his duties as superintendent or principal of the East Des Moines schools in 1867. After a short time at Des Moines he went to Fort Dodge from which place he was transferred to Ottumwa about 1874. Here he continued to serve as superintendent until his death in 1911 — a continuous service, one will observe, of about thirty-seven years. No other distinctly supervisory position in this State has been held as long by any one individual, although the instances already cited may be considered as extraordinary. One may add to these names those of Charles C. Dudley, who served at Maquoketa; John W. McClellan, at Marion and Vinton; John K. Sweeney, at Waterloo; James McNaughton, at Cedar Falls and Council Bluffs; Melvin F. Arey, at Fort Dodge; Daniel W. Lewis, at Washington; W. F. Cramer, at Waverly; Frank B. Cooper, at West Des Moines; O. J. Laylander, at Cedar Falls; and Dennis M. Kelley, at the same place; J. B. Young, at Davenport, and another J. B. Young, at Toledo; C. H. Carson, at Marengo, serving continuously for twenty-two years; L. T. Weld, at Cedar Rapids and Nevada; Jacob T. Merrill, also at Cedar Rapids; Joseph J. McConnell, at Atlantic and Cedar Rapids; W. F. Chevalier, at Red Oak and Muscatine; Amos Hiatt, at East Des Moines; Anson T. Hukill, at West Waterloo; Franklin T. Oldt, at Dubuque, and of many others who have given an impetus to the establishment of some standard by which city supervision might be recognized as a special work.

Nor should one fail to mention in this connection the first woman, Miss Phoebe W. Sudlow, to be appointed as city superintendent in Iowa. This position she held for some years in the city of Davenport. In 1876 she was chosen as the first woman president of the State Teachers' Association, being nominated with two others, Mr. Henry Sabin and Mr. Amos N. Currier, as was customary under the instructions of the Association. It may be noted further that the West Des Moines schools were under the supervision of Mrs. L. M. Wilson from 1884 to 1888, at which time she resigned and in company with her high school principal, Mrs. S. L. Morrow, determined to establish in Paris a school for American girls.[90] It should be said, however, that while women have not generally been employed in the larger superintendencies it has been common for them to hold the position of supervising principal. For example, Miss Lucy Curtis held such a position for twenty years at State Center.

About 1898 there appears to have been a marked increase in the number of those who were abandoning the work of supervision or were seeking a change in position. It was shown in 1903 that of the men so engaged in county seat towns for the six years preceding, not less than thirty-seven percent had left the work, while thirty-eight percent had changed locations, thus leaving but about one-fourth who were retained for more than six years. This may not have been extraordinary when it was estimated that ten thousand changes among all teachers occurred annually, but it stands in marked contrast to the long terms described above.[91]

In 1884 a city superintendent was defined as ''the chief executive officer of the board of education''; and for many reasons the most important functions of the board consisted in ''securing, keeping, and aiding an efficient executive at the head of the schools.''[92] Accepting this statement as authoritative it becomes clear that a large number of governing boards either had failed to discharge the very first of their responsible duties, or there was some greater inducement for experienced men in fields of endeavor other than those of the supervision of public schools.

In 1892 there were in Iowa twenty-four towns with a population of over 4000; in 1910 this number had increased to thirty-eight. If one may assume that this population represents an enrollment (varying from 800 to 1700) which warrants the employment of a superintendent who gives all of his time to such functions, and who possibly is assisted by special supervisors, there might be established some basis for differentiating the superintendent and supervising principal. On the other hand, if the population is reduced to 3000 or more, the enrollment then being as low as 500, there would be nearly sixty who would come under such a classification. There appears to be no authority for any conclusion of this character, and therefore no attempt has been made, as was suggested in the outset, to distinguish superintendents from supervising principals, of whom there are many hundreds.

PART II
STATE BOARDS

VIII

THE NEW CONSTITUTION AND THE EDUCATIONAL SYSTEM

UPON the organization of the constitutional convention in 1857 three propositions relative to educational matters were presented: first, the reorganization of the public schools; second, the withdrawal of the school fund from its distribution through small loans and its re-investment in some permanent securities; and third, a provision that would confine the State University to one place. Early in the proceedings, therefore, a resolution appeared which instructed the committee on education and school lands to make inquiry into the expediency of amending Article X of the Constitution of 1846 by providing for a Board of Education which should consist of ten or twelve persons, coming from different parts of the State, and who should possess the qualifications of interest in, and familiarity with the educational situation in this State. When selected they should be authorized to appoint a Secretary as their executive officer, who should be governed by such regulations as they might adopt. Furthermore, and this is noteworthy, when such an organization was completed the office of Superintendent of Public Instruction should be abolished.

It will be recalled that this constitutional convention followed immediately the report of the Mann commission in 1856 and the rejection by the General Assembly of the bill then proposed. Indeed echoes of the legislative action on that bill in 1857 are clearly heard in the constitutional debates centering about Article X of the Constitution of 1846. While all the interesting data which were presented in the arguments pro and con can not be reviewed in this connection, it is important that the reasons for such an innovation as a fourth department of government be summarized.

From the committee to which the resolution referred to above was committed there came two reports: first, a majority report in favor of a constitutional Board of Education which should possess powers equivalent in legislative capacity to those of the General Assembly; and second, a minority report differing from the former chiefly in subordinating this body to the General Assembly — that is to say, a board to be created, not by the Constitution, but by the General Assembly.[93] Upon this point the convention was divided. At the same time certain members were opposed to the creation of any such body either by the Constitution or by the legislature. The chief promoter of the proposed departure in the educational system, Mr. J. C. Hall, a native of New York, had been a member of the committee on education in the convention of 1844. To him more than to any other person the provision for a Board of Education, as found in Article IX of the new Constitution is due. Among those opposing the change Mr. James F. Wilson (United States Senator, 1883-1895), then a young man of twenty-eight, was conspicuous.

There were many attempts to reconcile the differences of opinion relative to the method of constituting this Board of Education, but these differences were so fundamental that all such efforts were unsuccesful. Some endeavored to show that the differences related only to the details; but it was clear that this could not be true. During the debates it was proposed to provide for a board of twelve members who should at the same time become the trustees for the State University and have general control over all the educational interests of the State. But it was pointed out that the proposed board would have no definite powers, such as would be conferred upon an independent body, and would become rather a ministerial agency, subject to the uncertainties of legislation. It was not believed by many that a board thus constituted would possess the necessary authority to make the public school system effective. On the other hand, by electing men from the districts — some sixteen as at first proposed — it was declared that the relation of constituency and representative upon such a board would establish a dignity which must ultimately result in permanency of organization.

Throughout the debate upon this proposed amendment sound reason was advanced for its adoption and for the creation of some means of independent legislation relative to education in the State. The majority, it appears, agreed that the legislature had neglected the problems of education and that some radical change was demanded. Indeed, Mr. Hall declared that he was acting in accordance with the wishes of many citizens with whom he had counseled. It was asserted also that the history of the legislation during the ten years just previous to 1857 was sufficient argument for the creation of a body with independent powers. It was shown, too, that the General Assembly had acknowledged its inability to meet the demands of the educational public when in the year preceding (that is in 1856) it had authorized the Governor to appoint a commission to revise the laws. Again, when the Governor had selected two eminent citizens of other States who were skilled in such work, and when they had made a carefully prepared report the legislature had failed to accept it.[94] It seems, then, that had the Mann commission bill become a law in 1857 the Board of Education might not have been considered in the constitutional convention — thus saving a great amount of time and avoiding some acrimonious debate.

Another element favorable to the amendment appears to have been the opposition to a continuation of the office of Superintendent of Public Instruction. But if the office were abolished the functions devolving upon it must be vested elsewhere; and so, to avoid the one-man power, a board of this nature would be acceptable — especially since through a secretary under its control, there would be an accountability which did not exist under the old law. In the original report of the committee provision was made for a "Chancellor" to be appointed by the Board, who should have jurisdiction over all questions that might arise under the laws of that body, and from whom an appeal might lie to the Supreme Court; but this proposition met with little favor. In fact the whole plan was attacked as the creation of an independent legislative body with a "Chancellor" of their own appointment to interpret their legislation. Nothing of the kind it was declared had ever before been proposed in the United States.[95]

While it was held that, theoretically, men qualified to serve on such a board would be glad to give their services for twenty days annually at a moderate compensation, it was pointed out by practical men that in all probability the persons best adapted to carry out the law would not be chosen. That is to say, the political factor in a general election would prevent such a choice. For, as some observed, those persons who had devoted their lives to the investigation of educational subjects were not accustomed usually to mix in political matters. It was suggested, therefore, that party questions be ignored in such elections.

Again, it was proposed at various times that the authority to appoint the members be delegated to the Governor or be made a function of the General Assembly. Governor Grimes, it appears, recognized the danger in popular elections, for in his biennial

message of 1858 he "presumed that they will be selected on account of their peculiar fitness for the
positions they are to occupy. They will bring to the
board their experience as educationists, and they will
be able to represent the true condition and wants of
every part of the State. They will stimulate the zeal
of the people in their several districts in behalf of
education".[96]

It seems quite certain that provision for a Board
of Education possessing full power to direct all the
educational agencies of the State, but organized
under the authority of the legislature, would not only
have been made a part of the Constitution without
extended debate, but it might have become in that
way a permanent institution and might have performed a notable work in the Commonwealth. The
very fact that the scheme was made as an integral
part of the Constitution, made it unchangeable without amendment; while the provision that it might be
abolished after five years was but inviting such legislation at the first opportunity. Doubtless the "five
year" clause was necessary in order to secure its
adoption. It is clear that the opposition displayed
was not so much against a Board of Education as
against the proposed method of its establishment
and organization.[97]

James F. Wilson was positive in his belief that
two bodies could not legislate on different phases of
the same subject without coming into conflict —
having in mind the fact that the General Assembly
would make appropriations in all cases. He com-

pared the relations of the two bodies to those provisions of the Constitution of the United States which had caused so much disagreement between the Union and the States. It was declared, however, by Mr. Hall, that the proposed veto power of the General Assembly would so control the legislation of the Board that radical differences could not occur. The principal object in view was the separation of the Board from the control of ordinary legislation so that educational matters might have that attention, which, it was felt, they had not secured and could not expect to have under the existing constitutional requirements. It was alleged further, and not without reason, that the minority report provided for ''no efficiency'' and ''no vitality'' and that ''it is just like what we have always had; and that is the reason given why we should adopt it.'' An appeal was made to the convention that it should not adjourn until ''a school department'' had been established.[98]

The proposition submitted was an innovation. Members were unable, therefore, to decide for themselves as to the action that should be taken. By some it was thought that while twenty days, fixed for the annual sessions, might be sufficient for the routine business the members of the Board should exercise supervision over the educational affairs of their district during the entire year. It was suggested also that they be empowered to establish such additional institutions as might be necessary to increase the efficiency of the schools in their respective sections of the State. For such services, and for visiting the different parts of the district, they should be compensated. It was finally agreed, however, that such provisions were not properly constitutional questions, but rather subjects for legislative action.[99]

The problem then before the convention was the adjustment of the legislative relations of two branches of government — that is, the General Assembly on the one hand, and the Board of Education on the other — so that one would retain the entire control over the financial part of the system, while the other would organize and promote the educational agencies. It was when this difficulty seemed impossible of solution that an effort was made to substitute a single section for the whole of Article IX as it now appears in the Constitution. The section proposed would have proved a more reasonable method of control, since it would have provided for a board with an executive secretary, which should control all the educational agencies of the State but which would have been organized under the authority of the General Assembly. Moreover, it would have compelled action on the part of the legislature and thereby satisfied the demands made in the convention.[100]

As originally proposed the Board would have included sixteen members; but owing to the accident of there being but eleven judicial districts and, as it appears, out of a desire to prevent duplication, the number was reduced to eleven with the Governor an ex officio member. He was to have a part in the discussions but no vote, although the veto power could be exercised by him as in the case of ordinary legislation. When the office of Lieutenant Governor was created and the committee in their final report made him the presiding officer of the Board, the veto power was vested in the General Assembly. Some fear was expressed in the convention lest the two ex officio members, the Governor and the Lieutenant Governor, would dominate the Board and thereby limit its independence.[101]

Nor did the experimental nature of this provision of the new Constitution escape attack. Indeed, the fact that its supporters had provided for its possible abolition after a given date was declared as evidence that they doubted its usefulness. Moreover, it was inquired "why try an experiment in the constitution of the State?" To incorporate details of organization in the fundamental law was declared to be foreign to the purposes of such an instrument. Nevertheless, to some any provision seemed to be better than the existing arrangement, and so they were willing to experiment, although it might be dangerous since there was need of "a change that will make a revolution in the present state of things". The public mind was not aroused on the subject of education, and the reasons for incorporating the provisions for an independent board in the Constitution were that it might have a constitutional standing independent of legislation and possess an authority that could not be destroyed by any legislative act. At the same time, however, the supporters of the amendment endeavored to show

9

that ordinary legislation prevented extreme measures on the part of the Board, inasmuch as all legislation initiated by that body might be "altered, amended or repealed by the General Assembly; and when so altered, amended, or repealed" could not be reënacted by the Board.[102]

The committee on education which had the matter under consideration was the largest of the convention, including one-fifth of the entire membership. Its chairman, Mr. A. H. Marvin of Jones County, urged careful deliberation, declaring that he was willing to "encamp in Iowa City, and stay until the first of June, if it is necessary, to perfect this [educational] system." There was a determined effort, as the debates show, to change the outlook for general education in the State. If the provision finally adopted by a vote of twenty-three to eight and as it appears in Article IX of the Constitution was not the best arrangement that could have been adopted, it can not be said that the constitutional convention was hasty in its action or insincere in its efforts to "revolutionize" the prevailing methods in school management.[103]

As finally constituted the Board of Education consisted of eleven members elected by the people of their respective judicial districts. Over this body the Lieutenant Governor was authorized to preside, while the Governor became a member ex officio. As provided by the Constitution the qualifications for membership were twenty-five years of age and citizenship in the State for one year. The term was fixed at four years, with one-half retiring every two years. Furthermore, after the first session, which was to be held in December, 1858, the General Assembly was authorized to determine their frequency, although not more than one session of twenty days could occur in any year except upon the recommendation of two-thirds of the members and a call by the Governor.

The Secretary of the Board of Education, appointed by the Board, was constituted an executive officer, and through him all laws as well as rules and regulations which had the force of law were to be "published and distributed". Finally, full authority was granted the Board to initiate legislation relative to "Common Schools, and other educational institutions" that were to receive aid from the school or university fund; and it was specifically required that provision should be made for the "education of all the youths of the State, through a system of Common Schools".

It will be observed that the Board was to "initiate" legislation relative to education only and in no instance to make a law appropriating funds. Indeed, the members were dependent entirely upon the General Assembly for their contingent expenses as well as for their compensation, which, according to the Constitution was the same as that of members of the legislature. This item of increased expenses in administration created some fear in the minds of certain members of the convention lest it endanger a favorable vote on the Constitution.[104]

IX

SCHOOL LEGISLATION UNDER THE BOARD OF EDUCATION

IN accordance with provisions of the Constitution and statute laws the Board of Education held its first session in the Senate chamber in Des Moines on December 6, 1858. It was declared to be "a grave and dignified body of men, who feel the responsibility that rests upon them, and who will not fail to meet the expectations of their constituents. The Lieut. Governor [Oran Faville] seems in his element in an educational assemblage." It was said that the members of the Board felt themselves much embarrassed, both by the action and non-action of the General Assembly. By its action the legislature had appeared to take the work of the Board out of its hands, and then by its non-action they had failed to make the necessary appropriation for the expenses of the Board. Again, more time should have been given for deliberation, the constitutional limit of twenty days being entirely too brief — especially for the first session. It was observed, too, that the law of the General Assembly (approved on March 12th) was viewed with favor by the Board and that they were inclined to perfect it rather than to remodel it in detail. Such action, if prudent, would

116

tend to insure their independence in future educational legislation —a result "much to be desired."[105]

Frequent mention has been made of the decision of the Supreme Court by which it was held that under the Constitution the General Assembly had no "primary power to pass laws providing for the public instruction of the state, until the board of education was elected and organized", and so the act of March 12, 1858, was "unconstitutional, and void".[106] In accordance with this ruling it became clear that with the exception of such parts of the law as related to school funds and school lands there had been no "legal school system" since the repeal of existing laws by the act of March 12th. The first need then was a "curative act" legalizing proceedings under the law since March 12, 1858.[107]

A petition, led by Washington and Cedar counties, was at once presented to the Board requesting the retention of the law in its general features. From Johnson County came a request for legislation relative to districts. Another petition from Keokuk County would have an act to compel a school term of nine months each year. These petitions are indicative of the recognition that was given to the authority of this body at the outset, although the Board itself made sure of its prerogatives by an appeal to the Attorney General for an opinion as to its status.

In the very beginning the members of the Board were divided upon the policy of electing a permanent Secretary, who should perform also the duties which formerly devolved upon the Superintendent of Public Instruction.   To substitute an officer selected by twelve men for one already chosen by the people was held by some to be entirely unjustifiable and repugnant to democratic principles.   Then on the old problem of districts there was also a division of opinion which continued as long as there was a Board of Education.   Moreover, it is apparent from the records that the Board consumed half the time allotted for the first session in an attempt to discover their real authority and to determine whether a new statute should be drafted, or whether the statute of the General Assembly should be reënacted.   In fact a new bill was introduced by Judge Charles Mason — which according to the opinion of the press was "a sort of mongrel", being composed in part of the old organization and the new system as provided by the General Assembly.[108]

Before the Board had adjourned at the conclusion of their first session some observations were made by the press on the blunders of the constitutional convention relative to the division of legislative authority.   Indeed, it was apparent that although the Board might provide the necessary educational machinery, the power to put it into operation was lacking.   Thus the Board might legislate wisely and outline a complete educational system, but every act would fall short of execution unless the General Assembly voted the necessary appropriations.   It was pointed out, months after the convention closed, that the object of creating the Board was to place educational matters beyond "legislative tinkering".   In the attempt to accomplish this, however, neither the Board nor the legislature was given authority to consummate its acts inasmuch as the former must initiate all educational laws and the latter alone could appropriate money. As early as December, 1858, there were suggestions for a constitutional amendment to remove this seeming inconsistency in authority lest, it was said, the educational system of the State should become more complicated and expensive than before.[109]

The members of the Board of Education were in doubt also as to their authority over the institutions which did not, as provided in Article IX of the Constitution, receive aid from the school or university fund. It was clear that the University was under their control and the public schools likewise, but as to their relation to the Agricultural College, then projected, there was uncertainty. Some were of the opinion that this institution should be included, while others were opposed to this view. Mr. S. F. Cooper, the member from the sixth district, declared that there was nothing educational about the Agricultural College and never would be, and hence it was his opinion that the Board had no jurisdiction. Mr. Connolly of the eighth district agreed with Mr. Cooper; while Mr. Hildreth of the tenth district was in favor of some action — at least the Board should make an investigation of the situation, for as the matter then stood he regarded the institution as a great ''leech'' upon the public treasury. While the language of the Constitution seemed plain, certain

members held that it would be advantageous for the
institution if the Board were empowered to act. It
was observed at the time that it was fully as essential that farmers have a special education for their
business as it was that doctors and lawyers be
trained for their profession. But whether this special education should be offered through an agricultural college or an agricultural bureau was a
matter of opinion. One member spoke at length upon
the necessity of a knowledge of chemistry in connection with agricultural pursuits. It was finally
decided, however, that the Agricultural College did
not come within the provisions of the Constitution
relative to the jurisdiction of the Board.[110]

Early in the session the Board had adopted a
resolution to the effect that ''the Educational interests of the State, including common schools and
other educational institutions which receive aid from
the School or University Fund'' were under its control, and therefore it should provide not only an
entire system of common schools but also ''such
other educational institutions'' as the future might
necessitate.[111] It seems certain, then, that the Board
would have proceeded to establish schools of divers
kinds to meet the needs of all the people had the
means at its disposal not been limited. Furthermore, the sentiment of this body as a whole favored
the unifying of the educational forces. But the opportunity to accomplish this end was lost because of
constitutional restrictions upon the agency.

During the closing days of the first session an

animated discussion occurred over the question of legislation on the use of the Bible in the public schools. It may be said that at this time the question was not confined to the Commonwealth of Iowa but had caused some stirring public comment throughout the Union. A resolution, which does not appear in the journal, was offered proposing to leave the matter to the people; but there were members who believed in "facing the question". Mr. Cooper declared that his constituents expected him to act in this matter. Judge Charles Mason was in favor of making the Bible a standing text-book in every school, but in no instance should one be compelled to use it against the will of his parents. The entire matter was finally disposed of in the act approved on December 22, 1858, which incorporated the sentiments expressed by Judge Mason and by Governor Lowe in that it prohibited the exclusion of the Bible from the public schools.[112]

Just before adjournment a memorial was submitted to the Board requesting an inquiry into the expediency of including academies and collegiate institutions in the State school system, but owing to the expiration of the constitutional term (twenty days) the committee on revision, to whom it was referred, was instructed to report at the next session. A careful study of the journal, however, reveals no report when the Board convened in its second session in 1859.

All assemblies which were called upon to formulate public laws, constitutions, or regulations in those

years were confronted with the race problem. The
General Assembly in 1857, having been divided on
this question, had failed, it appears, to legislate for
schools. The constitutional convention was wrought
up over the question. Nor did the Board of Education escape a consideration of the "colored youth"
in the public schools. At different times amendments were proposed which would have prohibited
the schooling of the negro, except in separate schools,
when any white patron objected. It was not, however, until the session of 1859 that the Board was
requested to pass upon the meaning of the law as it
existed. A communication from Pee Dee in Cedar
County (which does not appear in the journal) reads
as follows:

Dear Sir:—

Having much trouble in our Sub-District School with
regard to a Black man being crowded in with the white
children in opposition to one half of the inhabitants of said
District, therefore we call on the Board of Education for a
decision in the case as we think the law is not plain on all
points.

1st. Is a colored person allowed in a District School?

2d. How many hours are to be taught for a day?

3d. From what source shall the money come to pay for
making fires?

4th. What constitutes a legal voter in a District School?

As our school is doing little good, we would be much
gratified to have the Board say what shall be law. . . .

Signed G. FRAIN, *in behalf of said District*.[113]

Under the operation of the new law, considerable prejudice was aroused against the Board of Education previous to the session of 1859 — although the General Assembly had been chiefly responsible for the law then undergoing trial. It is evident that before the second session was held public opinion was strongly set against this form of educational legislation, and the hope was expressed that the deliberations of the Board would be marked by "prudence and a due regard for the great interests entrusted to its care." The good of the State demanded a fair trial of the law enacted in the previous year, and it was not considered wise to make any material change.[114]   It may be said that the deliberations during the twenty days centered about the report of the Secretary and the questions relative to the abolition of the office of county superintendent, the tax levy for school house purposes, district organization and elections, the expensive features of the school system in all its departments, text-books, and finally teachers institutes. While the law for public instruction was re-written it was not materially changed; and thus the hope that no radical measures would be taken was realized.

By the statute under which the Board of Education was elected, its sessions after December, 1859, were to be held regularly every two years; hence the third session did not occur until December, 1861. Previous to this time, however, there was agitation for its abolition, and a bill which would have had that effect, and which originated in the House, was promptly vetoed by Governor Kirkwood. He said in his inaugural address that under the Constitution the subject of education had been almost wholly removed from the legislature, and had been confided to a board especially constituted for that purpose. Since that body had just closed its second session (in 1859), wherein such amendments to the laws were made as seemed necessary, the General Assembly was advised by the Governor to interfere only in case of an "overpowering necessity" for so doing. Governor Lowe, also, in his biennial message of the same year (1860) had opposed the movement to abolish the Board and thus prevent a consistent attempt to carry out the provisions of the new Constitution. Likewise, Governor Kirkwood in vetoing the bill for that purpose said that such an act was in "conflict with the spirit, if not the letter of the Constitution." Such an act, indeed, was unauthorized and would result in great confusion.[115] The measure as proposed would have postponed further sessions of the Board until 1865, and thus an opportunity would have been given at a subsequent session (1862 or 1864) for the General Assembly to abolish it under the provisions of the Constitution.

It was, however, but a question of time when the effort to restore the control of educational legislation to the General Assembly would be successful. Public opinion on this matter in 1860 was revealed through the press, wherein it was declared that this part of the Constitution was regarded as an error, and a veto of a measure, as noted above, would but postpone the inevitable.[116]

The third and final session of the Board of Education was held in December, 1861. The period of twenty days was occupied mainly with the disposal of three questions: the codification of the school laws in force; the enactment of a new law which would have restored the independent district system; and the teaching of German in the public schools — one-tenth of the time being taken up with the discussion of the last named problem. To those favoring codification there were opposed those who advocated the restoration of the old independent district organization, although the majority at all times seems to have supported the new law as it stood. It was declared, indeed, to be the best law ever devised. Some thought that there was too much legislation, while others would consider the petitions and memorials presented and give them respectful attention. Governor Kirkwood approved the system established, but he would support necessary amendments. Moreover, there was a disposition to defer to the Secretary of the Board, Mr. Thomas H. Benton, Jr., as an authority on what changes, if any, should be be made in the laws.

The whole matter of organization, whether the district township should be retained or whether there should be a restoration of the former plan, was fully considered but failed to result in any change which would affect the township system with its sub-districts. It seems certain that, while there may have been dissatisfaction, the change desired was not due to any general complaint, for no petition of such a nature had come into the hands of the Board. The Secretary of the Board, who had been in all parts of the State, had not requested it; county superintendents in nearly every instance commended the law; and furthermore, teachers institutes and the State Teachers' Associations had given their testimony as to progress under it. It was pointed out by Mr. D. C. Bloomer, the member from the third district, that the bill before the Board would produce an entire change in district organization, and in fact would restore the system that had been tried and discarded. It was in this connection that Mr. Bloomer asserted that the law in force, namely, the act of the General Assembly of March 12, 1858, and reënacted by the Board of Education in the same year, was substantially the measure reported by the Commission of 1856, of which Horace Mann, the most able advocate of the common schools in the United States, was the chairman. The system adopted had been the result of his ripe experience, and in the opinion of Mr. Bloomer it was not the system that was at fault so much as its administration. It was the business of the Board of Education to correct these faults in the application of the statute.[117]

The whole matter relative to the teaching of German in the public schools seems to have grown out of a petition from citizens of Johnson County which was presented by Governor Kirkwood. To provide for such instruction a bill was introduced and ultimately passed, but not without some interesting suggestions as to its form. Originally the bill provided

that language should be taught on the written request of any director, but it was proposed to substitute therefor the words "upon the written request
of a majority of the electors" of any subdistrict, and
also in place of the German language "the German
or other language". The Governor objected to the
words "or other language", believing that the German was more extensively used in this State and was
almost indispensable to business success. On the
other hand, certain members would be liberal and
would treat all alike by including the language of the
Swedes and Norwegians and, indeed, of any other
people who might desire their own language taught
in the common school. Some members were so consistent that they proposed to include the Indians in
the western part of the State; while Mr. Perry, who
came from the district which included the settlement
of Hollanders at Pella, was determined that in their
case there should be no discrimination, although he
was opposed to the whole measure.

This was held to be a practical matter, and was
not to be considered a favor to any people but of
interest to all. At the same time it was shown by
Mr. Bloomer that no further legislation was necessary, since all needful authority had already been
conferred upon districts by the existing statutes. In
Council Bluffs — Mr. Bloomer's home town — Latin
was taught in one of the common schools. Why not
German or any other language dead or living? Then
it was shown by Mr. Perry that the bill as it was
proposed would allow a majority of the electors to

force the teaching of German upon a minority who
might be the parents of a majority of the pupils. It
was declared, too, that the common school was no
place for the teaching of any foreign language. Mr.
Viele, of the first district, was doubtful as to the
wisdom of this measure. It was his opinion that
"we ought to Americanize all coming among us —
that is our policy. . . . I hope the time will come
when we shall know nothing of the use of any but one
language among us in ordinary life."[118]

It is interesting to note that while the Board of
Education was endeavoring to draft a bill that
would provide for instruction in German a petition
came up from the settlement at Guttenburg requesting that the school laws be made more explicit, and
that they require the English language to be taught
in greater purity. The petitioners were not satisfied
with instruction conducted in broken English. It was
further suggested in the petition that county superintendents be penalized for granting certificates to
those who could not speak the English language and
give the sound of each letter and syllable.[119]

Before a conclusion was reached on the teaching
of German in the common school some opinions were
expressed as to what the term "common school"
comprehended. To some the common school was an
institution common to all who wished to patronize it,
and not necessarily a place where common branches
only could be taught. On the other hand, some would
extend it to include not only schools for all the youth
of the State in which the rudiments should be taught,

but in which there were also additional facilities which would carry the pupil "from the first lessons of an elementary education to the end of our University course." Such an extreme position did not go unchallenged. Mr. Chase, of the eleventh district, asserted that it must mean the ordinary school in which the great body of people obtained their education. One could not include, therefore, the State University which was at least academic in its courses.

In the common acceptance of the term "common school" it was believed to be beyond the power of the Board of Education to provide classic or scientific instruction. Moreover, the law required teachers to be qualified to instruct in the common branches, and this would not apply if German should be introduced. Nevertheless, the committee on revision prepared a measure which became a law on December 14, 1861. It gave the electors power to decide by vote as to the teaching of "German, or other language" in one or more schools of the district. All other branches, however, must be taught in English. As for instruction in these special subjects the teacher employed must satisfy the county superintendent as to his qualifications.[120]

There was other legislation relative to institutes, a State board of examiners, debts of districts previous to the new school law, and a department of military instruction in the State University. The act authorizing instruction in German, however, was probably the most important of the final acts of this Board since numerous petitions were presented from

10

different portions of the State requesting such legislation.

In 1864 Governor Stone directed the attention of the General Assembly to the expediency of abolishing the Board of Education. The period had arrived, he declared, when it was no longer needed. But if the Board should be abolished as recommended it would be necessary to restore the office of Superintendent of Public Instruction to perform the functions then devolving upon the Secretary of the Board.[121]

While the bill to abolish the Board was pending in March, 1864, it was amended in the Senate by a provision that the Governor should appoint the Superintendent of Public Instruction, but as finally adopted the General Assembly was authorized to elect this officer for the remainder of the biennial period. The bill elicited considerable debate. Its original provisions would have required the Superintendent of Public Instruction to travel about the State and to personally inspect the schools in fulfilling the duties of a supervisor of the county superintendents. This clause, however, was stricken out on account of the additional expense involved in its execution. But outside of the General Assembly the opinion was expressed that the time would come when the people would demand this very service. With the approval of the act on March 19, 1864, the Board of Education was abolished.[122]

Thus another experiment, conceived in the midst of stirring political events, yet having for its supreme object the creation of a complete educational system on broad lines, met with failure because of the division of authority, or because the provisions for its establishment were such that little opportunity was given to work out a well balanced system before the clamor for a change brought on a reaction. This is the common fate of innovations, especially in the field of public instruction.

X

THE STATE BOARD OF EXAMINERS

PREVIOUS to 1858 the examination of teachers was either a township function or it was dependent upon a local board of education. With the enactment of the school law of March 12, 1858, however, there was established a county board of examiners consisting of the county superintendent and two assistants appointed by him. The provision for assistants was made optional with the superintendent by the legislation of the Board of Education in the reënactment of the statute. Not until 1861 was there any State authority designated which should govern the licensing of teachers for service in any part of Iowa. In that year, through the influence of leading teachers and the recommendation of the Secretary of the Board of Education, that body enacted a law providing for a State Board of Examiners.

The official title of Educational Board of Examiners was conferred upon this body which consisted of the faculty of the State University with the "professor of the normal department" (D. Franklin Wells) as the chairman, the secretary of the board of trustees being ex officio the secretary of the board of examiners. They were required to hold one annual session of one week which should commence on the

132

first Monday after July 4th; but they were authorized to hold special sessions if necessary. All
sessions were to be held, however, at the State University, while in all instances the standard of qualification required should be equivalent to that of the
normal department of the University. The certificates issued by this Board were for life and good in
any school in the State without any further qualification; but the power of revocation was vested in the
Board. The members of this ex officio body were to
receive no compensation for their services in this
capacity, although the performance of the duty required at least one week in midsummer.[123]

On June 5, 1862, the Board of Examiners, or the
faculty of the State University, met, organized, and
adopted resolutions to govern examinations. It was
decided that all examinations should be "written",
and six series of subjects were adopted: (1) arithmetic, algebra, and four books in geometry; (2)
reading, grammar, rhetoric, and English literature;
(3) descriptive, mathematical, and physical geography, botany, and geology; (4) physiology, natural
philosophy, and chemistry, or advanced geometry;
(5) history, intellectual and moral philosophy; (6)
theory and practice of teaching, the constitution, and
school laws. Each question should have a specified
value and in each series the sum of the values should
be one hundred; while no one should be passed who
did not make fifty in any one series or who obtained
less than seventy-five as an average on the whole
number. This action of the Board seems to have

been in preparation for the first annual examination to begin on July 7th following, as the law required.[124]

There were two reasons given for constituting the faculty of the University an examining board: first, economy and convenience, and second, "unquestioned ability". Since the education of teachers was the business of the normal department of the University it was proper that the head of that department should be made chairman of the Board. It is noteworthy that the statute as enacted is almost verbatim the language of the Secretary of the Board of Education who made the recommendation, and in which he referred to other States which had established certain standards of qualification. This, indeed, was an effort to incorporate a professional element in the statutes governing the school system; but owing to the plan evolved the needs of the State were not wholly met.

At the first meeting of the Board in July, 1862, no candidate appeared for examination. It may be more appropriate to say that there were preparations for a meeting in case any one should appear. In 1863 there were three candidates, two of whom, Mr. Ben W. Clark of Scott County and Mr. Joseph McCarty of Mahaska, were granted State certificates — the first issued in Iowa. There were no fees in those days; but to reach Iowa City where all examinations were at first held required considerable outlay as well as some patience. With but three candidates and one of these rejected, it was clear that the examination was, as the chairman declared, as "*impartial* and as *thorough* as circumstances would permit." It was regretted that so few applied for State certificates, but unfamiliarity with the advantages of the law was held as a reason for the small number. The members of the Board were not fully satisfied with the act, but they hesitated to recommend any changes in 1863 after only two years of trial.[125]

While it was announced that these examinations would be written, as determined by the Board in June, 1862, it appears that they were partly oral, at least in later years.[126] One may inquire as to what influence this form (the written) had upon the county examinations of that period, since in those days it was not generally the custom to write examinations. For example, it was reported in 1864 that "several" county superintendents had adopted "the plan of written examinations."[127] It seems certain, therefore, that this method was inaugurated after the Board of Examiners had announced their plan. Again, the minute description of a written entrance examination to the new Des Moines high school in 1864 is suggestive of innovation. The committee, it was said, proceeded to examine in geography in the following manner:

Each applicant [for admission] was seated alone, and the printed questions placed on the desk before them. At a given signal they all with paper, pen, and ink, proceeded to answer what they could of the questions, not being allowed to turn in their seats or communicate with each other in any way whatever.

The observer was so convinced of the method's "fairness and utility" that it was recommended to others.[128]   It is quite certain then that the written examination was introduced at this time in different phases of educational work; and it doubtless was patterned to some extent after methods followed in the schools of the States farther east — notably those of Cincinnati.   Of course the announcement that a State board authorized to examine would employ this method was of itself more or less influential.

It was soon seen that to limit the State examination by law to one place was a great disadvantage; and so, in 1867 Superintendent Faville recommended a change whereby greater facilities would be offered teachers for undertaking the examination through its being held at other points in the State.   It was suggested then that a favorable time would be the meeting of the State Teachers' Association.   Moreover, the chairman of the Board should be empowered to appoint examinations in different sections of the Commonwealth and to call to his assistance qualified persons who were resident therein.   It was further recommended that the certificates thus awarded should not be based solely upon scholarship but upon actual successful experience as well.[129]

Although an effort was made to carry out these suggestions it was not so successful as to warrant the continuation of this form of examination; consequently one finds no provision for the Board of Examiners in the *Code of 1873*.   During the entire period of the first Board of Examiners — 1862 to 1873 — but seventeen persons presented themselves for examination, and of these eight were rejected. The names of the nine successful candidates are: in 1863, B. W. Clark and Joseph McCarty; in 1868, Wells A. Bemis, Phoebe Schofield, Ellen E. Johnston, Mrs. Tirzah F. M. Curry, and Jacob P. Lyman; and in 1870, Florella King and Anna M. Woodruff. It will be noted that more than half of these are women. But the men and women are divided evenly when the following, who were granted certificates by the Board on first grade licenses from other States, are included: Lavinia Davis, Josephine A. Cutter, Mrs. M. A. McGonegal, Mrs. Cynthia See, Miss A. C. Hollen, B. C. Hollen, W. E. Crosby, I. C. Lusk, Harriette S. Dickenson, Fanny Arnold, Hattie Coryell, Leonard A. Rose, T. H. Smith, James H. Thompson, Wm. F. Steigerwalt, Mary E. McBride, Benjamin C. Rich, Sarah F. Loughridge, Manily T. Brown and Samuel E. Beede. These came from the States of Massachusetts, New York, Pennsylvania, Ohio, Illinois, and from Canada. In addition to the persons named the graduates of the normal department of the State University up to 1862 were granted certificates for life upon graduation.[130]

This, briefly, is the history of the first State Board of Examiners. The statute providing for the Board was repealed, it was said, because of its "little value to the teachers of the state, and for the purpose of securing the enactment of one that should be more comprehensive in its operation."[131]   But following the repeal of this law no provision was made whereby any person could secure a State license in Iowa until nearly ten years later. Attempts were made, it is true, to secure such legislation but without results.

It was in 1874 that the State Teachers' Association, through a committee composed of Mr. Samuel J. Buck, Mr. Edwin R. Eldridge, and Mr. C. P. Rogers, recommended the appointment of a board of examiners to consist of the State Superintendent of Public Instruction and four professional teachers. This body was to have power to grant "professional life diplomas" which should be perpetual, and certificates which should be valid for "six, four, and two years"— all of these being indicative of a State-wide qualification.[132] In harmony with this recommendation a bill was introduced in the Senate in 1876 and again in 1878 providing for the appointment of the four professional educators by the Superintendent of Public Instruction for a term of two years. According to the provisions of the second bill they were to be authorized to issue life diplomas, good "until revoked", and certificates for five and three years. But these were not to be "free", as under the former board, since a fee of five dollars for the diploma and three and two respectively for the certificates was required. Furthermore, there was to be an additional registration fee of two dollars required from all applicants. All fees of whatever character were to be turned into the State treasury at the close of each session. There was also an effort

to accommodate the teachers in that at least two
examinations were to be held annually and not at the
same place; and when twenty or more expressed a
desire for an examination at a specified place, a
special meeting of the board was to be called. But
the proposed measure was indefinitely postponed,
although four years or more had elapsed since it was
first recommended.[133]

Governor Newbold had supported the measure as
recommended by the State Superintendent, believing
that some such law was necessary in order "to give
the occupation of teaching what would practically be
a legal recognition as a profession".[134] Moreover,
many of the county superintendents were desirous of
the establishment of some authority which would
relieve them of a part of the responsibility for the
certification of teachers. It was proposed by some,
as a measure of relief, that groups of adjoining
counties form a board of examiners composed of
the several county superintendents by which the
grading of papers might be standardized to some
extent, and at the same time the individual officer
might be saved "much personal abuse."[135] This,
it is clear, was but the first step toward county
uniformity which has since become an actuality.

Previous to the session of the General Assembly
in 1882 a petition was circulated among the teachers
of the State praying for legislation which would provide for a State Board of Examiners. The General
Assembly heeded this request and the present Board
was established. As constituted in 1882 the Board

differed from the original plan in having three ex officio members instead of one. The presidents of the State University and the State Normal School and the State Superintendent, with two persons to be appointed by the executive council were to compose this Board. It was provided further that one of the appointive members must be a woman and neither of them could be reappointed. Contrary to previous recommendations only two classes of credentials could be issued by this body, namely, a life diploma, and a five-year certificate — the fee for the former being fixed at five and for the latter at three dollars. In case of either diploma or certificate registration with the county superintendent before the holder entered upon his work was required. But there was no fee for this registration when the act was first passed.[136]

The appointive members of this Board for the first term of two years were Mr. John W. Rowley of the *Keosauqua Republican* and Mrs. J. W. Rich of Vinton; and the first meeting was held in Des Moines on Friday, October 13, 1882. All members were present except Mrs. Rich, whose attendance was prevented by a delayed train. It was determined at this preliminary meeting to hold the first examination at Cedar Falls on December 25, 1882, for State certificates, and for diplomas in the same week, provided five persons made application for the same. The second examination was appointed for the last Wednesday in March, 1883, to be held simultaneously at Des Moines and Burlington.

No applicant under twenty years of age nor one
having less than two years of successful experience
would be admitted to these examinations, while a
"certificate of good moral character" from the
county superintendent and two citizens of good reputation of the county in which he resided must be
presented by each candidate.   As stated above there
were six groups of subjects in 1862.   Now, twenty
years later, there were three groups specified; while
the standing required appears to be quite different.
State certificates would be granted on a general
average of eighty-five, but diplomas required an
average on regular certificate studies of ninety, with
eighty-five on all others — provided, however, that
neither would be awarded when the candidate fell
below seventy-five in any one of the group consisting
of arithmetic, grammar, history of the United States,
orthography and geography; or below sixty-five on
reading, writing, book-keeping, physiology, algebra,
botany, natural philosophy, drawing, civil government, constitution and laws of Iowa, and didactics;
or below sixty on geometry, trigonometry, chemistry, zoölogy, geology, astronomy, political economy,
rhetoric, English literature, and general history.
There were, then, twenty-six subjects on which a
candidate for a diploma must stand an examination;
while the first sixteen named above constituted the
field of preparation for the State certificate.   In the
first instance the preparation of questions was divided among the members of the Board, and it was
the duty of the member preparing the questions to

read the papers on that subject. After being graded all papers were to be sent to the State Superintendent's office for preservation and recording.[137] Thus the machinery of the Board of Examiners was set in motion, and since then its powers and functions have varied — with a large increase in recent years.

As announced the first examination was held at Cedar Falls commencing on Christmas Day, 1882, and closed two days later. Six candidates were present, all of whom wrote the examination; but three were denied certificates. The three successful candidates were Mr. W. I. Benham of Manson, Mr. Edgar T. Bedell of Applington, and Mr. Ernest R. Nichols of Charles City — the last named being in recent years the president of the Agricultural College of Kansas. At the two examinations held in March, 1883, at Des Moines and Burlington eleven applicants were present, only four of whom received certificates, namely, Mr. M. J. Pusey, Mr. A. B. Carroll, Mr. Oscar McKim, and Mr. Nicholas Messer.[138] Thus there were seventeen candidates within a year, whereas the same number had appeared before the first Board in a period of ten years.

After two years of trial Governor Sherman observed that the law appeared to be a good one, since it had a tendency to make a higher grade of teachers. Although not as many had taken advantage of the State examination as had been expected, that was no evidence of the unpopularity of the law, and therefore he hoped the statute would be retained. It did remain without amendment until 1890 when the

Board was authorized to issue State certificates to the graduates of the State Normal School upon the evidence of thirty-six weeks successful teaching. Furthermore, after five years of actual school experience a life diploma might be obtained upon the completion of a thesis prepared under the direction of the Board.[139] Again, in 1897 the Code contained an additional provision permitting the recognition of certificates and diplomas from other States and gave authority to issue special primary certificates. It will be observed that up to this time no provision had been made for issuing any special credential. Moreover, this authority was extended in 1900 to include music, drawing, penmanship, or other special subjects — these being valid, to be sure, in the one department only. Another function imposed upon the Board in the same year required the listing of books for public school libraries from which county officers should make selections.[140]

Some of these amendments were brought about, it appears, through the recommendations of a committee composed of President Seerley, President Schaeffer, and Mr. E. E. Blanchard, who were requested by the Board in 1895 to suggest needed legislation for the more effective working of this body. Their report recommended that the Board be given power to appoint a permanent clerk or secretary, so that the members might be relieved of details. This was shown to be possible without adding any expense for administration, since the Board had collected in fees an amount above ex-

penses sufficient to pay for such clerical service.
That is to say, the State of Iowa was making money
by requiring teachers to pay fees for professional
recognition, and by requiring that the heads of State
institutions take from their executive duties valuable time to examine candidates who could be disposed of as well by a competent clerk.   This
committee recommended also the legislation which
authorized the special certificate, and likewise the
granting of power to take the initiative in revoking
State certificates.[141]

By an act approved in 1902 the Board of Examiners was required to inspect and supervise institutions which sought recognition from that body as
being qualified to prepare teachers for the common
schools.   It was not until 1906, however, that the
long desired county uniformity plan of examination
and certification was endorsed by the legislature and
the Board of Examiners was given full authority
over the scholastic qualifications of all the teachers
of the Commonwealth.   It should be said that the
biennial report of Superintendent Riggs had presented this desirable action to the General Assembly
just previous to its enactment.   In this report it was
shown that there were up to 1906 but two kinds of
certificates obtainable, namely, a State license of a
single grade good in any district and a certificate of
the county limited by county lines.   Furthermore,
neither of these, under laws then in force, could be
issued except upon written examinations.   That is to
say, no recognition of diplomas or certificates of

scholarship from any institution was permitted after the repeal of Section 2630 of the *Code of 1897* in 1900.

Nor was there any authority by which the Board of Examiners could treat the certificates issued by other States with decent respect and thereby secure reciprocal consideration. Probably the most effective argument for the enactment of a law providing for uniformity of certification was the fact that it could be inaugurated without additional expense to the State, while the additional burden of labor would fall upon the Board of Examiners and the office of the Superintendent of Public Instruction. The next year after this general law became effective the Board was authorized to issue, under certain conditions, five-year State certificates without examinations to graduates of "regular and collegiate courses" of the higher institutions of the State.[142]

Acting under the legislation just cited the Board of Examiners prepared to carry its provisions into operation notwithstanding the fact that there had been no provision for expenses in organizing the system. There were also other difficulties to be overcome; and regulations governing the conduct of examinations were to be adopted. Nevertheless, after one year of trial it was shown that the advantages were all on the side of the new method of certification. It was fully recognized, however, that time would be necessary to carry the law into effect so that the changed conditions could be traced directly to its influence. Moreover, among the 26,000 persons

11

affected there would necessarily be some dissatisfaction; and pending the complete application of the
law some provisional arrangements might become
necessary. At the same time, it was generally agreed
among county superintendents that the single year's
experience pointed to the success of the plan.[143]

By the provisions of the law the Board was required also to devise some basis of classification for
the institutions which were to be recognized in the
granting of certificates without examinations. In
this, it was said, they found great difficulty in complying with the letter of the act; but interpreting its
intent they proceeded to arrange these institutions
in three groups, adopting regulations to that effect.
Eight items that should enter into the system of
standardization were selected: (1) class hours, (2)
faculty qualifications, (3) library facilities, (4) laboratory equipment, (5) endowment or means of support, (6) salaries paid faculty members, (7) number
of departments or chairs, and (8) the character of
requirements for graduation. Any college fully
meeting these eight points and a general definition
of an institution which should be entitled to recognition was classified as in the A group; one meeting
not less than five of these required conditions fell
into the B group; while one having satisfied but
three came under the C group. The last group was
declared to be temporary and would be discontinued
after a reasonable time to permit the institutions so
classified to advance into the B group.[144]

Such was the method of inaugurating the final

effort to provide a State recognition of the preparation of teachers without the traditional formality of an examination, or indeed the humiliating experience of submitting to a questionnaire on subjects that were entirely foreign to the purpose of preparation. Thus a recognition was given also to experience as well as to permanency in occupation, for the law of 1906 encouraged continuation in service and an effort to advance in grade. And this movement has shown its effectiveness while costing the State nothing, if not, in fact, acting as a source contributory to the State treasury. For example, for the two years ending June, 1911, 47,000 applications were received by the Board of Examiners, 2500 of which were for State certificates. For the labor in passing upon these papers the teachers paid $25,500; while the expenses were less than that amount by over $2700 — which sum was turned into the funds of the State.[145] Although in the beginning (and for probably ten years thereafter) advantage was not taken of the services of the Board of Examiners in a very large way, there were issued, nevertheless, during that first decade 170 life diplomas and 700 State certificates, which must have supplied some leaven to the whole lump. Moreover, there was a steady increase in the number applying for the State certificate.[146] Since 1900 there seem to have been few requests for the diploma; and these will in all probability grow less. The Board of Examiners came into its true relation to the certification of teachers when all necessary authority was conferred upon it.

PART III
TEACHERS INSTITUTES

XI
THE TEACHERS INSTITUTE

ORIGINATING in the city of Hartford, Connecticut, in the late forties, these assemblies of teachers, patrons of the schools, professional men, and citizens generally were first called "institutes" in the State of New York. They were not intended as a substitute for academic training, but were established as a supplementary agency to provide a brief course in the theory and practice of teaching adapted to the common schools. They presupposed, therefore, a well-laid foundation of knowledge acquired elsewhere.

It is necessary to differentiate the "teachers institute" and the "teachers association" very early in the history of education in Iowa, although it is apparent that they were not in fact so distinguished at first. It may be shown, indeed, that in some instances the association grew out of the institute, or that they were combined in a single session with a distinct procedure in each. As to the characteristics of these assemblies the following paragraphs probably will be sufficiently suggestive without further illustration.

Dr. J. L. Pickard, known so many years as Superintendent of Public Instruction in the State of

Wisconsin, as Superintendent of the Chicago schools, and then as president of the State University of Iowa, has written recently that the first institute in Iowa was held in Dubuque in 1849, being one of a series of three organized by the "Mining Region Teachers' Association". That is to say, the association provided for an institute in which certain of its members took part. Dr. Pickard said that he well remembered the event, and that Thomas H. Benton, Jr., a young man of attractive personality, was prominent on that occasion. This first institute in the State was a direct result of the first one held "west of the Great Lakes" at Chicago in October, 1846. The "seed sowed there by three men from New York sprang up in the Mining Region."[147]

The presence of Superintendent Benton at the institute in Dubuque and elsewhere may have influenced his declaration in 1850 that these were the most effectual means that could be adopted to increase the efficiency of the Iowa schools — although their practicability was doubted owing to the consequent expense. He therefore recommended a State appropriation of one hundred and fifty dollars annually for three years to assist in defraying the expenses of three such assemblies in the State at points designated by the Superintendent. Each of these was to receive fifty dollars to be applied as a majority of the members — that is, of the institute — might determine. By this arrangement it was estimated that all teachers in the State would be able to obtain the advantages of at least one institute in each of the three years; and a favorable opportunity would thus be offered each of them to present their views on text-books and methods of instruction.

As early as October, 1850, an effort was made to organize a "regular institute" in Jones County, when "several lectures were delivered, however, by gentlemen present". In the same year it was said that an "association of teachers" had been formed in Henry County, thus conveying the impression of a similar purpose in both instances. The terms "institute" and "association" were not definitely distinguished in 1850. Moreover, it is certain that the outlined "complete national system of instruction", as presented by Superintendent Benton on his return from Philadelphia, after participating in a national movement, placed the "institute" as a State institution where the State Teachers' Association is now; for he included the "district school, the normal school and the teachers' institute" in the States as contributing delegates to form the national organization.[148]

Although full information relative to the character of these first organizations is not available, a catalogue of an institute held in 1856 in Cedar County has been preserved. It was called by the board of education of the Tipton Union School; and five instructors are specified, who were to be assisted by the same number of lecturers. Mr. C. C. Nestlerode was the "Instructor in Charge", or the "conductor" as this individual later came to be designated. But the organization of this institute (under a form which continued for many years) included a president, vice presidents, a secretary, assistant secretaries, and finally a treasurer. The board of education, being chosen as a committee on arrangements, recommended "daily exercises" in the following subjects: orthography, reading, mental and written arithmetic, English grammar, geography, and physiology. Following this schedule the persons assigned to the special subjects entered upon their duties. Miss Sibbel Maynard conducted the exercises in mental arithmetic; Mr. William McClain in written arithmetic and grammar; Dr. Joshua Maynard in physiology; Mr. B. L. Boynton in geography; and Mr. C. C. Nestlerode in orthography and reading. There were daily lectures upon the "theory and practice of teaching"; while the subject of graded, free, and union schools was carefully considered. Among the evening lectures Dr. Maynard spoke on "Educational Advancement During the Last Fifty Years" from his personal observation; Rev. G. D. Porter spoke on "Moral Education"; Mr. S. Dewell discoursed on "The Teacher's Profession"; Rev. M. K. Cross talked on "Universal Free Education"; and Rev. S. Ritz discussed the "Co-operation of Parents with Teachers". Following these lectures there were discussions each evening on some educational subject. While this was announced as a teachers' institute and was clearly conducted as such, the attendance thereon included twenty-four teachers and nearly seventy "friends of education"— meaning of course the citizens of the community and of outlying townships, or of places as far distant even as Iowa City and Davenport.

Such was the plan of the mutually organized institute at the conclusion of which a constitution was adopted, providing for a county teachers' association, and permanent officers were chosen. The first meeting was appointed for February, 1857. This action, moreover, suggests a difference between an institute and an association. The former undertook to provide instruction in subject-matter and discussion on the same, while in the latter there was more formality in organization and the presentation of papers. Lectures were adapted to both. The custom of adopting a series of resolutions covering a great variety of educational wants or ills seems to have been established with the institute; for on this occasion, as for years after almost without exception, such are the resolutions appended to the proceedings.

No less than sixteen separate "reasons" expressing pleasure or regret are suggestive of the large place the interests of that time gave to the educational awakening in Iowa. There was commendation of the institute in general; a well conducted educational journal was demanded; the prospective revision of the school law (the Mann commission bill) was hailed with satisfaction, while it was hoped that the measure would contain a provision authorizing what was known to some older States as "union schools"; the pernicious habit of using tobacco was condemned; it was urged that all honorable efforts be used to induce the building of comfortable school houses; women were regarded as fully equal to men in performing the duties of a teacher; and finally thanks were tendered to the citizens for their "generosity in boarding all Teachers free of charge" during the session.[149] This institute was typical of many which were held during the period preceding the establishment of the statutory normal institutes. Legislation did little to encourage or limit in any way their action.

Superintendent M. L. Fisher at the suggestion, he said, of "many distinguished teachers" recommended in 1857 that a liberal provision relative to institutes be incorporated in the new school law which was anticipated from the General Assembly in 1858. The success attending institutes in other States as well as the conviction that all possible means should be employed to provide competent teachers were other facts which supported his suggestion.[150] For the first recommendation on this subject one must go back to the report of the Mann commission in 1856, wherein it was clearly set forth that "your commissioners could not deem the educational system of any state complete without a liberal provision for Teachers Institutes. This feature gives to the systems of Massachusetts and New York a decided superiority over those of other States, and from its highly beneficial effects as there displayed, every new State should be admonished of the propriety, nay, the necessity of its adoption." The recommendation of the Mann commission did not provide, however, for a complete organization but rather left the movement to originate with the teachers and to be encouraged by them. Moreover, the teachers should bear their own expenses, unless places where these institutes were held should agree to make the necessary provisions, while the State should appropriate funds for instruction and incidentals.[151] This report, moreover, is the source of suggestions offered later in support of legislation for institutes.

The general school law of March, 1858, made provision for institutes practically in agreement with that proposed by the Mann commission, since the Superintendent of Public Instruction was authorized to appoint a time and place for such an assembly when he was reasonably assured that not fewer than thirty teachers were desirous of it. It was in this act that the six days minimum session was established — a provision which remained unchanged until 1913 — while the Superintendent of Public Instruction was empowered to receive from the State Treasury not to exceed $100 for a single institute, the entire amount appropriated being $1000 annually. As amended by the Board of Education in December, 1858, the $100 should be forwarded immediately to the county superintendent, who was authorized to pay out the same "as the Institute [that is, the members] may direct".[152]

Under the provisions of this act the Secretary of the Board of Education in 1859 appointed fourteen institutes in as many counties. It would seem, therefore, that each institute would receive its pro rata share only of the $1000 appropriated, since the Board had no power to add a single dollar to the amount. The one remedy, that of recommendations by the Secretary to the General Assembly, remained and was employed at the first opportunity. Secretary Benton suggested that, in addition to a provision for an increased amount which the State should appropriate, the county judge be required to provide a place of meeting for the institutes. All such assistance, it was declared, was essential to the encouragement and training of teachers, although the Superintendent was of the opinion that it would be unnecessary "if the profession of teaching were as lucrative as it is laborious".[153]

It is noteworthy that the Board of Education at their second session in 1859 called attention to the fact that the reduction made in the salaries of county superintendents would make possible a four-weeks' institute in each county without any increase in the the total expenditure for educational purposes. The arrangement by which this could be accomplished was not within the power of the Board, and was left, therefore, for action by the General Assembly. Accordingly, the legislature in 1860 proceeded to cut in two the previous amount of one hundred dollars, giving thereafter fifty dollars to each institute. The payments were to be made as before for one such institute in each county, thus placing no maximum on the amount appropriated.[154]

As a result of this legislation thirty-four institutes were held in the State in 1860, and thirty-five in 1861. No agency, it was declared, had done more to promote interest and efficiency in the schools; and it was made clear that it would be agreeable to the friends of education everywhere if further encouragement could be provided. At the same time, some county superintendents reported that at no time of year was it possible to hold an institute without interfering with schools then in session. Indeed, it was said that some directors refused to permit the closing of the school under such circumstances; and so it was proposed that a law requiring such action be enacted. This demand met with the approval of the Board of Education, and at their final session in 1861 they enacted a law which enforced the closing of schools during institutes and provided for compulsory attendance before a certificate would be issued.[155]

Just before the adoption of the compulsory attendance act the teachers of Polk County had voluntarily proposed to secure the same practical result by their own efforts. At a preliminary meeting those present declared it to be their intention to hold an institute in the public school building on the West Side during the last week in March. Each one was charged to use all diligence in securing the presence of others in the county and thereby to aid in elevating the standard of education in the public schools. They pledged themselves, furthermore, to use their "utmost endeavors" to obtain pleasant homes, free of charge, for all who might attend, not only for those from their own community but also for any one in attendance from adjoining communities. It was proposed that Mr. J. L. Enos of Cedar Rapids be employed as conductor at a compensation of not more than twenty-five dollars for the session of one week.

The program of the Polk County teachers was carried out as proposed, lectures being given by Mr. J. L. Enos, Mr. E. D. Hawes, and Mr. Thomas H. Benton, Jr. Thus was demonstrated the application of the principle advocated by Horace Mann that the institute movement should proceed from the teachers themselves.[156]

It was about this time that the State Teachers' Association put an agent into the field to arouse interest in education generally, to assist in conducting institutes, and to deliver lectures at association meetings. It was the opinion of the leaders that this general agent, in conjunction with an efficient county superintendent, would "constitute a perfect machinery" for carrying into effect the free school system. There was nothing "legal" in this arrangement; but it was an undertaking approved by a voluntary organization which supported its agent through the contributions from its members.

While such a personal representative had been authorized at the annual meeting of the Teachers' Association none was appointed until the following year, owing to failure to make a schedule by which he would be continuously employed without too great expense for travel. A committee having the matter in charge proposed to arrange a circuit of forty counties in the eastern half of the State, so that institutes could be held successively in each according to statutory provisions. At the same time the State agent would thus be able to economize in time and distance. The scheme was planned perfectly on paper, but the county authorities did not coöperate. It was felt, however, that such an agent, if of the right type, could accomplish much for education. Mr. Lorin Andrews of Ohio, once elected to the presidency of the State University of Iowa, was pointed out as a person fully fitted for such a task.[157]

In 1861 the project was realized by the appointment, through the executive committee of the State Association, of Moses Ingalls, "a man of thorough education, a teacher of many years experience, and during the past year [1860] edited the Literary and Scientific department of the *Iowa Instructor*." He was required to give all his time to the work, and for his accommodation a plan similar to that mentioned above was devised and the coöperation of school officers solicited. That he entered upon his assigned duties with success is evidenced by the commendatory items which appear from time to time in the newspapers and the educational journal of that date.[158] But the efforts to secure an unbroken chain of institutes failed a second time, very few of the forty-four counties included complying with the request, for the reason, as it appears, that schools were in session a great part of the year. The agent declared that it was nothing but prejudice which pre-

12

vented coöperation, since there was no better time to hold institutes than under such circumstances.

The conclusions of Moses Ingalls relative to the manner in which these institutes were conducted were not flattering, for in his opinion but one purpose should dominate the session, namely, how to present the subjects taught. Methods of instruction and not academic work, he declared, was the true function of the institute. Having been continued in the office, he reported in 1863 that he had conducted sixteen institutes in which he had kept constantly in view a purpose to increase the number of graded schools, endeavoring on every occasion to show their superiority both in efficiency and economy. He had lectured also on such subjects as "Public and Private Schools Compared", "Ventilation", "Superintendency", "School Records", on "Reformatory Education", as well as on many other topics.[159]

Of the 8500 teachers employed in the State more than half, it was said, attended some county institute during the year 1863; and this was declared to be indicative of genuine satisfaction with the law requiring attendance. Whether the other half was excused for cause or changed their occupation is not clear. The State contributed in 1862 the sum of $2600 for institutes, and in 1863 over $3000. It was the opinion of the Secretary of the Board of Education that the instruction given was either by persons who gave all their time to such work or by practical teachers. The employment of the latter was preferable to what was called by Superintendent J. J. E.

Norman of Dubuque County in 1864, the *"fashionable mode* of conducting Institutes"*, by which paid lecturers occupied most of the time to the exclusion of "live teachers".[160]

That these institutions were appreciated by those for whom they were established is evidenced by their growth from year to year. For example, there was not only an increase in the number held but also in the attendance upon each; while favorable comment by the press of the State was not uncommon. During the year 1866 not less than sixty institutes were held in as many counties, with an enrollment of over 4800 teachers. In the succeeding year there was a slight increase, the total attendance for the two years in seventy-three counties being nearly 10,000, while the State employed in 1867 but 10,343 teachers. There were not enough teachers in fifteen of the counties to secure an institute, inasmuch as the law as amended in 1864 required at least twenty before an institute appointment could be made.

It is an interesting fact that on the basis of attendance, the State was contributing during this period sixty-three cents for the training of each teacher. Up to this date (1867), a decade since the school law had been enacted, 431 institutes had been held, there being twenty in 1858 and sixty-two in 1867; and for the attendance of 28,000 teachers during that time the Commonwealth had paid $21,600. There was no control, however, exercised by the State nor by the Superintendent of Public Instruction by which institutes might be properly supervised and competent individuals be recommended as instructors and conductors — a very desirable provision in the opinion of Superintendent D. Franklin Wells. It was his suggestion, moreover, that four counties be permitted to unite in a single institute, and that those employed therein be required to submit to a thorough examination by the proper authorities — presumably the State Board of Examiners.[161]

The county superintendent was the compelling force in securing attendance, since persons refusing might suffer the revocation of certificates or be refused one at the outset. Indeed, from one county at least it was reported that every refusal had met with such a penalty. While this was the extreme punishment, certificates were made to expire usually at the opening of the first succeeding institute, which would necessitate attendance thereon. Nevertheless, there was a uniform tendency to adjust the annual sessions to the needs of those for whom they were held, while a friendly rivalry seemed to prevail among the counties in the matter of attendance. In 1866 one hundred was considered a large enrollment for any county; and so, in November of that year when Linn County secured two hundred it was said to excel any in the State. Mahaska County with an attendance of one hundred and thirty-five was especially mentioned. At the same time, the Lucas County teachers had voted to hold two sessions annually, and to require an extra fee for their support. The county of Franklin also, by an agreement of the teachers, appointed a six weeks' institute to commence about the middle of September, 1867, while the law required but six days. The support of such an extended meeting must come wholly from the persons in attendance — provided the county authorities did not see fit to provide aid from the treasury. The Superintendent of Public Instruction appointed fifty-two institutes in 1867, and declared that in no State of the Union were more such meetings held than in Iowa, and in none were they more faithfully sustained.[162]

No institute during these years closed its session without recording in a series of resolutions the belief of its members on educational questions. From these expressions of opinion it appears that the legal term of six days was considered as entirely too limited for schools of instruction — four weeks being the most common period suggested. An institute in Muscatine County in 1867, composed of eighty women and fifty-two men, declared in favor of the recommendation of Superintendent Wells relative to institute control by State authority. Experience, too, should be considered in the granting of certificates; and salaries should be granted according to the grade of certificate held. Normal training schools were held to be necessities of the age, and personal influence should be employed in the effort to secure such institutions in Iowa. Davenport deserved much commendation for establishing an excellent training school in that city, and other cities were urged to do likewise. Compulsory attendance was deemed advisable; a State reform school was demanded; while approval was given to the recommendation that Congress fix an early date for the obligatory use of the metric system.[163]   These resolutions, moreover, are as distinct a feature of the early institutes as the enrollment or the instruction. They reveal much of the sentiment then prevailing in reference to education.

In 1868 a four weeks' normal school was opened at Newton in Jasper County under the supervision of county superintendent Mr. S. J. Moyer, and the instruction of Mr. D. Franklin Wells, Mr. Leonard F. Parker, Rev. E. N. Bartlett, and Mr. S. B. Martin. In this instance the county board of supervisors appropriated two hundred dollars for support — the purpose being to offer a thorough review in all the subjects taught in the public schools, as well as giving attention to the "art of teaching". It was Mr. Jerome Allen who asserted on this occasion that the "establishment of local normal schools" was a good sign, and thus the way was being prepared (in 1867) for a "Normal University such as Illinois possesses."[164]

During this adjustment of instruction and management to the needs of the several counties more or less opposition was aroused against institutes in general. This is illustrated by the comment relative to one held in Linn County in December, 1868, with Mr. Jerome Allen as conductor. It was declared that thereafter "much of the prejudice against institutes, previously existing in the minds of the people, was removed." Clearly the institution was not as popular in Linn County as in Lee County, where it was reported that there were present daily nearly a thousand persons, not only teachers of course, but "friends of education" as well.[165] A total of 12,000 teachers attended the institutes of the State during the two years of 1870 and 1871, while single counties enrolled two hundred and forty or more. This was regarded as indicative of a prosperous growth.

It was suggested by Superintendent Kissell that the large attendance provided an opportunity for the introduction of "school jurisprudence" which should become a feature of the institute course of study, as it had of the course in normal schools of other States. It was felt, indeed, that above all teachers should understand the civil relations under which they worked, as well as the "drift of recent legislation" on the general subject of education. While formal lectures might be provided, it was held important that there should be general discussion and class exercises in this course.[166]

About this time (in 1871) there were indications of a clear distinction between a "teachers institute" and a "normal institute". For instance, Decatur County had announced in 1870 a "normal institute" of three weeks and a "teacher's institute" of one week, while in the following year the former was extended to four weeks, the latter remained as before. Floyd County had a quarterly meeting of an "Educational Society"— which was probably of the nature of a county association. For wholesome inspiration Hardin County depended upon the normal institute at Iowa Falls, of which two sessions had been held under the direction of Mr. Jerome Allen. Jackson County inaugurated a system of Saturday institutes, apparently for academic instruction only; but later they were designated as normal institutes. The procedure therein was later adopted in the county institute, in which the instructors were to "teach the teachers, and not to tell them how to teach — were to give little of theory and much practice." During 1871 three of the instructors in this county normal institute were persons trained in the normal schools of New York.[167] Mahaska County provided in the same year a four weeks' normal institute conducted by Mr. R. G. Gilson and Mr. Amaziah Hull; and this was followed by the statutory teachers' institute of one week. A school called "select" was in session for twelve weeks preceding the institute in Ringgold County. This was a sort of summer school. As an experiment which was declared to be successful Scott County instituted monthly meetings which were characterized as local institutes, since the usual exercises included essays, orations, music, and discussion by teachers, school officers, and citizens generally; while the succeeding Saturday was devoted to a meeting exclusively for teachers.

Similar informal meetings were a feature of the local interests in Tama and Van Buren counties, although in the latter they were held during the school session, each teacher being "required to bring a class of his own school and conduct a recitation" in accordance with a previously arranged schedule. On such an occasion, it was said, pupils, teachers, and parents assembled together for the evening session during which a lecture was delivered. Such meetings were described as "auxiliaries" to the county institute. Again, a "normal class" was conducted in Wapello County during August, 1871; and this was followed by the week of institute. Such was the popularity of the longer session that a desire was expressed for its continuance in the following year. It is noted that President Richard Edwards of the Illinois Normal School at Bloomington was in charge of the regular institute of that year in Wapello County. Washington County, through its superintendent, Mr. Edwin R. Eldridge, provided a regular institute of two weeks duration in November, 1871, which was probably preparatory to the development of the strongest "normal institute" in the State. On this occasion the teachers were organized into classes for the purpose of exemplifying the "Theory and Art of Teaching."[168]

It was in 1872 that the normal institute established by Mr. E. R. Eldridge maintained an attendance of one hundred for a session of four weeks. Again, in 1873 one hundred thirty-five remained for two months; and it was announced that two sessions would be held in 1874 under the management of a board of directors and the teachers of the county. The features of the instruction in this county included "school organization, management, discipline"; while in the review of the branches taught "extra work on physiology, the new study" was required.[169] It is an interesting fact that this institute became a popular resort for teachers from far beyond the limits of Washington County.

It seems clear that the one week institute was fast becoming the exception at this time, several counties having extended, not only the time, but also the opportunity for more frequent sessions. For example, Clinton County was divided into five institute districts, in three of which a ten days meeting was held in 1873. In these a course of study for "ungraded schools" and the methods of presentation of the same were prominent. In Davis County also methods were of chief interest in eighteen township institutes during the same year; while a normal institute of four weeks was provided in Delaware County just previous to the regular session as required by law. It is of interest to note that Professor Jacob Wernli, "late principal of the 'German-English normal school' at Galena, Ill.", was employed in this normal institute. Other counties were adopting a similar plan, Mahaska being one in which the session was extended to six weeks in the months of July and August, 1873; while the county superintendent, Mr. E. Baker, would have the normal term not less than eight weeks, to be conducted by "workmen" and not by "theorists".[170]

Commencing with a voluntary organization for their own betterment, the teachers had continued to exercise some originality in providing for the means of instruction in the affairs of their own occupation, notwithstanding the limited aid granted by the State and the short period of a six days session. The situation was developing its own agencies to satisfy the demands, and, as it appears, forcing a statute for uniformity of action in all counties by the law of 1874.

XII

THE NORMAL INSTITUTE

It was not until 1874 that a normal institute was required in every county and that the compulsory attendance feature of the law of 1861 was eliminated. That is to say, the statute of 1874 provided that the sessions should be held at "such times as the schools in the county are generally closed", which was intended, it appears, to leave no excuse for non-attendance. It was this legislation, moreover, which established the fees of one dollar for each certificate issued and one dollar for institute registration which, together with the State appropriation of fifty dollars and whatever amount the county board of supervisors might contribute, should constitute the "institute fund" from which all expenses of the sessions must be paid. The management and control of these annual meetings devolved upon the county superintendent who was authorized to employ, "with the concurrence of the superintendent of public instruction" such assistance as might be necessary.[171]

That this law was well received by the persons affected is demonstrated by the generally increased attendance and by the large number who pointed out the advantages under it. There was a suggestion, however, offered by the State Teachers' Association, to the effect that the work of these institutes should be made uniform through an adopted course of study outlined for each year; and further, that the conductors employed should be commissioned for that service by the Board of Examiners. Thereafter the State should be districted and an authorized conductor be assigned to each district with a sufficient number of assistants to manage all the institutes in that district — it being understood that the county superintendent would become an ex officio assistant. No person, it was held, should be qualified for the office of institute conductor who was not the holder of a life diploma or State certificate in Iowa; and in all cases they should be subject, at the call of the Superintendent of Public Instruction, to attend a meeting of the Board of Examiners to plan the work for the several counties.[172] It will be noted that these recommendations presupposed the institution of a State Board of Examiners during the following session of the General Assembly, which, as is shown in a preceding chapter did not occur.

During the biennial period ending in 1877 county normal institutes followed a definite course of study prepared by a committee selected for that purpose, namely, Mr. Carl W. von Coelln, the Superintendent of Public Instruction, Mr. J. W. Stewart, representing the county superintendents convention, and Mr. C. P. Rogers, representing the association of principals and city superintendents. Two State normal institutes, composed of conductors, instructors, and county superintendents, were also held within these

two years. Since the law had become effective the
growth in these institutes in attendance was shown
in 1877 to have been as follows: 6774 in 1874; 7579 in
1875; 9548 in 1876; 11,929 in 1877. During the same
time the expenditures had increased from about
$16,000 in 1874 to over $33,000 in 1877. Of these
amounts the State contributed $50 to each county,
while the county appropriations had dropped from a
total of $3000 in 1874 to $335 in 1877. Thus it appears that the teachers provided almost the entire
support. It is not surprising, then, that doubt was
expressed whether "equal results have ever been
reached for so little outlay" on the part of the
public. It is interesting to note further that the
attendance in proportion to the number engaged in
teaching was greater than at any time under the old
compulsory institute attendance law.[173]

The State normal institute was an important
factor during the seventies or until it was merged in
1879 with the State Teachers' Association. Some of
its sessions have already been referred to, but an
extraordinary occasion brought its members together in July, 1878, at Iowa City. By action of the
University faculty the institute was invited to take
advantage of the summer school of science inaugurated by the institution for a session of two weeks.
Perhaps this session might be called a joint association or convention of the State institute, the association of city superintendents and principals, the
county superintendents, and the summer school of
science. Each of these groups provided an inde-

pendent program, but with the institute alone is this chapter concerned.

Superintendent Daniel W. Lewis of the Washington (Iowa) schools officiated as chairman, while Principal Leonard A. Rose of Davenport performed the duties of secretary. Professor Nathan R. Leonard opened the program with a consideration of the "Metric System" in relation to its presentation in county institutes. "Reading" was the subject assigned to Mr. J. R. Bowman of Davenport; while Dr. Riley of Jefferson demonstrated the instruction in physiology through concrete examples, using the eye of an ox as dissecting material. This subject was further discussed by Mr. Homer H. Seerley of Oskaloosa. The chief exponents of didactics were Mr. James H. Thompson of Des Moines and Mr. Henry Sabin of Clinton, each of whom was a recognized authority in that field. Mr. Thomas Irish of Dubuque had the topic of penmanship for special treatment; while Mr. William J. Shoup, from the same city, discoursed on grammar, commenting upon the institute course in that subject as it had been presented by the committee on course of study. Nor should one fail to note that on the last day of this institute, which was July 4th, the veteran institute worker, Mr. Jonathan Piper, then of Chicago, was called upon for a "Fourth of July Oration". He declared in his response that the creation of citizens was begun in those neglected portions of the public school system which were included in the primary departments.[174]

In his inaugural address as president of the State Teachers' Association it was asserted by Mr. Henry Sabin in 1878 that the State normal institute should be planned to meet the needs of normal instructors, to become in fact a real school of instruction for such persons and to be made a professional school in every particular where general principles should be taught and not only facts of local importance; and it was on this occasion that Professor R. Graham, institute manager for Wisconsin, addressed the teachers upon his special work. The Association, moreover, went on record in approval of the sentiment expressed by its president in declaring that the State normal institute should control and direct the institute work in the State, and a committee was appointed to arrange for the next meeting of this organization. Notwithstanding the fact that annual meetings were provided for, Mr. W. J. Shoup in his address as president of the Association in 1879 proposed a union of the State normal institute and the State Teachers' Association, which proposal was acted upon and approved at once.[175] In the following year, therefore, a half day of the session of the State Teachers' Association was given to institute matters, the leaders on that occasion including, among others, Superintendent von Coelln, E. R. Eldridge, S. N. Fellows, N. W. Boyes, W. J. Shoup, Governor John H. Gear, and United States Commissioner of Education John Eaton. It was out of this discussion that the four years course of study for county institutes finally evolved.[176]

Two years later it was said that a good degree of uniformity was recognized in institute management and instruction throughout the State. Much more attention was given to methods, school organization, and control — thus providing that which should constitute the real work of a normal institute. There was, however, the ''gradation and organization'' of the institute itself, which as yet had been undetermined and which had prevented, it was observed, the greatest ''usefulness'' of the work. That is to say, a person completing the four years in one county had no assurance that the same procedure would not be required of him in a neighboring county should he make the change. Nor was there any agreement as to the scope of the work accomplished in the different jurisdictions so that certificates might be evaluated. It was agreed (in 1885) that some recognized standard should be established whereby the completion of a definite course in one county might be credited in another — a result which thus far had not been attained because of the indifference in many instances of county superintendents. Some of these, casting aside all the good which had been accomplished by their predecessors, began a new experiment in applying the old course, which was not so faulty in itself as in the method by which it was used.

Again, in 1884 the State Teachers' Association requested the Superintendent, with the assistance of his advisory council provided by the Association, to revise the former course; and thereafter it is noticeable that the old syllabus was abandoned, an outline

13

only being submitted. Thus a fundamental form was
established, but details were relegated to the several
counties. Furthermore, it was recommended in the
instructions issued with the new plan that upon the
completion of the four years work a diploma should
be issued as evidence thereof. The Board of Examiners (created in 1882), it was declared, would arrange matters so that holders of such credentials
might "pass a limited examination" and obtain a
State certificate. At once, it appears, this suggestion
proved popular for it was adopted in more than half
of the counties during the first year and it was assumed as certain that all would be under the same
standard by the succeeding year. Just how these
"diplomas" might become a legal credential did not
appear. Neither was there any provision for further
institute attendance after the completion of the sixteen weeks comprised in the four sessions. It may
be shown, however, that this latter complication was
obviated in some counties by the organization of a
"professional" group.

In the beginning it was not foreseen that a time
would come when the large attendance upon institutes would be detrimental to the best results.
Nevertheless, it was suggested in 1885 that it would
be wise to provide in many instances for a preliminary meeting, "a kind of training school for be-
ginners", to be held in advance of the regular
institute so that persons of immature years might be
excluded from the annual session. The State, it was
thought, might "well afford to assist in defraying

the expenses of such schools'', which if provided by law should be left to the discretion of the county superintendent. The same year in which this was proposed a ''State Institute'' was recommended, but differing from the former one in organization and purpose, in that it was to be a strictly professional body which might command the assistance of the ''latest and most valuable experience and attainments of the ablest educators of the Nation.''[177]

The ultimate aim in these recommendations appears to have been the segregation of the inexperienced and untrained, and the preparation of a competent body of instructors for the common annual institute. Again, in a subsequent report Superintendent Akers proposed another plan by which the influx of the immature might be controlled — namely, a county normal school of twelve weeks which should provide a course of twenty-four weeks to be completed in two years. According to this plan the county superintendent should be required to act as the principal teacher, but he might call in one assistant. Both county and State should provide the support, the former supplying the necessary quarters and all apparatus and the latter appropriating not less than fifty dollars to each of such schools annually. This would necessitate, to be sure, certain fees from those attending, who, it was suggested, should include all persons intending to teach and also others having less than one year's experience.

Furthermore, no one should be permitted either to teach or to attend the normal institute until after

the completion of twenty-four weeks' preparatory
work. By this plan two things would be accomplished: first, applicants for examination would be
more mature and possess a better academic training;
and second, the regular institute would be less un-
wieldy and would require fewer instructors.[178] It
may be noted that this is suggestive of the provision
recently adopted (1913) which will require a certain
amount of training before one may be admitted to
instruct in the public schools.

While these changes were desirable and probably
possible, there was at the same time a disposition to
base success upon numbers; and so, many persons
were induced to attend the institutes who might well
have been excluded. It is certain, too, that there was
a large increase following the adoption of the course
of study with the granting of a diploma at its conclusion; and the greatest enrollment seems to have
been from about 1885 to 1896 — the attendance in the
latter year being nearly 23,000. There may have
been other inducements also in the new features
provided. For example, one does not observe that
primary work as a special subject appears in a
general way until 1887, when several counties employed specialists and even established a "model
school of primary pupils"— the earliest attempt of
this kind having been made, it appears, in Cedar
County in 1878.

There was, however, no escaping from the necessity of providing some academic work in these
institutes, notwithstanding the emphasis constantly

placed upon methods by the professional authorities. In the newer counties more especially this need of academic work was felt, it being granted that larger established communities might conduct such training schools on a different plan. A solution of this problem would have been possible under the organization proposed by Superintendent Akers, but a more general and independent arrangement was instituted in Polk County in 1887, when nearly five hundred teachers were instructed in two departments, namely, the "summer school of methods" and the "normal institute". In the former, special departments — primary, intermediate, and grammar — were provided for those engaged in such work; while in the latter, the State course was pursued. This institute was patronized by many from different sections of the State, as the Washington County institute had been in 1872 when nearly a thousand, it was said, were present at a great convention called an institute and which proved to be the beginning of normal institutes in the State.[179]

When the law of 1874 was passed the provision of the former statute continuing the pay of teachers in attendance was not incorporated, while the two fees of one dollar each, as mentioned above, were imposed, thus taxing the teachers for the support of the institution. Superintendent Sabin in 1889 called attention to this injustice and also to the small State appropriation. Repeatedly has the amount set aside for institutes, $50 for each county, been compared to that of $200 for county agricultural societies, but with little effect. It was the opinion of many that the institute should be "free to all actual teachers", and Superintendent Sabin recommended the immediate removal of the "tax", without, however, having an opportunity to commend such legislation.

Reference has already been made to the proposed licensing of institute instructors by some State authority. Further suggestions were made in 1891 by Superintendent Sabin, who enlarged upon the whole subject of the qualifications which such an individual should possess. It has been shown also that there was no State authority which could control the employment of any instructor, and no power, furthermore, by which the teacher could be protected from imposition in this respect, and therefore the recommendation relative to the requirement of legal qualification was appropriate. Again there was no action on the recommendation, and sharp criticism was made later because of the indiscriminate methods pursued in the counties of the State whereby the incompetent obtained important positions as instructors. In this connection the Superintendent of Public Instruction had suggested that the State University should provide during a summer session "a section devoted in the main to the interests of those who desire to work as instructors in institutes." Moreover, as in other States, means should be provided in Iowa for the inspection of institutes and for this purpose the Superintendent should be empowered to appoint both men and women especially qualified.[180]

As indicated in previous pages, the greatest emphasis had been placed upon the grading of institutes and of the instruction therein when, in 1897, the Superintendent of Public Instruction made the observation that by such a strict classification as had been developed teachers were often prevented from reviewing subjects which they most desired to cover. He had reached the conclusion, therefore, that "the graded normal institute needs reorganizing in the direction of greater freedom of choice on the part of teachers in attendance." At the same time it was foreseen that such a change would destroy the scheme of "graduating" from the county institute; but even this was considered advantageous, since it had produced a false notion relative to the purposes of institutes.

The normal institute had scarcely been established under the law of 1874 when there were suggestions for its abolition. Again, in 1897 this sentiment was expressed, with the provision, however, that training schools with short courses be substituted. It was asserted, nevertheless, that the time would never come when the teachers of the county should not be called together, at least once annually, for "mutual consultation and advice".[181] While there were advocates of the summer school and adverse criticism of the institute as then conducted, there were others who defended the system, pointed out the good it had done, and declared for greater efficiency through the same means. It was clear, however, that summer schools were about to interfere with the previous patronage of the institute, and that a new effort must be made in the adjustment of these agencies.[182]

Not until 1903, it appears, was there a noticeable decrease in institute attendance because of the opening of summer schools. Although the difference was small it was sufficient to call attention to this growing interest. Probably 3500 of those who might have been enrolled in institutes were in summer schools in 1903, and the attendance in succeeding years compelled an arrangement whereby such attendance might be substituted for the usual county institute. It was clearly only a matter of time when the "six day" minimum institute provided for in the original free school law of 1858 would be outgrown or outlawed in some form, and therefore the recommendation of the "Better Iowa Schools Commission" in 1912 was not unexpected. By that body it was proposed to abolish the institute as previously conducted and provide in its stead "short inspirational" institutes to be held during the school year with the "compulsory attendance of teachers without loss of pay". In accordance with this recommendation the institute law of 1913 permits, after July 1, 1914, not more than two such meetings in each county, and requires at least one which shall remain in session not less than two days. Furthermore, all teachers must attend or forfeit the "average daily salary" during the time of non-attendance. The statute authorizes, also, a summer school of "four to six weeks" in counties where it is considered advisable by superintendents — thus providing for academic instruction.[183]

In 1861, as noted in the preceding chapter, Moses Ingalls had said that there was no better time to hold institutes than when schools were in session. In 1908 the same opinion was expressed by President Homer H. Seerley; and both would continue the pay of teachers in attendance. It is evident, therefore, that the provisions of recent legislation are not altogether new ideas.[184] Indeed, there have been many advocates of compensation during these sessions, while frequent mention has been made of the omission of this provision in the law of 1874 which fixed certain fees for attendance and examination. It was Mr. Jonathan Piper who pointed to the fact that States paid the militia to learn how to shoot, but taxed teachers for the privilege of learning how to teach.

For more than a half century the original provisions as to minimum term and the sum contributed as State aid have prevailed, and the time seems opportune to record the history of the old institute. The conductors and lecturers may continue to be employed under some other title, but the inspirational institute will only repeat the history of those early meetings when the enthusiasm displayed required three sessions daily to satisfy its demands. There will be no more public announcements of available instructors, nor as much personal sacrifice to accommodate those in attendance as on some occasions in the past. Many of the counties are worthy of mention as the homes of pioneers who originated and promoted these institutions; but however interesting such facts might be, individual accounts cannot be admitted in this connection.

PART IV
TEACHERS ASSOCIATIONS

XIII

PIONEERS PERFECTING AN ORGANIZATION

WHEN the call was issued for a national meeting of the friends of education in 1849 at Philadelphia for the purpose of perfecting an organization, Thomas H. Benton, Jr., of Iowa was one of the signers. Again, when the American Association for the Advancement of Education matured from this call he was made a member of the business or executive committee.[185]   Later, in 1857, when upon the initiative of the teachers' associations of the several States a convention to organize a national teachers' association was summoned to assemble in Philadelphia, James L. Enos of Iowa wrote that the time had come when a movement to be truly national must embrace the West; and so, he was skeptical as to the success of such an undertaking when summoned to meet in the East.   Nevertheless, he advised that the State of Iowa should coöperate and that the real nation, the Valley of the Mississippi, should be represented.[186]

After such an assertion it must have been somewhat disconcerting (or gratifying) when, upon his arrival in Philadelphia, Mr. Enos of Iowa was nominated by Mr. William Roberts of Pennsylvania for temporary chairman, which, being agreed to, made

an Iowa man the presiding officer at the organization
of the National Teachers' Association. As such he
appointed the committee which drafted the first constitution and signed the proceedings of that organizing convention. Moreover, he became one of the
vice-presidents of the permanent organization.[187]

Between the two events just mentioned the
teachers of Iowa met in convention at Muscatine in
1854 at the call, it has been said, of D. Franklin
Wells, who was then in charge of the schools of that
city. While this has been considered the first session
of the Iowa State Teachers' Association one must
consider that it was not fully organized on that occasion — although seventeen other teachers had joined
Mr. Wells in the request for such a meeting. The
officers chosen at that time included four ministers
and only two or three public school men, the others
being engaged in academies or private work. The
first session having been held in May, a second was
provided for December, 1854, at Iowa City, when the
president, Mr. J. A. Parvin, a member of the legislature, delivered an inaugural address on "The Necessity of Universal Education". Mr. Jerome Allen,
then of Alexander College, Dubuque, came across the
prairies to speak upon "The Utility of Chemistry".
D. Franklin Wells of Muscatine, James L. Enos of
Cedar Rapids, William Reynolds of Iowa City, and
Samuel Howe of Howe's Academy, Mount Pleasant,
were also among those participating in this first
meeting of teachers in the Old Stone Capitol.[188]

A side-light on this Iowa City session is obtained

from the debates of the constitutional convention in 1857, when Mr. J. C. Hall in defending the report of the committee on schools, observed that two years before (late in December, 1854) he had attended a meeting in Iowa City held for the purpose of taking into consideration the subject of education. Although it was in the dead of winter during severe weather, there was assembled in the Old Stone Capitol one of the largest and most respectable conventions that had ever come together. It was said further that gentlemen from all parts of the Commonwealth, volunteers in the cause of education, manifested an enthusiasm which had not been supported by the legislature. Moreover, the members of this educational convention gave evidence of abundant information on questions relative to the cause they represented.[189]

For reasons not specified there was no session in 1855, although one had been appointed at Davenport. But in June, 1856, another meeting was held in Iowa City when a permanent organization was effected, not, as has been said, under the constitution presented at the former meeting but under a new constitution prepared by a committee appointed for that purpose. It is distinctly stated that ''a motion to re-organize the Convention [in June, 1856] under the Constitution of the State Teachers' Association was discussed, and finally withdrawn.'' Thereupon a new instrument was presented and adopted, and later at the Muscatine meeting in the following October it was amended.

It was during the June meeting in 1856 that measures were proposed for the establishment of an educational journal under the auspices of the Association to be edited and supported by its members. The first number was not to be issued, however, until there was a sufficient amount secured to guarantee the expenses for one year. There were to be one local editor and ten assistants located in different sections of the State, and by these monthly contributions were to be submitted. Not less than four of the twenty-four pages should be set apart for the use of the "Iowa Phonetic Association". Moreover, this journal was to be made also the organ of the State Superintendent of Public Instruction.

In October, 1856, another session of the State Teachers' Association was appointed at Muscatine, where, it appears, the constitution was first published as finally adopted and the name of the organization was determined. The advancement of the general interests of education, but more especially of the common schools, was to be the aim of the Association; and any person might become a member by subscribing to the constitution and, "if a male", paying one dollar. Women were not taxed at this time for the support of any feature of the Association, except through subscriptions which they might make to the journal. It is noteworthy, also, that free entertainment for all members was invariably provided during these days of organization and for many subsequent years.

Under the constitution of 1856 the officers consisted of a president, five vice-presidents, a recording secretary, a corresponding secretary, and a treasurer. In 1856 the following persons filled the offices of the Association: D. Franklin Wells, then of Iowa City, was president; Jerome Allen of Dubuque, George W. Drake of Oskaloosa, John F. Sanford of Keokuk, W. Duane Wilson of Fairfield, and D. Lane of Davenport were vice-presidents; James L. Enos of Cedar Rapids was corresponding secretary; Frederick Humphrey of Iowa City was recording secretary; and George B. Dennison of Muscatine was treasurer. There were six members of the executive committee: Chandler Childs of Dubuque, S. McNutt of Muscatine, and J. H. Sanders of Oskaloosa, in addition to the president and the two secretaries already mentioned.

An immediate duty imposed upon the corresponding secretary would require him to obtain from the several States and foreign countries copies of their "school systems", or other information of interest to the State Association. The executive committee was instructed to arrange for the publication of the new journal, *The Voice of Iowa,* on certain prescribed conditions, and to appoint a general editor. The final action at this meeting provided for a subsequent session at Dubuque in April, 1857, which, it will be observed, would make the third within a period of twelve months — and that, too, within a region where the means of transportation were mainly by boat on the Mississippi, or overland by stage coach.

14

The Dubuque meeting was unique in that it combined a State institute with the recently organized Association. The former was to have daily exercises similar to those described in the chapter on county institutes, and the latter was to occupy the evening hours with lectures. Although the time was unfavorable for those living at a distance, at least fifty persons assembled in the third ward building in Dubuque under what were declared by President D. Franklin Wells to be changed conditions. The first attempts to maintain the organization had failed, he said, because of insurmountable difficulties; while now the means of transportation would soon improve (trains then were running to Iowa City), and an organ of communication (*The Voice of Iowa*) had been established which would aid in uniting the educational interests of the State. It was at this meeting in 1857 that the first steps were taken to urge upon the General Assembly the establishment of a reformatory institution for juvenile offenders, a committee being appointed for that purpose. It is worthy of note that the committee persevered in their presentation of this need until it was finally met in 1868. There was also another committee appointed to confer with publishers relative to "phonetic type" text-books — a system of printing which is illustrated in certain pages of *The Voice of Iowa* during the three years of its publication.[190]

The annual meeting of 1857 was held at Iowa City in August in the Old Stone Capitol. When the Association assembled there was no officer present authorized to preside, nor secretary to chronicle its proceedings. In this emergency Mr. A. S. Kissell of Davenport called the meeting to order; and W. E. Ijams of Iowa City, who, owing to the ill health of the Superintendent of Public Instruction, took his place at the session, was chosen to preside. After a statement by Mr. S. S. Howe relative to the causes which led to the failure of the first State Teachers' Association, it was determined that all who had been identified with the former should become members of the new organization by signing the constitution, without the payment of any fee. Certain gentlemen who were present from Illinois, Ohio, and Canada were made honorary members. One of these, Professor D. Wilkins of Illinois, proposed during the meeting that the Iowa Association should support a movement to organize "The Mississippi Valley Educational Association", and that a convention for that purpose be held in Davenport in the following year. This, along with other resolutions, was adopted; but the proposed western organization, it appears, did not reach the convention stage, although it was resolved to meet in Davenport on the second Thursday of August, 1858, for that purpose.

That the purposes of the Association as expressed in the beginning were not formal is clear from the proceedings at this meeting when subjects for reports at a subsequent session were assigned as follows: Professor Sanford of the Medical College at Keokuk was requested to point out the best method of developing the physical powers of the

pupil; Professor Humphrey was appointed to outline the course of study which would most advance
the "mental and moral capacity of the pupil"; Mr.
C. Childs of Dubuque was to indicate the proper
kind of school architecture; Mr. A. S. Kissell was to
be responsible for some general conclusions relative
to compulsory attendance for a specified time during
minority; and upon Professor Stone of the State
University devolved a general history of the "origin,
progress, and present state of the modern and recent
reform in the preparation of text-books" for all
phases of education. Finally, the "Phonetic System" was recommended by the Association for a
fair trial by the teachers of the State.[191]

Although it had been agreed to assemble at
Davenport on the second Thursday in August, 1858,
there is no available account of any such meeting.
Moreover, since the third regular session of the
State Teachers' Association was held at the same
place in September, it may be concluded that the
former convention was postponed. It will be noted
that this session occurred after the new school law
had become effective and previous to the decision of
the Supreme Court declaring it to be invalid. It is
clear that the provisions of the new statute were
uppermost in the proceedings of the convention and
that the training of the teachers through county high
schools with normal departments therein was
thought feasible under that law. Furthermore, an
independent State normal school was advocated, the
question earnestly debated, and finally disposed of

by the adoption of resolutions which were quite unlike those originally passed.[192]

Again, late in August, 1859, the Association met at Washington and there decided upon a new plan of conducting their journal — *The Voice of Iowa* having failed to receive sufficient support to warrant its continuance. There were proposals from the *Iowa School Journal,* published at Des Moines, and also from the *Literary Advertiser and Public School Advocate,* published at Iowa City, to operate as the organ of communication; but the sentiment for an independent journal was against such propositions. During this session a resolution declaring that "females should enjoy the right of suffrage in school matters" was laid upon the table and seems never to have been revived. At the same time the subject of co-education was prominently before the convention. A committee, to which the matter had been referred, approved the suggestion made in the president's address that a truancy law, similar to that of Massachusetts, should be passed by the Board of Education. Moreover, a compulsory institute law requiring sessions of not less than two weeks in every county was recommended. Vocal music, it was declared, should become a part of the public school curriculum; the Bible should be read daily in the public schools; and a central State normal school to accommodate not less than three hundred teachers, which should stand as the acknowledged head of the common school system, was demanded. Finally, the Association took special notice of the death of

Horace Mann in a series of resolutions relative to his work and in voting a temporary adjournment out of respect to his memory.[193]

From Washington the Association adjourned to meet at Tipton in 1860, an inland town that must be reached by stage from the Mississippi & Missouri (now the Rock Island) on the south and from the Chicago Iowa & Nebraska (now the Chicago & North-Western) on the north. From the former it was fourteen miles, and from the latter twelve; yet conveyances were provided by the entertaining community through private or public accommodations. Even under such unfavorable conditions members were present from as far west as Polk County, the total enrollment being reported as two hundred and seventeen, more than one hundred of whom were from a distance. Among the prominent members on this occasion were D. Franklin Wells, who was serving as president for the second time, Thomas H. Benton, Jr., United States Senator James Harlan, Mrs. M. A. McGonegal, director of the model school in the normal department of the State University and later in charge of the Davenport training school, Moses Ingalls, A. S. Kissell, C. C. Nestlerode, twice the president of the organization, and Dr. William Reynolds, the Territorial Superintendent of Public Instruction in 1841–1842.[194]

Before adjournment the Association commended the arrangements of Dr. Reynolds to enter upon a lecturing tour throughout the State on the subject of geography in its "political, physical, and mathe-

matical'' phases. It was learned with satisfaction
also that he was in possession of the necessary apparatus to thoroughly illustrate his subject, thus
being able to interest the general public.[195]   Addresses were delivered by Thomas H. Benton, Jr.,
the Secretary of the Board of Education, and by
Senator James Harlan. Only one speaker from outside the State, Mr. C. T. Chase of Chicago, appears
upon this program, and it is of interest to note that
he addressed the convention upon ''Agricultural Instruction''. In the selection of officers it was customary in those days to appoint a nominating committee
consisting of one from each county — a plan which
was feasible when not more than ten or twelve counties were represented as in 1860, but scarcely practicable in more recent years.[196]

For convenience the executive committee of the
Association was called together at Wilton at least
twice during the year 1860–1861. Owing to the excitement preceding the outbreak of the Civil War
some doubted the wisdom of an Association meeting
in 1861, which had already been appointed at Muscatine. But others felt that ''ignorance is a more
formidable enemy than *rebel secessionists,* and
hence, should be met as promptly'', and so the usual
annual session was not omitted. It was announced
that for the first time the men would be expected to
pay for the entertainment, and it was anticipated
that no member would object to bearing his share of
the burden during war times. Moreover, the arrangements provided for accommodations at first

class hotels, which at the rate of "fifty or even seventy-five cents per day" were not considered expensive.

One hundred and seventy persons were in attendance at the 1861 meeting — largely, it may be said, from counties adjacent to Muscatine which registered forty-two, while Scott sent forty-five, Cedar twenty-seven, Louisa eight, and Johnson twelve. Washington had but six, Jefferson and Lee three each, and Van Buren, Des Moines, and Henry one each. There were two each from Linn, Poweshiek, Benton, and Clinton. Other States contributed thirteen, certain persons being named as "delegates" from Mississippi, Tennessee, Pennsylvania, and Minnesota.

No session of the Association had ever occupied itself with more serious business. The problems of a State board of examiners, of permanent certificates, of the State school fund and its management, of the efficiency of school officers, of sustaining the public school, of normal training classes in "higher Schools and Academies", of the county superintendency and the powers lodged therein, of teachers' institutes, of provision for a "State Agent", and of the maintenance of a school journal, and of a revision of the constitution of the Association were all assigned to competent committees for immediate or subsequent disposition. Thus, the sixth annual session of the State Teachers' Association set an example for succeeding conventions of its members, and it closed, as was customary, with the doxology and a benediction.[197]

The women in attendance at Mount Pleasant the next year (1862) outnumbered the men for the first time. The events of war had made this possible. Moreover, the proceedings during the period of civil conflict are interspersed with expressions relative to the missing members and the sacrifice they were making. Indeed, it is probably true that no more loyal body than the State Teachers' Association of the sixties ever assembled. At this, the seventh annual meeting, the committee to which was assigned the duty of transcribing the records of the Association reported that duty as performed, the proceedings from the first meeting in 1854 — with the exception, it was said, of two, those for June and October, 1856 — having been "recorded in detail". Furthermore, the names of all the members, men and women so far as they could be obtained, were also transcribed. But subsequent events seem to indicate that this record was lost, notwithstanding the care which was taken in its preparation.

The chief addresses at this session were given by Mr. W. H. Wells, superintendent of the Chicago schools, Rev. William Salter of Burlington, Rev. M. K. Cross of Tipton, Professor N. R. Leonard of the State University, Professor H. K. Edson of Denmark Academy, and by the president, C. C. Nestlerode. The session was concerned chiefly with reports from its State agent, Moses Ingalls, and from a committee appointed to investigate the State University, with the questions of the county superintendency, the educational journal, the holding of teachers institutes, and with amendments to the constitution of the Association. The publication of the *Iowa Instructor* had been productive of a debt which at this date was nearly $500 — a large part of which had been advanced by the executive committee. Furthermore, the small balance in the treasury from the preceding year had been deposited in a bank that failed, and so the Association was financially embarrassed. The field of membership of the Association was extended now by an amendment to include ''any active friend of Education'' who would sign the constitution, pay the initiation fee of one dollar, and contribute the annual dues of fifty cents thereafter — the latter provision applying to all after 1862.[198]

The next year (1863) the Association moved westward to Grinnell for its eighth session, this being possible by the increased facilities for transportation. Rev. M. K. Cross, the only ''pastor'' up to that date to hold the position, was the president, while Professor L. F. Parker seems to have been responsible for the local arrangements. During the preceding year the State agent, Moses Ingalls, had carried out the designs of the Association, which have been referred to in the chapter on county institutes; and on this occasion he made a full report of his operations. As noted above, the women had not been required to pay any fees up to this time, but now three of them being appointed a committee on amendments recommended that no distinction be made as to sex; that since they would claim equal pay for equal labor, on account of being counted

worthy to take the place of the *"brave boys* who
have gone to teach rebels the consequences of secession'', they should be permitted to share in the
support of the Association.   Since no objections
were recorded it is concluded that the recommendation was unanimously agreed to.   Thus, since 1863
women have been paying their portion of the annual
expenses.

The meeting at Mount Pleasant had revealed a
debt of nearly $500 which in 1863, through sales of
the bound volumes of the *Iowa Instructor* and
through the collection of fees, had been reduced to
about $260.   It was determined, therefore, to
''liquidate the debt of the Association'' by dona-
tions, among which were two contributions of $88
each by Barnes & Burr and by W. B. Smith & Co.,
text-book publishers.   It should be said that the
members of the executive committee, which had paid
the current expenses, made, aside from the book
companies, the largest single subscription.   The
Association adjourned in 1863 free from all indebt-
edness.

It was during this session that preparations were
made to memorialize Congress relative to the establishment of a National Bureau of Education, and to
''invite the co-operation therein, of other State
Teachers' Associations''.   Professor D. Franklin
Wells of the State University offered this resolution,
and its language suggests an original movement for
such an institution.   There was also another recommendation which requested the Association to indi-

cate its choice of a man for Secretary of the
State Board of Education, or Superintendent of
Public Instruction, as the General Assembly might
determine. Although there were protests against
such a proceeding, a ballot was taken resulting in an
almost unanimous vote for Mr. A. S. Kissell. It is
noticeable, however, that out of a total registration
of one hundred sixteen only sixty-five ballots were
cast. This appears to have been the first ''political''
event in the history of the Iowa State Teachers' Association.[199]

Although it had been proposed in 1863 to hold the
next session in Des Moines, the matter was finally
left to the executive committee who located it at
Dubuque. While ninety persons were present from
at least twenty counties there were but fifty members
of the Association in attendance. Thus, only about
half of those counted as delegates were supporting
the Association. The president, Mr. H. K. Edson,
sent from Boston his regrets in which he declared
that ''while visiting the Schools and Colleges of
Massachusetts, boasted as they are, I can but feel
that we in Iowa are *just* behind them — if in some
respects we are not in advance of them.'' It became
the duty of Mr. Oran Faville, a vice-president, to
preside. During the session he delivered an address
upon the ''History of the School Legislation of
Iowa'', following which he made a ''masterly argument and appeal for the creation of an Iowa State
Normal School''. His position then, that of Secretary of the Board of Education, made his utterances

official; and it may be added that the Association was in harmony with his views.

Again the State agent of the Association made his annual report in which he pointed out the enlarged work of the office and the importance of its continuance; and he suggested the proper remuneration of the person who would succeed to the office from which he (Moses Ingalls) was about to retire. Among other important recommendations he urged the construction of more attractive buildings, both outside and inside, not only for the sake of the children but also for the good appearance of the town and its reputation. He was not speaking, it appears, about the rural school houses of Iowa. In the immediate future, as it developed, the State was to be divided into two districts for the work of two agents, Mr. A. S. Kissell and Mr. Jonathan Piper, who were to be assigned to the field with the expectation that county superintendents would adjust their institutes to accommodate the time of these representatives of the State Association.[200]

The difficulties surrounding the meeting in 1864 were due to some extent to the location; accordingly, Oskaloosa, a more central point, was selected for the session of 1865. This, moreover, had been previously announced as a very important session which would have more important questions to decide than any former convention of the Association. It was declared to be a critical period in the educational life of the State, which would demand the counsel of the wisest and soundest among its membership.[201]

Oskaloosa, like Tipton in 1860, had no railroad in 1865; and to make the trip from the northern portion of the State instructions were given to proceed to the Mississippi by rail, thence down the river to Burlington or Keokuk, from which one could travel again by rail to within a short distance of his destination. A "line of omnibuses", by means of which all could be accommodated, ran regularly from the station to the city. The usual rate of full fare going and a free return on all railroads, and two-thirds of full fare over the lines of the Western Stage Company were obtained. Under favorable arrangements which had been made the attendance was larger than in several years before, but the persons who came were mainly from the counties in the southern part of the State.

The meeting brought to the State as special speakers Principal William F. Phelps of the Minnesota State Normal School and Superintendent Newton Bateman of Illinois. The question of a State agent was up again, the office having failed to meet with sufficient financial support to warrant keeping the two men previously appointed in the field — unless they had been willing to remain in positions that offered no assurance of a living. The matter was finally disposed of when Mr. Piper resigned in favor of Mr. Kissell. At the same time there was no certainty of the compensation being sufficient to maintain one man, inasmuch as his traveling expenses were largely increased owing to the lack of county coöperation. Other matters which the Association sought to adjust included the teacher supply, the district library, amendments to the school law, and the position of the organization on the temperance question.[202]

Cedar Rapids entertained the State meeting in August, 1866. While this was called the tenth year of organization by some it has since been recognized as having been the thirteenth, counting from the first meeting in 1854. One evening of this session was devoted to an address upon the "New Decimal System of Weights and Measures" (that is the Metric System) by Mr. John A. Kasson, at the conclusion of which the Association tendered the gentleman a vote of thanks for his "lucid exposition" and declared its purpose to secure the early introduction of the system in the schools of the State. At this meeting the State agent, it appears, made his final report, wherein it was shown that further attempts to provide for such an officer would not succeed without some State aid. Indeed, after consultation with the Superintendent of Public Instruction the arrangements proposed at the Oskaloosa meeting had been deemed impracticable, and the agent, Mr. Kissell, had resigned, although under protest from the executive committee. Although D. Franklin Wells was named at the Cedar Rapids meeting to succeed to this office, it is well known that he had scarcely entered upon his duties when he was appointed to the office of Superintendent of Public Instruction to succeed Mr. Faville. Thereafter no further action relative to a State agent is recorded.[203]

Thus a chapter in the history of the State Teachers' Association was completed, with a final effort to support by voluntary contributions a movement which all must have felt should devolve upon the State. The organization had seen the enactment of a free school law and witnessed its effects; had survived and had met annually through the exciting period of the Civil War, contrary to the general experience of the similar associations in other States; had overcome the difficulties of insufficient means of transportation; had stood for advancement in all educational endeavor; had established a journal at a financial and personal sacrifice; and had been instrumental in arousing the General Assembly to enact needed legislation. But this was done by the leaders, the enthusiasts: the rank and file were not yet sufficiently interested.

XIV

A FEDERATED INSTITUTION

THE thirteenth annual meeting of the State Teachers' Association had more than the usual number in attendance, thus requiring some special activity on the part of the entertaining city, Cedar Rapids, to find accommodations for the delegates. As a result of this experience the executive committee was warned of what the attendance might be at the session of 1867, which for the first time was appointed at Des Moines. Certain towns, also ambitious to entertain the Association, were cautioned lest they should "get an elephant" on their hands. At the same time attention was called to the fact that for the twelve years since the organization of the Association the burden had been borne by a comparatively few teachers, while there were hundreds equally qualified and able to aid in its management. Especially was this said to be true of presidents and professors in colleges and of men prominent in public school positions who seemed indifferent.[204] It was a time of reconstruction, it appears, when an effort was being made to create a wider influence for the Association.

As in the case of the meeting at Oskaloosa, so now specific directions were given for reaching Des

Moines in August, 1867, when it was hoped that the
Mississippi & Missouri Railroad would be completed
to that city. From the south one could reach the
city by rail, and from the north by way of the Western Stage Company's line from the Nevada or
Boone station on the Chicago & North-Western Railroad, while the same accommodation would be available from the western terminus of the Mississippi &
Missouri Railroad provided it had not yet entered
the city. The headquarters and place of meeting on
this occasion were located at the court house, where
the sessions were ''largely attended by the representative teachers of the State, and by other friends
of educational progress.''

Again the action of former meetings relative to
institutes was affirmed; while the executive committee was authorized to continue their efforts to
promote this form of instruction. The normal
school under State patronage and support was once
more before the Association for approval; and vocal
music was recommended as a component part of the
public school curriculum, which should be recognized
also as a requirement in the qualification of teachers.
Furthermore, a system of supervision which should
be complete for the State and its subdivisions was
outlined with suggestions for a liberal compensation
of all officers including those of the district school.
It was considered the duty of the State not only to
provide competent teachers but also to see that they
were paid ''according to qualifications and labor''
and not according to sex.[205] Thus, each session while

affirming the position of the Association on questions long before it was taking a stand on new problems.

At Keokuk in the following year an attempt was made to increase the paying membership by refusing credentials to returning delegates until the fee was paid, but the movement failed to secure sufficient support. Perhaps the effect was satisfactory, for instead of enforcing such a regulation it was concluded to "earnestly invite" all persons present to enroll and thus share in the support of the organization. For the future, however, it was agreed to grant return certificates to such only as were properly enrolled. Other recommendations would provide for permanency in the office of secretary, thus insuring a continuity of interest in carrying on the business of the Association.

It is noteworthy that, after ten years of effort on the part of a committee of the Association, a "Reform School" was established by legislative action — this result being due, in great measure, to Mr. W. A. Bemis of Davenport, who made a final report during this session of 1868. There were present also representatives of the academy who spoke for it and its province in education. Mr. H. K. Edson of the Denmark Academy was conspicuous in this field. President W. F. King of Cornell College defended the utility of the classical course in providing a liberal education and opposed that which was falsely called the practical. Mr. F. M. Witter of Muscatine declared that the common schools should occupy all the ground held by the academy as then conducted and that on the completion of courses therein pupils should be prepared to enter college.[206] This, indeed, was but forecasting the accredited high school which has since become a prominent factor in the public school system.

When the Association met in Marshalltown in 1869, Allen Armstrong, superintendent at Council Bluffs, and Jerome Allen of Monticello had just returned from the National meeting at Trenton, New Jersey, and therefore it was deemed appropriate that some time should be devoted to a report from these gentlemen. It may have been because of this information relative to national education that early in the session a committee, consisting of A. S. Kissell, the Superintendent of Public Instruction, F. M. Witter, S. N. Fellows, and T. S. Parvin, was appointed "to compile a history" of the Iowa Association "from its organization".[207]

More attention was given the high school at this session than on any previous occasion, it being considered an opportune time to promote the township high school as well as a uniform curriculum for such institutions throughout the State. Before adjournment nine men were appointed as a committee to act on the call of the Superintendent of Public Instruction in the preparation of such a course of study. Again the normal school as a separate institution was recommended, while the General Assembly was urged to appropriate not less than $3000 to the normal department of the State University. Finally, a memorial service for D. Franklin Wells occupied the larger part of an afternoon session, his personal friends setting forth his contributions to the educational growth of the State and the excellence of his character and labors as principal of the Muscatine schools, as head of the normal department of the State University, as State agent, and lastly as Superintendent of Public Instruction.[208]

The Association during these years was not established in one city, but seems to have selected a new place of meeting each year. In 1870 Waterloo was chosen; and at this session there were several departures from earlier customs. For instance, the college men were in evidence, having held a preliminary session preceding that of the Association proper, and before the adjournment of the latter they had requested the executive committee to provide a section devoted to their interests in subsequent programs. Again, provision had been made at this meeting for primary, grammar, and high school divisions which, however, became impracticable because only "one or two gentlemen engaged in high schools were present". It appears, therefore, that a combination then formed resulted in the organization of what has since come to be the elementary and graded department of the Association.

The president on this occasion, Mr. Jonathan Piper, presented in his address the subjects which had interested the State for many years, namely, normal schools, institutes, township districts and the abolition of the subdistrict, the school journal, and the use of the Bible in the public schools. Among

these the township unit of organization occupied a
leading place, and to secure favorable legislation
relative thereto a committee was selected to serve
for two years. They were to carry on a campaign
through local papers and public meetings which
should set forth the advantages of the township
system of organization. It was at this time that the
association determined to assume no further responsibility relative to a school journal, it being determined that thereafter the periodical should be
considered a private venture and that it must stand
as other journals, on its merits.

The practical phases of the teachers' work were
demonstrated by Mrs. M. A. McGonegal of the
Davenport training school in outlining a course of
study for primary schools. Mr. C. G. Kretschmer of
Dubuque illustrated the method of teaching by objects; while Miss Emma Quintrell of Sioux City, by
means of a class of thirty pupils, gave a model reading lesson before the Association. There was much
interest manifested also in the matter of school reports and statistics, which at that time were apparently neglected — a fact that accounts, in a
measure, for the failure to secure accurate information relative to the school system.

Reference has already been made to an address
by Oran Faville on ''School Legislation'' at the
Dubuque meeting in 1864. Now, in 1870, Mr. A. S.
Kissell addressed the Association upon the ''School
Legislation of Iowa: Past, Present, and Future.''
He declared that since 1858 the State had made no

improvement in school legislation and that the laws were so ''enigmatical'' that the intent was at times difficult to determine. A gentleman from Pennsylvania being introduced at this juncture said that since he had heard of the great State of Iowa and her excellent school system, he had read the State's laws relative to schools and was forced to conclude that if the system was good the laws did not reveal it. Indeed, he pronounced them an ''incongruous mess'', and incidentally referred to the disadvantages of the subdistrict system.

An energetic committee, of which Professor S. N. Fellows was the chairman, had been at work since the meeting at Marshalltown the preceding year in arousing throughout the State a full discussion relative to the establishment of a State normal school. The whole matter was summarized in a memorial to the General Assembly in 1870, when by the joint action of the House and Senate committees and the personal attention of the chairman of the Association committee a bill incorporating the wishes of the Association was prepared. For a time it seemed certain that this bill would pass, and its subsequent defeat could not be explained by its promoters. Nevertheless, the Association determined to continue the agitation until such an institution was secured to the State. A new committee, consisting of Henry K. Edson, Finley M. Witter, Samuel Calvin, Stephen N. Fellows, C. C. Chamberlain, and John K. Sweeney, was appointed for that purpose. Here, then, the aims of the Association were clearly defined, and there was abundant evidence of a desire to place the State in a better relative position educationally. This was shown at the conclusion of the session in Waterloo, when through the endorsement of a formal request the National Teachers' Association was invited to meet at Davenport in 1871.[209]

In 1871 the State Association assembled on the western limits of the State, meeting at Council Bluffs in August. Three sectional meetings had been provided — primary, grammar, and high school. Mrs. M. A. McGonegal presided over the first of these, Mr. C. P. Rogers over the second, and Mr. F. M. Witter over the third. The separation of these divisions was not, however, very distinct at this time, since it appears that papers appropriate to each were read before the general Association. There was a college division also in accordance with the request of the year before, and this was presided over by Professor L. F. Parker.

It might be said that the Council Bluffs meeting was devoted to high schools, since that department of the school system received the greatest attention. The committee appointed in 1869 had failed to cooperate, and therefore a new committee appointed at Waterloo had formulated a report for 1871. It directed attention to the fact that conditions then (in 1871) demanded at least three special courses of study: one suitable for villages and small towns, another for populous districts, and a third for cities where there would be a large regular attendance and a well graded system.[210] The position of the high

school in the educational system was again the theme
of a paper in that section, while the president of the
Association, Professor S. J. Buck, dwelt upon the
province of the institution as a college preparatory
school and suggested that its curriculum should be
arranged with that in view. Finally, it was the
opinion of some that the law should require the
establishment of a high school in every county which
had a population of seven thousand or more.[211]
Serious consideration, therefore, was certain to be
given to this phase of public education in subsequent
meetings.

From the banks of the Missouri the Association
returned to Davenport where but eighty teachers
assembled in August, 1872. Among the first events
of this session was an inquiry relative to the records
of the organization. A "long discussion", it was
said, ensued, resulting in the appointment of a committee to "investigate". It was discovered, too, that
parts of the constitution were lost with the records,
necessitating another search for or restoration of
certain amendments. This was accomplished by submitting a complete document which was adopted at
this session. The first committee, however, recommended the establishment of a "special committee
and a special appropriation from the funds of the
association to carry on the work" of publishing a
history of education in Iowa from the beginning,
which was to be completed before the succeeding
sessions.

During this convention the school system was severely criticised, indicating dissatisfaction with conditions, more especially in the rural districts. Superintendent Abernethy declared that the great mass of the people were so opposed to supervision that there was danger of its entire abolition. Sharp reforms were needed to correct prevailing conditions which were produced, it was asserted, by wrong principles of education and not by any kind of institution. Some differences of opinion were expressed by college and public school men as to where the responsibility for the situation should rest. Some would endorse a truancy or compulsory attendance law, while others would vigorously oppose such a measure because the people were not prepared for such legislation. It may be noted that the proposed law was recommended by Mr. James C. Gilchrist, then principal of the Cedar Rapids Normal College, and was opposed by Mr. William M. Wilcox, a prominent city superintendent.

It was on this occasion that President A. S. Welch of the State Agricultural College was summoned by telegraph to fill a vacancy on the program. He spoke upon the "New Education", which was defined as including such industrial features as were taking form in the kind of institutions which he represented, where the aim was "to help the industrious", not to "elevate the professions". During the session many of the former recommendations of the Association were repeated, while a more recent suggestion would amend the law relative to the licensing of teachers so as to include an examination in physiology and hygiene. Finally, it was determined to urge upon all educational assemblies the importance of educating the people to the need of a township system, normal schools, and more effective county supervision.[212]

In 1873 the annual meeting was again appointed at Iowa City, but on this occasion the Old Stone Capitol as an assembly hall gave place to the new University Chapel where all the sessions were held. One need summarize only the conclusions of this meeting since in general they were not new. The province of the hoped-for normal schools was outlined to include the training of teachers already employed, those expecting to instruct in the common schools, and others who wished to qualify for principals and superintendents. As before, the office of county superintendent was declared to be of great importance. There was also a recommendation that three boards of examiners be established — a State, a county, and a city board — under general laws. The first should consist of the Superintendent of Public Instruction and four others; the second, of the county superintendent and two others; and the third, of the city and the county superintendent and one other. A recommendation was made also that a competent commission be authorized to "simplify and harmonize" the school law.[213]

The next year (1874) Des Moines entertained the Association for the second time; and it is noticeable that among those invited to appear on the program were the editor of the *Davenport Gazette,* Waldo M.

Potter, a farmer and stock raiser, Colonel John Scott, and a member of the law faculty of the State University, William G. Hammond. The "Press and the Free Schools" was the subject of the editor; "The Demand of the Producing Classes for a more Practical Education" was the topic of the farmer; and "The Right of the State to Establish Schools for Instruction in the Higher Branches in Education" was the theme of the law professor. While all departments of education were represented there were no speakers from outside the State.

A large attendance of the "leading teachers of the state" and also of "prominent educators from abroad" composed the meeting of the Association at Burlington in 1875. This was the first time that the annual meeting had been held during the holiday season, or so late in December. Professor W. F. Phelps of the Winona, Minnesota, Normal School addressed the Iowa teachers for the second time. With Superintendent Duane Doty of Chicago, he represented the outside talent employed. By the provisions of the executive committee all grades of work were included, while the coming international exhibition (in 1876) was presented for immediate action. The legislative committee of this year, consisting of Mr. S. J. Buck, Mr. E. R. Eldridge, and Mr. C. P. Rogers, made more than the ordinary number of recommendations which included the following: (1) the appointment of a State board of examiners, concerning which reference has been made; (2) the election of the county superintendent by a board of education; (3) that no pupil should be admitted under six years of age; (4) that natural philosophy and drawing should be added to subjects for examination of all teachers; (5) that a sanitary board for districts be established; (6) that a truant law be enacted; (7) that better control of institutes be provided; and (8) that the General Assembly make a liberal appropriation for the State educational exhibit at Philadelphia.[214]

On December 26, 1876, what is now considered the twenty-second session of the State Teachers' Association assembled in the Congregational church at Grinnell. Not since 1863 had it met in this city. On the second day it was proposed by Mr. T. S. Parvin that the proceedings along with the leading papers be published at the expense of the organization. This proposition was finally approved the third day of the session — provided the amount expended did not exceed $100. Once before, in 1869, the proceedings had thus been distributed, but there seems to be no record as to the authority for the action on that occasion. It is, therefore, possible to cite an independent publication in referring to the session of 1876.

The centennial exhibition had just closed, and from it the president of the Association, Mr. C. P. Rogers, drew some practical lessons in his inaugural address. While the value of these addresses and papers may well be recognized it is not within the scope of the present work to review them in detail. The president dwelt upon the demands then present.

These included thoroughness in instruction, a union of the educational forces of the State, the recognition of secondary schools, and supervision. In this address Mr. Rogers made a radical recommendation in which he proposed to "abolish the office of County Superintendent, root and branch." Moreover, he would substitute a plan which would "let the presidents of the several township boards constitute a county board of education, clothed with power to legislate for the welfare of the county schools. This board should have power to *appoint* a superintendent and to fix his salary." Furthermore, in order to obtain the best qualified person such a superintendent should be selected either from without or from within the county.[215] Thus there was outlined in 1876 the very plan subsequently adopted by the commission of the Association in 1912 and incorporated into the law of 1913.

For the first time, it appears, the subject of "political science in the public schools" was presented to a State convention of Iowa teachers. For the first time, also, the principal of the Iowa State Normal School, Mr. J. C. Gilchrist, appeared before the Association — that is to say, in his official capacity to present the scope and methods of normal school instruction. And finally, it was the first time that a woman was chosen for the office of president, Miss Phoebe W. Sudlow of Davenport being elected for the succeeding year. The metric system was taken up again, and once more it was proposed to make due preparation for its adoption which seemed about to occur.[216]

Just before the next annual meeting, which was held at Cedar Rapids, it was said that "probably no agency has done more to inaugurate educational reform in Iowa than the State Teachers' Association." It was said further, that in no Commonwealth was there greater harmony among the educational forces. These conclusions were presented to induce a more complete organization at the approaching session. It appears to have been the practice at that time to use home talent in the preparation of the annual program, for on this occasion but one speaker from abroad, Superintendent J. L. Pickard of Chicago, was present to discuss "The Education of Women".

While all departments of the Association were represented much attention was given in executive sessions to the reconstruction of proposed legislation. There was the usual procedure in the election of officers under the constitution as revised in 1872, by which the nominating committee was no longer composed of one from each county. The association of principals and superintendents was granted one hour for special problems. The papers before the Association included the subjects of moral training, the English language, the intermediate grades, political science, rural school architecture, mathematics in the high school, normal schools, and a report on the metric system by Professor N. R. Leonard who illustrated his paper by apparatus. The last subject was further discussed by Professor Philbrick, who sketched the "origin, introduction

and progress of the metric system.'' Others advocated that the members do ''active work'' to bring
about a change in this State. Just at this time the
''Metric Bureau'' was in session in Boston, and
communication by telegram was established bringing
the following response:

To P. H. Philbrick:

Greetings, and the strongest active co-operation from
the Bureau. The largest and best meeting yet held — three
hundred present. Let Iowa keep abreast.

M. Dewey, Sec.

It was during this session that the plan of collecting comparative reports from city school systems
was inaugurated, Mr. W. J. Shoup of Dubuque
having made the suggestion which was actively supported by Mr. R. G. Saunderson of Burlington. Out
of this movement there developed a system of reports under uniform rules, which was adopted by
every progressive district. Then, there was a proposition submitted to hold an ''educational congress''
in Iowa, but under the increasing number of conventions and associations it was considered as
impracticable. Indeed, it was just at this time that
several organizations had arranged to hold a joint
meeting at Iowa City in conjunction with a summer
school of science supported by the University.[217]
Since instructions were given at this meeting to
preserve twenty-five copies of the proceedings for
the archives of the Association one may conclude
that their publication was authorized, but as to the
location of the ''archives'' there was no specification.

Although the associations of city superintendents and principals and county superintendents, which were component parts of the State Teachers' Association, met during the summer of 1878 their deliberations must be incorporated as a part of the State meeting at Marshalltown in December of the same year. Indeed, the same questions were arising in both the general and the auxiliary associations. One is impressed with the advocacy of the use of the public press as an instrument to create public sentiment favoring the schools and its employment by school men. There are also evidences of the approaching commendation or condemnation of examinations and of the "red tape" exercised in supervision. Furthermore, the right of the State to certain definite results from its system of public instruction was presented for earnest consideration; while the relative educational value of Greek and Latin and the sciences was a subject in harmony with the tendencies of the period. It was the good fortune of the Association this year to secure the assistance of Dr. W. T. Harris, superintendent of the schools of St. Louis, who spoke on the "Theory and Art of Education"; while Judge George G. Wright of Iowa gave a practical address "full of advice and experience, applicable to the teachers' profession."[218]

During the summer of 1879 three branches of the Association met at Clear Lake — the State normal institute, the county superintendents, and the city superintendents and principals. Among these groups, however, were many college men who were

16

not identified with any one of them. Wisconsin was drawn upon at this time for instruction, Mr. Robert Graham, an expert in institute management, being present from that State; while President Newton Bateman of Knox College was called from Illinois.[219]

Six cities contested for the privilege of entertaining the State Association in 1879. Against the protests of some in the southern portion of the State the meeting was located finally at Independence. It was shown that during the life of the organization it had been held north of the center of the State but three times, while it had gone south for eighteen years. Although there were threats of secession, such folly was at once condemned. There was, however, an "inter-state" meeting at Allerton, near the Missouri line, while the State convention was in session at Independence — an action which was interpreted as a reflection on the wisdom of the executive committee.

Dr. Mark Ranney introduced a new subject to the teachers of Iowa at the Independence meeting, for never before had any one spoken of the possibilities of education in counteracting the tendency to insanity. Aside from this there was no new feature presented during this session, although the social program might be considered as setting a new standard for entertainment on the part of the city visited. But this was not vital to the school system of the State. No one, it appears, came from beyond the borders of the Commonwealth to present theories or to inspire to new effort.[220]

Des Moines was chosen for the annual meeting in 1880. Here the attendance was larger than at any former time. There was an apparent demand on this occasion for a more active service on the part of the Association in organization, in legislation, and in providing for the educating of public opinion through local interests, as well as through means of communication that would make the general Association influential. It was here, too, that the advisory council for the Superintendent of Public Instruction was appointed. But the only event out of the ordinary seems to have been the address of the United States Commissioner of Education, General John Eaton.[221]

It was in 1881, at Oskaloosa, that recommendations were made for section meetings the following year, in order that common interests might be discussed, the previous effort in this respect having failed to become permanent. Several sections met for preliminary organization before final adjournment, and thus prepared for the succeeding session. It should be mentioned that one paper on this occasion caused some excitement in the ranks of the Association, namely, the one on "The Psychology of Crime". There seemed to be none who were friendly to the speaker's opinion — which was an uncommon occurrence.[222]

Somewhere in the series of annual meetings previous to 1880 the long established custom of closing with the doxology and benediction was abandoned. In 1882, however, the doxology was sung at the beginning, and thus the session was opened at Cedar

Falls — which was a new meeting place. The executive committee of this period had invited suggestions relative to the subjects for consideration, and thereafter set a new example in distributing the proposed program broadcast over the State. It was the opinion of many in this convention that the constitution of the Association should be revised, and action was taken with that end in view. It will be remembered that it was necessary in 1872 to restore the constitution, parts of which had been lost, and in so doing certain changes had been made in that document in harmony with the growth of the organization. The committee for the purpose of this second revision in 1882 included S. N. Fellows, G. L. Farnham, W. J. Shoup, M. W. Bartlett, and S. T. Boyd.

It appears that the Association through its executive committee had taken an active part in aiding Iowa College in restoring some losses caused by the great cyclone of 1882. Owing to the great interest of the members in that event Professor H. K. Edson, by request, gave a vivid description of what occurred in the catastrophe which left the college without a class room. It is noted, too, that the incident of the previous year, when the paper on the psychology of crime was so severely attacked, was revived in another instance which served to provide, to some extent, for a further study of unfortunates. Then, "The Legal Rights and Duties of Teachers", presented by Professor Emlin McClain of the State University, seemed timely; while that on "Industrial Education'', by Mr. C. P. Rogers, was more or less prophetic. It was in 1882, moreover, that the movement to secure Federal aid for common schools was before Congress, and the members of the Iowa Teachers' Association, at the suggestion of the National Association, requested Iowa members of the House and Senate to support the measure.

Previous to the adjournment of this session the city superintendents' and principals' section arranged for a committee conference on the revision of the constitution, in which the matter of the appointment of an ''executive council'' should be considered. Another committee, also from this section, was instructed to confer with a similar body from the college section relative to a course of study preparatory to entering college. Finally, the Association pledged its support to the prohibitory amendment to the State Constitution.[223] Thus, for ten years, the Association had operated under the second constitution and had developed certain new phases of effort by which there was a growing tendency toward unification of purposes as a whole, yet with a decided demand for specialization through departments.

XV

INCORPORATION AND EXPANSION

THE twenty-ninth session of the State Teachers' Association when assembled in Des Moines in 1883 was without a president or a first vice-president, both having left the State. The former, Mr. W. W. Speer, had become identified with the schools of Chicago; while the latter, Mr. G. D. Farnham, had become connected with the schools of Nebraska. Thus, it became the duty of the second vice-president, Mr. L. L. Klinefelter, to preside. A proposal of the executive committee, composed at this time of Homer H. Seerley, Charles E. Bessey, and Leonard W. Parish, favored the establishment of the Association at some permanent meeting place, thus providing a central point favorable to all teachers in the State. Although the Association had always been represented in national meetings, now for the first time it appears, a small appropriation, not to exceed twenty-five dollars, was recommended for the use of the Iowa delegate or director of the National Association.

It was in 1883 that the committee chairman reported the new constitution, which after some consideration was adopted. Thereafter, three departments — the county superintendents and normal

230

department, the graded and high school department, and the college and university department — were to compose the Association; while provision was made for the organization of other sections upon the written application of twenty members. The new document made provision also for an educational council. Furthermore, under the requirements of the by-laws enrolled members only were to be permitted to vote, and receipts for annual fees might be demanded before the casting of ballots.

The first educational council, consisting of twenty members from the general Association and the several departments, was organized this year. Indeed, the entire session was arranged in accordance with the new constitution. It is worthy of note that previous to this time a contract had been made with the *Iowa Normal Monthly* to publish the proceedings, which thereupon became available to enrolled members. Thus the valuable contributions of numerous papers were preserved.[224]

The next session (in 1884) was also held at Des Moines, but on the west side of the river. Thus the custom of moving from year to year was not broken. Plymouth church, the scene of so many sessions of this organization, housed the meeting which enrolled a largely increased number, or a total of 336. The chairman of the executive committee, Professor C. E. Bessey, like the president and vice-president before, had left the State. He had become a member of the faculty of the University of Nebraska, but remained loyal to the Iowa Association. He sent his enrollment fee by mail and telegraphed his registration. The State University faculty, being detained by a late closing of the fall term, sent regrets through President Pickard who gave the reasons for their non-attendance. Superintendent J. W. Akers, Professor T. H. Macbride, and Professor Samuel Calvin, who were at the exposition in New Orleans in the interests of the Iowa educational exhibit, forwarded a message relative to the outlook at that place.[225]

In 1885 six hundred teachers were in attendance at the Association meeting which for the third time in succession was held at Des Moines. Over four hundred of those present were enrolled. The feature of this session was the address by Mr. Jonathan P. Dolliver on "Public Virtue as a Question of Politics". No one was called from outside the State to assist in providing instruction or entertainment, and it was declared that more interest was manifested than for several years. This year, too, the proceedings were issued as a separate publication, a practice which has ever since been followed.[226]

The annual meeting of 1886 was distinguished by the appointment of a woman to the executive committee. It had been pointed out that while three-fourths of the teaching force was composed of women only one appeared upon the program among forty participants — which seemed to be a sufficient reason for a radical change. Superintendent J. M. Greenwood of Kansas City was the only one in addition to Iowa teachers who had a part in the program. Governor William Larrabee gave the Association an entire evening in an address upon the "Ideal School". It was this convention, which, upon the suggestion of Mr. T. S. Parvin, decided to present the matter of State recognition of the Association to the executive council, and if necessary to the General Assembly.[227]

It was in 1886 also that the section devoted to secondary instruction held its first session and became a recognized department of the Association; that the movement for a reading course for children was inaugurated; that graded and supervised township schools were proposed; that the Association ordered a congratulatory letter to be forwarded to Berryman Jennings, Iowa's first teacher; and that the educational council urged the more extensive establishment of county and city high schools, or, if these could not be provided, endowed academies, in order that the "youth of Iowa" might have advantages beyond the district school.

After several successive meetings at the capital of the State, the session of 1887 was called at Cedar Rapids where more than four hundred were enrolled. Instead of one woman, as in 1886, there were now eight who shared in the literary proceedings — thus fulfilling the predictions made the year before when a woman was elected to the executive committee. Again the entire program was provided by home talent, the chief address being given by Mr. S. M. Clark of Keokuk, a favorite speaker among Iowa teachers. At this session the articles of incorporation, prepared by a committee appointed the pre-

ceding year, were adopted. By the terms of this
document the principal place of business was fixed
at Des Moines, Iowa, and by it provision was made
for five departments — a department of penmanship
and drawing being added to those already established.[228]

During the annual meeting of 1888 the women
teachers of the State perfected an organization, not
as a part of the Association, but to meet yearly at the
same time. Of this organization Mrs. L. T. Weld
was the first president. For the second time a
woman, Miss Lottie E. Granger, was chosen president of the Association; and in order to make sure
that a woman would occupy the executive office at the
next meeting, another woman was selected for first
vice-president. Again the Association determined
to meet at the capital of the State. Indeed it was
clear that the time would soon come when Des Moines
would be made the permanent meeting place for these
annual conventions. Once more, too, the matter of
preserving the early history of the institution, now
an incorporated body, was presented, with the result
that authority was given to proceed with such preparation as might be necessary to place this material
in the souvenir number of the *Iowa Normal Monthly*.
This suggestion had been made, it appears, through
Mr. George B. Dennison of Muscatine, a member of
the first executive committee (1854), and Mr. C. C.
Nestlerode, twice president of the Association while
he was in charge of the Tipton Union School from
1856 to 1862.[229]

While but five hundred had identified themselves with the Association in 1888, the next year witnessed a remarkable increase, when more than eight hundred registered as members. For the first time, it appears, the session extended into the New Year. Moreover the convention of that year established a noteworthy record, not only in attendance but also in the reports submitted, the most complete report being that of the committee on "Educational Progress", which included information from many sources relative to legislation, higher education, associations, industrial education, judicial decisions, co-education, and text-books. Furthermore, the educational council presented the draft of a compulsory attendance bill for the consideration of the general Association, by which it was approved although a minority of the council had reported adversely.[230]

When the Association met in annual session in 1890 attention was directed toward the preparation that would be necessary for the approaching Columbian exposition; whereupon action was taken to coöperate with the Iowa commission. But no exceptional movements mark the session of this year, although it is noticeable that two outside speakers, Dr. E. E. White of Ohio and Superintendent George Howland of Chicago, were placed upon the program.[231] There was a tendency at this time to subdivide the organization into small sections — a movement which threatened, it was said, to destroy some departments previously established. Subsequent events will illustrate this point.

In the convention of 1891 Dr. Andrew S. Draper gave the principal evening address. Indeed, the custom of drawing upon other States for such support seems to have been practiced from 1890 to date without exception. Preparations were now under way for the coming exposition, and the claims of that great event upon the schools of Iowa were presented by Professor Thomas H. Macbride. Within a period of ten years it had fallen to him to supervise the installation of two school exhibits — one at Madison, Wisconsin, and one at New Orleans — and so his suggestions were authoritative. It is worthy of mention also that the section of city superintendents and principals held its first independent session this year.[232]

A special feature, limited, however, to one hour of the entire session of 1892, gave recognition to the pioneers who established the Association. While but two members, Mrs. George B. Dennison and Mr. T. S. Parvin, of the original Association organized in 1854 were present on this occasion, papers of great interest were sent by others who were personally acquainted with the facts of thirty-eight years before. Henry W. Lathrop, C. C. Nestlerode, H. K. Edson, Jerome Allen, and E. R. Eldridge, each submitted reminiscences which have been preserved in the published proceedings. Although this session had been called at Cedar Rapids, after several successive meetings at Des Moines, it is noteworthy that an amendment to the constitution was now proposed which would fix the meeting permanently at the capital of the State. Another event of more than ordinary interest was recognized in the retirement of Mr. D. W. Lewis from the office of treasurer after a quarter century of continuous service.[233]

Since 1893 the State has published the proceedings of the Association. The first action taken on this matter appears to have been during the session of the year just mentioned, when the executive committee was instructed to secure the necessary assistance through the department of public instruction.[234] There were in 1893 seven section meetings in addition to the educational council, and also nine ''round table'' groups; but to cover the growth of these and the development of the Association along lines that have included every phase of educational activity would require an entire volume.

The enrollment had increased in 1894 to over nine hundred, and the sections of library and school officers were recognized as component parts of the institution, while the rural teachers had arranged for a round table in conjunction with the other grades of work. It had been said by Deputy Superintendent Ira C. Kling, an authority on this matter, that the organic school law had not been changed in any fundamental way since 1858, when country schools were the only ones in operation. Therefore, what ''round table'' was more appropriate than that for rural school teachers? It was in 1894, also, that the Iowa Society for Child Study came into existence, under the direction of a few leaders, notably, H. E. Kratz, O. C. Scott, and C. P. Rogers.

The events of 1895 and 1896, when the enrollment

of nearly eleven hundred showed something of the possibilities in attendance, included a revision of the constitution which seemed to be so outgrown that changes had become quite necessary. The constitution was adopted as revised in 1896, and thereafter under its provisions the district and county organizations were to be recognized as "subordinate associations". As such, moreover, they were to provide for united action through county delegates who should meet in district conventions; and in this joint meeting provision should be made for two members from each county in the several districts as official representatives to the State meeting. The difficulties surrounding the growing number of sections and round tables were partly obviated by the revision.

But the revised articles of incorporation adopted in 1896 were so reconstructed the next year that the somewhat complicated provision for delegate representation from counties and districts was removed, thus giving no real opportunity for a trial of its operation. There were four prominent speakers from other States before the session of 1895, namely, Commissioner W. T. Harris of Washington, D. C., David Starr Jordan of Leland Stanford, Jr., University, and John M. Coulter and Miss Florence Holbrook of Chicago. In 1896 there were but two outsiders — Mr. C. B. Gilbert of St. Paul, and Mr. Booker T. Washington of Tuskegee — while in the years before 1890 the Association had generally made up the entire program of persons from within the State.[235]

The convention of 1897 was noteworthy on account of the unanimous expression of good will toward Henry Sabin, who retired from eight years of service as State Superintendent. By resolution of the Association he was made "Superintendent Emeritus" as long as he should live, and, furthermore, upon him was conferred "in perpetuity the freedom of the state teachers' association."[236]

Although large inducements had been offered by other cities, the meeting for 1898 was appointed at the capital where, on this occasion, the main subject for consideration seems to have been: "Do the schools meet the reasonable demands of the people?" For the third time, it appears, this subject had come before the Association and it was officially recommended for consideration by all departments and round tables during the session.[237] Again, in 1899 a general discussion was featured in all departments relative to the desirability of greater efficiency and power of the Association in the State. At this session the noted journalist, Murat Halstead, was probably the greatest attraction.[238]

It was in 1900 that provision was made for a reserve emergency fund of $1000 by instructing the executive committee to set aside $100 annually until such sum had been accumulated. This sum was to be used only in emergencies and then only under the authority of the Association. It was made the duty of the executive committee to submit thereafter an annual report relative to the principal and interest in this fund and to make inquiry as to the will of the organization when the principal amount had been reserved.[239]

On December 20, 1901, the committee of twelve of the State Teachers' Association, which had been engaged for some months in the work, completed the high school manual and submitted it to the Association on the 28th of the same month. Although full consideration of this valuable effort must be deferred, it may be said in this connection that the Association at the session of 1900 had provided for financial support in placing the manual in the hands of high school authorities in the State. Another recommendation relative to "teachers examinations" made by the educational council in 1901 was an important contribution to the studies on that subject and probably influenced subsequent legislation. A notable experiment of the convention was the provision for its continuation over Sunday with a suitable series of events appropriate to the day. On this occasion Bishop J. L. Spaulding delivered an address upon "Moral Education", while the afternoon was given up to the Sunday school as an educational factor.[240]

Again in 1902 the Association had under consideration the proposition for another exposition for which a committee was appointed to coöperate with the State department of public instruction. The next year the plans already matured were approved. At both these sessions an advanced stand was taken on the new compulsory attendance law, as well as on some needed legislation relative to the certification of teachers and to a substantial provision by which their compensation might be more equitable. It was in fact declared that a campaign of education should be instituted to accomplish these results. It was in 1902, furthermore, that an effort was made through an amendment to the constitution to abolish the educational council, but the support for such a movement was not of sufficient strength to bring success.[241]

It was fitting that the convention of 1904 should include an observance of the fiftieth anniversary of the life of the Association. That nearly a full day devoted to a review of education in the half century should not be held as too much of the session to commemorate suitably the events of these years is worthy of note. Indeed, the 1904 meeting will remain as one of the most important for that reason alone, although the great winter storm prevented the fulfillment of all the plans of the executive committee.[242]

It has been said that a new spirit of progress and unity marked the annual meeting of 1905, when more than thirteen hundred members were registered. It was determined on this occasion to use all the forces of the Association in an endeavor to secure legislative action on at least one desired reform, namely, the certification of teachers, for which the legislative committee had provided a measure. Heretofore, it appears, there had not been a united effort in such instances.[243] The results of this movement are well known. In coöperating a real influence was brought to bear upon the General Assembly.

17

In 1906 and 1907 the movement for further reform and advancement was continued, and to encourage it many prominent leaders in educational thought were brought from distant States. It is noticeable, too, that industrial training was receiving attention in making up the annual program. Indeed, a careful study of the growth of the Association will reveal the educational innovations as they were recognized as meeting in some measures the demands of the time. In 1907 the executive committee sought to discover the preference of the teachers of the State relative to the place of meeting, but with little satisfaction as to interest in the matter. It was therefore retained at Des Moines. Again, in the spring of 1908 a vote relative to changing the annual meeting from the holiday season to an earlier date was taken, with the result that beginning with 1909 the convention has assembled in November.[244] Thus the way was opened for a large increase in the attendance.

The convention in 1908 approved the work of the commission appointed to revise and codify the school laws, and the measures proposed by that body were supported before the General Assembly by members of the Association. In 1909 the effort to establish a larger district unit was endorsed, and, although previous legislation was accepted with a purpose to make it effective, the necessity for amendment in the near future was well foreseen. It was in 1910 that the last revision of the articles of incorporation was submitted, by which the legislative committee was established on the basis of three representatives from each congressional district — that is to say, thirty-three in all, one-third of whom should retire from office annually.

The business of this rather large representation thereafter was to consist mainly in recommending subjects for consideration by the educational council, and in presenting to the General Assembly such legislation as the council might direct. There were, furthermore, some minor changes in the designation of the departments recognized as composing the Association, while an important provision made all persons, who had maintained membership in the Association for three years in succession, members also of the educational council. One should note likewise the effect of the change in the convention season; for, although in 1909, the first year of the change, the enrollment as indicated by fees was less than 1500, it was shown to have reached nearly 3900 in 1910, and more recently has exceeded 5000.[245]

With more than $2000 in the permanent fund, in accordance with amendments to resolutions heretofore mentioned, and with more than $3000 at the command of the treasurer, some field of operation could well be financed by the organization. It was therefore appropriate that a most important piece of fundamental work should be undertaken for which the Association in 1911 set aside $2000 of its accumulated funds — not to pay men, indeed, but to further the cause of education, thus exemplifying the old-time spirit of the pioneers of the institution

whose words had so recently been made a part of the
Association records. This movement, pronounced as
one of the most significant in the history of the
Association, had in view an "educational campaign"
which should seek, first of all, for definite information relative to conditions which might form a basis
for subsequent action. From this there resulted the
appointment of the body known as the "Better Iowa
Schools Commission", which in 1912 presented to the
Association, and subsequently to the General Assembly, a number of important conclusions as well
as some radical recommendations relative to legislation.[246] While this accomplishment may be viewed
as but a beginning of the true effort of the organization, it would seem to be a fitting conclusion to so
many years of activity during which no session has
ever been wholly abandoned.

Thus, from the call of less than twenty teachers
in 1854 when rate bills were yet the fashion, when
there were no free schools, when great sacrifice must
be made to reach a given destination by primitive
methods of transportation, when a half hundred was
a large attendance, when debts were met by subscription, and when enthusiasm was the chief reward for
the investment of energy and hard-earned dollars,
the State Teachers' Association has come to 1914
with thousands of members, and thousands in the
treasury — with members who know little of the experience or of the names of pioneers or of rate bills
or association debts. A volume, dedicated to the
pioneers who founded it, should be devoted to the
history of the Iowa State Teachers' Association.

XVI

COUNTY AND DISTRICT ASSOCIATIONS

WHILE the greater number of minor meetings among teachers of similar grades of work and also of conventions of a general nature but local in organization are of recent origin, there are some that were instituted at a comparatively early day. For instance, on February 21, 1857, the first session of the Cedar County teachers association convened at Rochester, where the first subject under consideration, the "Cause and Cure for the present Apathy on the subject of Education", was discussed by William McClain, H. Starr, C. C. Nestlerode, and Samuel Dewell, all of Cedar County, and by D. Franklin Wells of Iowa City. That this was not a temporary organization is shown by the fact that it held its thirteenth session in 1861 and that it had been so well maintained that county school matters were practically dictated by it.

At its first session measures were taken to establish a local standard of qualification for teachers; and for that definite purpose three persons were appointed as a county board of examiners, who were authorized by this self-appointed agency to examine and certificate teachers "in the name and on behalf of" the association. This board was instructed,

245

moreover, to fix the standard of qualification just as high as the demand for teachers would permit, and to establish three grades of licenses. It is noticeable that all persons should be examined in "physiology", irrespective of whether such a subject was required under the laws of the State. It was ordered further by the association that two annual examinations should be held, while the treasury of the organization would become responsible for expenses incurred in providing record books and for "printing plain, neat certificates." Other committees were charged with the examination of text-books for the information of the association; to correspond with publishers relative to prices "wholesale, retail and [for] introduction"; to draft a plan for organizing and conducting a county library for teachers, with township branches; and to investigate the various kinds of school furniture.

Later, in 1861, after the authority of the county superintendent to visit schools had been repealed, it appears that this association through its committee on superintendency, employed the county superintendent, Mr. James McClung, to visit schools at the expense of the organization which had guaranteed him two dollars per day. Again, it is observed that the coöperation sought by the Secretary of the State Board of Education in holding the series of institutes, as outlined in a former chapter, was not agreed to on account of the unfavorable time of year (July) which had been assigned to Cedar County.[247] Other counties, doubtless, were fully as ambitious as Cedar, but one account will suffice to indicate the local activity at a time when the State Association was developing its primary resources.

Out of such beginnings there have grown in subsequent years many, not to say numerous, combinations known as township associations, round tables, district associations, bi-county, tri-county, or other groupings, until the four quarters of the State have succeeded in establishing meetings that rival or even excel in some particulars, the State organization. Among the earliest of these smaller groups the "School-Masters' Round Table" of eastern Iowa may be cited. It included superintendents and principals in the territory from Clinton to Boone on the east and west, and from Hampton to Des Moines on the north and south. This one round table arranged meetings at Marion, Marshalltown, Cedar Rapids, and Cedar Falls, all within a single year, thus reviving the custom of the State Association in 1857. Moreover, it should be understood that these were not formal gatherings, but conferences where men learned of each other through personal contact. The fellowship there established made the meetings of great value, while at the same time they were productive of State movements which were planned in these smaller councils.

In 1888 the principals and superintendents of the fourth congressional district formed their own association arranging for at least two meetings within a period of six months. Some well-known names appeared in that group in October, 1888 — for example

Mr. J. B. Knoepfler, who was afterwards State Superintendent, and Mr. Edwin G. Cooley, later superintendent of the schools of Chicago. During the same month a "big-four" meeting, which included counties about the town of Sheldon, discussed, among other subjects, science in the grades, fractions, primary language work, the relation of school work to the development of moral character, Scotch methods of education, and music. Nor was the important question of the day, how to teach the effects of stimulants and narcotics as the law required, neglected on this occasion.[248] These subjects suggest a program of the usual type.

A year later the women teachers of southeastern Iowa met in a "round table" in Cedar Rapids. This movement was clearly in harmony with the association of women formed in conjunction with the general State Association. It is noteworthy that the old question of equality in compensation was recognized in the slogan, quality and quantity of work, not sex, the standard for wages. During the same year there were other new "round tables" that came into public notice, notably, the central Iowa group meeting at Boone; the west central educators round table meeting at Carroll; the school masters round table of the "blue grass region" meeting first at Council Bluffs; and the Mississippi round table which included men from Illinois, all of which maintained an organization for a limited period.[249]

During 1891 Superintendent Sabin recommended that these several forms of educational gatherings should undertake to formulate plans for the approaching Columbian Exposition.   Thus all units were employed in furthering the cause then being promoted by the general Association.   It was through a call issued by Superintendent Sabin in 1894 that the first of the large district organizations was summoned at Storm Lake.   He expressed at the time a desire to see not less than three hundred present in May of that year.   Soon after he issued another call for a similar assembly of the northeastern section at Waterloo, this time in November, 1894, where he anticipated an attendance of five hundred, urging especially the presence of rural teachers.   In this second call there was a definite declaration of a purpose to agitate reforms, and to educate the public until they were obtained.[250]   The attendance at these sessions which were originated by the State Superintendent did not disappoint him.

With the northern half of the State thus committed to the district plan, it was but a brief period before the same arrangements were completed in the southern half.   Indeed, before the adjournment of the State meeting in 1894 both the southeastern and the southwestern associations were provided for through executive committees, the former having designated Fairfield as its first point of meeting while the latter selected Council Bluffs.   It is worthy of note that these district meetings paid special attention to a division for school officers which later came to be a feature also of the State organization.[251] The attendance upon the southern district associations at the first session in each instance was over seven hundred, indicating that a greater opportunity was afforded through four such organizations than through a single State meeting which had not yet considered the advisability of selecting some earlier period than the holidays for the annual convention. It was granted, furthermore, that the talent secured in the former was equal to that offered by the latter; and it became the policy of the graded schools to close so that teachers might attend.

While the southern district associations were being established those of the northern were increasing in popularity, more than eight hundred having enrolled at Sioux City in April, 1895. The northeastern section was equally successful in October of the same year. In the meantime the "round tables" were losing their former place, since the larger and apparently permanent sections had become well established. Indeed, it was at this time that the final meeting of the round table in the northeast was held at Charles City, its members arranging then to unite with the large district association. It was prophesied in 1896 that the State Association would soon be overshadowed by the district meetings, and there was reason to think that this prediction would be fulfilled.[252]

It must have been gratifying to the originator of these district meetings to observe their immediate success and their effect upon the educational interests which he was endeavoring to promote. It was appropriate, too, that on the occasion of Superintendent Sabin's appearance before the northeastern meeting at Dubuque in 1896, where he gave an address on Horace Mann, that at its conclusion a little girl should hand to him a great bunch of roses presented by the fifty-five hundred pupils of the Dubuque city schools.

One might follow these district associations through subsequent sessions, but their general procedure was very much like that of the State convention described in previous chapters. Often the same speakers appeared in all of the four districts, and usually some were brought from abroad as the "special feature". It is noticeable, however, that the presidents of the State Normal School and the State University were heard on all occasions, and always on questions most nearly related to the actual educational needs of the Commonwealth. The president of the State Agricultural College likewise participated in this general educational revival. The number attending the territorially subordinate meetings continued to increase until, under the old custom of the holiday session, the State Association could no longer equal their attendance. Indeed, in 1909 at Cedar Rapids the northeastern division broke all former records of any State Association meeting, when nearly fifteen hundred were registered, the same district having passed a thirteen hundred registration two years before. Other districts had reached one thousand, but none had approached the attendance recorded in that quarter of the State.[253]

While these greater conventions are illustrative

of what may be accomplished in bringing opportunities nearer to those interested, the cause of their popularity may be found in the large number of minor groups which were often represented in the larger assembly. For example, it was pointed out that during the year 1895 eighty-six counties had well organized associations for teachers, while fifty-seven of these had township conventions as well, which meant that, including the larger divisions, there were during the year a total of eleven hundred meetings. It was shown further that the number had nearly doubled in the biennial period, which indicated to some extent the effect of the larger organizations upon local interests. For this no one individual may be given the credit, since leaders were active everywhere. At the same time there were some who were more conspicuous than others; and it is a fact that the teacher in the ranks was showing signs of growing into an appreciation of these mutual improvement organizations.

It was Henry Sabin who had written in 1895 that ''a dead teacher in a live community is out of place. A live teacher in a dead community becomes disheartened and fails to do good work. But a dead teacher in a dead community, God pity the children.''[254]

PART V
MISCELLANEOUS ACTIVITIES

XVII

EDUCATIONAL JOURNALS

BEFORE the enactment of the free school law in 1858 a journal, which sought to provide the means of communication between the educational agencies and also to promote generally the interests in public instruction, had been provided. Broken files of this early publication, as well as of other journals subsequently established and abandoned, have been preserved. For example, it is of interest to note the contents of number eight, volume two, of the *Iowa Journal of Education* issued in August, 1854, at Dubuque by R. Spaulding, editor and proprietor. This publication had been established in 1853 as the *District School Journal of Education for the State of Iowa,* but at the beginning of the second volume the title had been changed. It appears that one R. R. Gilbert was the first editor, while R. Spaulding, a book-seller, was the publisher and later also the editor.

The issue here referred to was more than educational in its scope, since it contained general information relative to agriculture as well as miscellaneous news items. There were, indeed, but two items of State school news, namely, a mention of the catalog of Denmark Academy for 1853 and a reference to the *Iowa Medical Journal* — the publication of the medical college at Keokuk which was at one time affiliated with the State University of Iowa. While the *Iowa Journal of Education* seems to have had a fair circulation it was, nevertheless, suspended at the end of the second volume.[255]

That some permanent support might be given to such a publication, which it was clear would be patronized by an interested element in the population, Superintendent James D. Eads recommended legislation authorizing his office to subscribe for a sufficient number of copies to supply each district in the State. With such encouragement it was believed that private enterprise would undertake the publication. At the same time it was declared that this "medium of communication", which should contain all laws and instructions of the Superintendent relative to schools, should be under the general control of that officer.[256] It remained, however, for the State Teachers' Association to inaugurate a movement to provide the desired means of communication.

In 1857, therefore, *The Voice of Iowa*, edited by Mr. James L. Enos under an agreement with the executive committee of the Association, was begun and continued for a year and a half or through three volumes. The financial support thereafter would warrant no further contracts on the part of the committee; and so for nearly a year, or until October, 1859, the State was without an educational journal. It appears, then, that *The Voice of Iowa* was the second Iowa journal devoted to the interests of education. It was in the first issue that the editor made the observation that "history must treasure our growth as a State, and in no form can it be more conveniently referred to than in this. We shall therefore seek to gather all of interest in our early history and seal it from decay." In this connection reference was made by the editor to the assistance that might be available through the organization of a State Historical Society then contemplated, and which he hoped to see effected "early in the present year" (1857). *The Voice of Iowa,* he declared, occupied a new field.[257]

The recommendation made by Mr. Eads in 1854 was enacted into law in 1858, when *The Voice of Iowa* was recognized as the official educational journal and when school district clerks were authorized to subscribe for one copy for the use of the district. Moreover, upon the formation of a school library the statute required the librarian to protect the copies of this journal as in the case of other property. The aim in this legislation, it will be observed, was the distribution of official communications and decisions of the Superintendent of Public Instruction.[258] The enterprise was also privately encouraged by Mr. Andrew J. Stevens of Des Moines, who, "with a view to lend it some pecuniary support as well as to disseminate educational intelligence among our people", proposed to send the publication free of charge to each school district and literary institution in Polk County.[259] Within three months of the first issue *The Voice of Iowa* had found its way into nearly every county in the Commonwealth as well as

18

into many other States; while a majority of the districts had acted under the statute authorizing subscriptions by the clerk thus assuring a circulation of about one thousand copies.[260] Nevertheless, it was suspended at the conclusion of the third volume.

The State Teachers' Association in 1859 again undertook the publication of a journal through the management of the executive committee, and in October of that year the first number of *The Iowa Instructor* appeared. It was edited by the chairman of the committee, Mr. C. C. Nestlerode, who for some time bore the greater part of the necessary expense of publication. This journal was maintained under unfavorable financial conditions until 1862, when it was united with *The Iowa School Journal,* which had been published by Mills Brothers of Des Moines from July, 1859. Of *The Iowa School Journal* Mr. Andrew J. Stevens was the first editor. There were good reasons for the combination of these two journals for it was recognized, it seems, that only by this means could the educational interests of the State be united. It was said, indeed, that such a union was quite necessary in order to heal ''a division that was unhappily springing up among us'' — an expression which suggested an ''East'' and a ''West'' within the borders of the Commonwealth. Some diplomacy was exercised, it appears, in bringing about this consolidation, for an entire day was spent in conferring before a plan was fully completed and the title, *The Iowa Instructor and School Journal,* agreed upon. In September, 1862, the executive committee of the State Teachers' Association at a meeting in Muscatine ratified the arrangement by which only one publication appeared in the following month, with Mills Brothers as publishers. The editing of this publication was provided for through the coöperation of the Teachers' Association, the publishers, and the Secretary of the State Board of Education.[261]

In May, 1859, Mr. S. S. Howe had ventured to establish at Iowa City a small journal known as *The Literary Advertiser and Public School Advocate,* which, although begun previous to the other two of that year, was the least pretentious, its form being that of a quarto of eight pages. It was published monthly at twenty-five cents a year. Moreover, when *The Voice of Iowa* suspended publication its subscription list was transferred to this new journal; and so, it came to pass that the editor claimed the support of the law of 1858 which authorized the district clerks to provide a copy for each school, because in the statute *The Voice of Iowa* was specified. When all three journals offered their pages for the use of the Board of Education and its Secretary, it was ordered that each should become a "medium" of communication, one of which was located in Des Moines, one in Iowa City, and one wherever the executive committee of the State Association should determine.[262] After the consolidation of the two journals above named there was no disagreement since *The Literary Advertiser and Public School Advocate* had gone the way of its predecessor, while an act of 1864 recognized *The Iowa Instructor and School Journal* as the official organ of the State Superintendent and authorized him to distribute copies thereof to all county superintendents, provided it contained his decisions and instructions.[263]

It was not until 1868 that the long title produced by the consolidation of the two journals was abandoned for that of *The Iowa School Journal,* which was retained until 1875 when the publication was transferred to the *Common School* journal projected in 1874 by Mr. W. E. Crosby, superintendent of the Davenport schools. For sixteen years, from 1859 to 1875, *The Iowa School Journal* was edited by persons of ability who gave their services, for the most part, to the State Teachers' Association — at least until that organization determined in 1870 to assume no further responsibility relative to any journal.

The Secretary of the Board of Education and the State Superintendent were charged at different times with the editorial management. It was in 1868 that, owing to the increasing duties of the office, Superintendent Wells declined to continue as the editor, declaring that such duties were incompatible with official functions imposed by law. Although he resigned in May the State Association refused to accept the resignation at the subsequent session; and Mr. Wells was retained as resident editor. At the same time he said that, "for whatever of confidence and appreciation the election may indicate, I am profoundly grateful. The honor and emoluments I would gladly resign to another; for the honor is vanity, and the emoluments, vexation of spirit.''[264] Mr. Jerome Allen had been selected as editor in 1869; but owing to absence from the State he resigned his office, thus making it necessary for the executive committee of the State Association to substitute others, among them Jonathan Piper, S. N. Fellows, William H. Beach, and Major Hamill.[265]

It was in 1872 that a second consolidation of *The Iowa School Journal* occurred, this time with *The Manual,* a publication which seems to have been begun in 1871 in Keokuk under the management of Mr. C. M. Greene who, by the union, assumed the control of the *Journal* until its transfer to the *Common School* as mentioned above. The latter publication appears to have been short lived, since in 1877 there was a distinct demand for a new undertaking in educational journalism.

At a meeting of the State Institute in 1877 there was begun a movement which had for its object the establishment of a journal upon a new basis. Mr. L. B. Raymond of Hampton was requested to undertake the editorial management, but owing to official duties he declined, the more firmly he declared, when he learned that Mr. W. J. Shoup of Dubuque was prepared to assume the responsibility. It was in August, 1877, therefore, that *The Iowa Normal Monthly* was founded with Mr. Shoup as editor; and from that date until 1912, under the patronage of Iowa teachers it was issued each month. Its first editor fostered and successfully maintained a vigorous publication. Indeed, the files of this journal will remain the source not only of very much of State educational history but also of the views of educational leaders as expressed from time to time through formal papers. Since it was the official journal of the Superintendent of Public Instruction it became important also to preserve it in all educational and general libraries. It is fortunate, indeed, that such a journal was projected and sustained during this period of Iowa history.[266]

It was in 1877 that the *Central School Journal* was established at Keokuk under the management of Mr. J. W. Rowley. Several editors succeeded him before the *Journal* was purchased in 1883 by Miss L. G. Howell, who was to have the editorial assistance of Mr. S. M. Clark of the *Keokuk Gate-City*. The *Central School Journal,* it appears, was maintained until 1895. But there were yet other publications, *The Normal Index,* edited by Mr. E. R. Eldridge of the Eastern Iowa Normal School, together with *The Iowa Teacher,* appearing in 1882 at Marshalltown under the management of Marvin, Morissey, and Churchill, would seem to have provided school journals enough for one State. Nevertheless, *The Northwestern Journal of Education* was projected in 1885 in Des Moines by Miss Ella Hamilton as editor and Mr. G. S. Cline as business manager. The latter publication took over in 1886 *The Iowa Teacher,* which had suspended publication in that year. Although *The Northwestern Journal of Education* had announced the consolidation in May, 1886, it, too, before the next issue had transferred its subscriptions to the *Teachers' Institute* of New York, thus clearing the field for those remaining.[267]

The Iowa Teacher had championed the "new education"; while *The Northwestern Journal of Education* was ambitious to occupy a territory much larger than the State. On the other hand, *The Iowa Normal Monthly* was established as an Iowa journal and designed to occupy that field more especially. It was said by Henry Sabin in 1893 that Mr. W. J. Shoup was "absolutely fearless as an editor, and did not hesitate to express his opinion upon the educational vagaries of that day. He edited his own paper in every sense of the word."[268]

Of the publications above named, not one is now published. *Midland Schools,* the only surviving school journal in Iowa, was not established until 1889 under the title of *The Iowa School Journal,* which was changed to *Iowa Schools* in 1892, when for two years Henry Sabin was its editor. Later Mr. F. B. Cooper occupied the position of editor and was followed by a number of men who at some time have been actively identified with the public school work of the State.

A journal of special interest to school officers, *The Directors Round Table,* was undertaken by Mr. J. H. Richards at Iowa Falls in 1894. A stock form for counties consisting of general educational matter was issued for several years under the name of *The Iowa Teacher,* at Charles City. This publication was distributed through the county superintendents who supplied the local matter for one or two outside pages.

Although the school journals of Iowa had been many in number and quite different in character, according to the particular field to be reached, it was the opinion of Henry Sabin, expressed in 1895, that the educational journal most needed in Iowa was one that would "reach the people in their homes as well as the teachers in their school rooms." That is to say, such a publication should aim to shape public opinion in favor of certain important measures which were necessary to improvement. Moreover, "the directness of its utterances should command the respectful attention of other papers"; while all questions should be discussed from the standpoint of public utility. He granted that such a paper would be voted "dull and uninteresting" to such as were unprepared for the higher views of educational work, but this was but an indication of the training yet necessary before persons should be permitted to enter the teaching profession.[269]

For sixty years, therefore, individuals as well as the State Teachers' Association have attempted to promote the interests of education through the publication of periodicals with the certainty that a time would come when each would be abandoned for a new venture. Whether the profession has been at fault, or whether the courage of the promoter, editor, or publisher has failed at a critical time is not clear. Nevertheless, the record reveals the fact that in Iowa several types of educational journalism have been attempted, encouraged, and finally abandoned.

XVIII

SCHOOL LIBRARIES

AMONG the provisions of the educational laws of Michigan, from which Iowa drew one of her earliest statutes, was one authorizing districts to levy a tax "for the purchase of a suitable library case", and also an amount not to exceed ten dollars annually for books which were to be selected by the district board when so directed by the electors. This provision became effective in Iowa by the adoption of the general school law of 1840, and was applied in some of the earliest organized districts. Where and by whom this public property should be cared for was also to be determined by the district but under rules defined by the Superintendent of Public Instruction.[270] To be sure, there was no general effort to apply such a statute in its entirety, as has been frequently observed, but it is significant that such a provision was not forgotten when in May, 1846, the constitutional convention included in its proposals to Congress that "one quarter section of land in each township be granted to the State for the purpose of purchasing a common school library for the use of such township."[271]

Subsequent legislation encouraged the formation of libraries, although other equipment was held to be

265

more important by those responsible for the administration of the schools. While it was said in 1857
that attention was being drawn to such means of
education, it was declared by the county superintendents in convention in 1858 that good buildings
should precede everything else while text-books and
apparatus should follow. Furthermore, it was the
opinion of that body that the tax for libraries should
be assessed upon the township rather than upon the
district.

While the statutes provided abundant authority
for district action it remained, nevertheless, for the
teachers again to take the initiative in arousing
public interest and in contributing the funds for the
maintenance of a working equipment; and so, what
were designated as teachers educational libraries
were collected in several counties. As early as 1877
Keokuk County reported four hundred volumes,
valued at $700 — the voluntary offerings of more
than one hundred teachers aided by a few enterprising citizens. At that time the income of the
library association amounted to twelve dollars per
month, which was applied to its support through the
county superintendent, Mr. H. D. Todd. In 1879 this
collection had increased to six hundred volumes —
all available to the teachers of the county. A similar
plan was pursued in Mahaska County, where three
hundred volumes were provided through branches in
convenient places.[272] This arrangement was made
possible through a county association with a township organization. Other counties also adopted the

same methods, among them being Cerro Gordo, which organized a library association in 1878. Grundy County organized a similar association in 1880, Polk County in 1882, while the Mason City public and the county teachers library were placed under one management in the same year — both libraries being made available to teachers for a moderate fee.

While this movement was in progress certain communities were providing more liberally for the districts. For instance, in 1883 Jasper County reported more than twenty schools with independent libraries, while as much as $200 was voted for a township library in Jackson County. About the same time (in 1884) there were in the State, it was declared, not more than ten townships and seventeen cities and towns with libraries of more than three hundred volumes.[273] During the decade from 1881 to 1891, however, there was an increase of nearly 72,000 volumes in the district libraries of the State — that is to say, from about 27,000 to nearly 99,000 — while all of the schools in the twenty-four cities of four thousand or more in population possessed a library of greater or less value, varying, it is true, from 4300 volumes in the highest to thirty in the lowest. In 1897 there were one hundred and ninety districts with libraries above two hundred and fifty volumes, the cities of Marshalltown and Clinton being far in the lead in this respect.[274]

By the provisions of the *Code of 1897,* which authorized boards to expend twenty-five dollars for this purpose without a vote of the electors, it was hoped that an impetus would be given to the selection and purchase of library books. To assist in this matter, Superintendent Sabin issued a circular of information concerning the names, list prices, and the publishers of not less than two hundred choice books, each of which was briefly described as to content so that all might understand the nature of the volume purchased. Again, the General Assembly in 1898 requested the State Superintendent to make, during the succeeding biennial period, a full investigation of the question of free school libraries in other States. Accordingly, that officer compiled and submitted a report to the General Assembly in 1900. The conclusions from this investigation, conducted by Mr. Richard C. Barrett, led to the recommendation of an act requiring the withholding, for the purchase of library books, of a definite annual amount from school money received, thus providing a legal minimum that must be expended for books in all districts.[275]

While the *Code of 1897* permitted the expenditure of a given amount without a special vote, the statute of 1900, passed in accordance with the recommendation above mentioned, required the withholding by the district treasurer of each school township and rural independent district of a sum equivalent to "not less than five nor more than fifteen cents", as the board might determine, for each person of school age. The fund thus withheld should be expended under the direction of the president and secretary of the board in conjunction with the county superintendent in the purchase of books selected from lists prepared by the State Board of Examiners. It became the duty of the district secretary to distribute these volumes among such districts, and thereafter, at least semi-annually, to collect and redistribute the same. That is to say, the secretary became ex officio the township librarian, while the director in sub-districts and the secretary in rural independent districts were required to act in that capacity.

At the same time there was created a State Library Commission which should assist in the formation of school and public libraries by advising as to their establishment and administration.[276] Thus an opportunity was not only offered to each district to provide library facilities, but the law required action relative to the accumulation of choice books, which, in the opinion of the best informed, was the only method which would improve the taste for good literature.

Although it must be said that some boards refused to enforce this act, it was very generally observed — but probably not at the maximum amount which the law specified. In this connection it is worthy of mention that a citizen of O'Brien County, Mr. Geo. W. Schee, employed his wealth in encouraging districts not only to use the full amount allowed but also to raise additional sums by offering prizes to those most successful in northwest Iowa. His own county was so well managed that in 1901, after a period of five years growth, it possessed

10,500 volumes representing an expenditure of $6300 for the rural schools, or an average of eighty books for each district in the county. At the same time the graded school libraries of that county included 4000 additional volumes; while a special collection of 650 volumes for teachers was maintained through the generosity of Mr. Schee, who gave $100 annually for five years for this purpose.

Other counties in the northwest were pursuing similar plans. Osceola County reported an average of sixty-four volumes for each rural and ninety-four for each of the graded schools, while 400 volumes constituted the professional library for teachers. Here, also, the influence of the money and inspiration of Mr. Schee was apparent. During the biennial period ending in 1901 the county of Palo Alto had raised $9000 through private subscriptions for library purposes, while Calhoun County increased its library equipment by 3000 volumes during the same period. Webster County likewise had a teachers library of 1200 volumes, with a central station from which eight traveling sets of about one hundred volumes were sent over the county for local groups of readers.[277] No section of the State was able to equal these counties in the rapid improvement in library equipment.

Previous to the legislation for and also before great attention was given to the instituting of libraries, the teachers reading circle was established under the direction of the State Teachers' Association. The reading circle was inaugurated, it appears, through a suggestion or recommendation made by the president of the Association, Mr. Homer H. Seerley of Oskaloosa, in 1884. The committee on president's address proposed in their report the appointment of nine members to arrange such a course of reading.[278] Immediate action seems to have been taken, resulting in the adoption of the plan by more than half the counties of the State before June, 1885. The county superintendents had become the leaders in the organization of such circles. While the institution seems to have been begun in the proper spirit, it was said in 1889 that the reading circle had not prospered as in other States; and so, a reorganization appeared to be necessary. It had been suggested, furthermore, that the Superintendent of Public Instruction should be authorized to name certain professional books as the basis of an examination on the reading course, thus providing an incentive which would result in greater interest. While it was true that some counties had not neglected this matter it was considered that uniformity in the course and some method of testing the thoroughness of the reading was desirable.

It appears, then, that in 1889 the reading circle board, composed of six members selected from the county superintendents section of the State Association with the Superintendent of Public Instruction as chairman, established a uniform course with a definite working plan for the four years. From the commencement in 1889 with a small enrollment it was shown that by 1895 "nearly 30,000 teachers" had profited by such reading.[279]   The plan originated in 1889 has prevailed practically to the present time; and, moreover, while this movement was in progress that for the extension of library facilities was also being developed, the two thus supplementing each other doubtless to the advantage of both.   It is in accordance with the original design, too, that teachers are required by the certificate law now in force to pursue a course of professional reading before certain licenses will be granted.

Another agency which for a time influenced the growth of libraries originated in 1891 and was designated as the "Iowa Pupils' Reading Circle".   It was modeled to some extent upon the plan provided for the teachers.   There was much machinery connected with it, and numerous inducements were offered to secure activity upon the part of pupils, while books were prescribed for grades from the second to the twelfth of the graded systems.   Four years from the time of organization more than 50,000 children were registered in these reading circles.[280]   With the increased facilities offered by library equipment, however, the purchase of the books required through the pupils reading circle was no longer necessary, and therefore such a scheme had no place in the economy of administration.

Such a combination of effort as these forces represent has resulted in the accumulation of a great collection of books in numerous libraries and at a large outlay.   Indeed, it has been said that $100,000 annually is expended in additions to these free libraries, while the total accumulation in 1910 was estimated at nearly 1,100,000 volumes. Of this number the greater part, or 644,000, were in the rural schools. Although, as mentioned above, the State Board of Examiners provided lists from which selections were to be made, their authority did not extend any farther; and there was not then, nor is there at present, any general State supervision over this feature of the educational equipment. It has been recommended, therefore, that the Library Commission be given authority over such libraries so that expert advice may be available in their selection and maintenance.[281] Finally, it is observed that the most recent tendency is toward a consolidation of school and free public library interests either through management or coöperation.

19

XIX

INDUSTRIAL TRAINING

IT was in 1808 that Father Richard on the Michigan frontier provided that the schools which he established for girls should instruct in "sewing, spinning, knitting, and weaving", while at the same time the young men in other institutions should devote themselves to Latin.[282] Such provisions were in accordance with the views of a day when higher education consisted in classical training adapted to men, and when the domestic duties of women required a knowledge of certain household industries.

Nearly forty years later when Iowa was admitted to the Union, the Constitution contained a section which required the General Assembly to encourage "agricultural improvement"— it being foreseen that the people must for some time devote themselves largely to that pursuit. Such a provision was as much adapted to the needs of those who would till the soil as the industrial training of the school of Father Richard was suited to those taught therein. Moreover, this reference to "agricultural improvement" did not pass unnoticed, for Governor Ansel Briggs in his biennial message of 1850 called attention to the fact that no steps had been taken by the

274

General Assembly since the adoption of the Constitution, for the advancement of agriculture. "This portion of the Constitution", he declared, "is as obligatory and binding as any other. It was probably inserted for the reason that our State has every facility for becoming, in an eminent degree, an agricultural State. The best method of cultivating the soil is, and it is believed ever will be, a subject of the first importance to a large majority of the citizens of the State. The greater portion of those who attend our Common schools will become agriculturists, when the term of their education expires; and consequently, any knowledge which they may obtain, touching that branch of industry, will be to them of the most essential service. It would therefore seem to become your duty to enquire whether books relative to agricultural science, can, with propriety, be introduced into our Normal and Common Schools. I feel confident that, if introduced, the most beneficial results may be anticipated."[283]

It was not, however, until ten years later that the State undertook any movement in this direction; and it is well known that agriculture in the common schools is of such recent introduction that it can hardly be regarded as established. Moreover, it remained for one of the first colleges founded in Iowa to introduce scientific instruction in agriculture in connection with what was designated the *"Manual Labor Department"*. This institution, now known as Leander Clark College, but then as Western College, selected its location with the view of providing such instruction. Indeed, when the institution was organized in 1857 Professor S. S. Dillman had been engaged "to take charge of the College farm, to furnish work to students, and conduct the whole, upon scientific principles". It was said further that this arrangement would afford to students "not only the privilege of becoming scientific farmers, but of paying a considerable part of their current expenses, in labor."[284]

Through some unknown philanthropist a half section of Iowa land was offered at the State Teachers' Association in 1857 to be appropriated to the purpose of establishing a manual labor school that should be a model for similar institutions. A certain writer, commenting upon this offer, cited as an example of what might be done in Iowa the practical results derived from an institution of this character in another State from which it was said every boy was discharged at sixteen "a practical farmer, and some are shoemakers besides", while girls learned "housework, and to measure, cut out, and make all garments worn by both sexes."[285] Moreover, it was about this time White's Iowa Manual Labor School was projected under the auspices of the Friends in Lee County, and had its plans succeeded the results would have been equal to those of similar institutions in other States.[286] To be sure these undertakings were largely dependent upon the land for their development; but it was clear that the time was approaching when a different training would be demanded.

Indirectly the General Assembly of Iowa provided for the introduction of industrial training in the common schools of the State in 1874. That is to say, in authorizing the "board of directors of independent school-districts, and the subdirector of each subdistrict" to provide at their discretion for industrial expositions "in connection with each school under their control", there was the implied authority to promote instruction in the preparation of the material for such a display. It is noteworthy also that the statute was specific in requiring that these exhibits should consist of useful articles made by pupils "such as samples of sewing, and cooking of all kinds, knitting, crocheting, and drawing, iron and woodwork of all kinds, from a plain box or horseshoe to a house or steam engine in miniature; also, all other useful articles known to the industrial world, or that may be invented by the pupils in connection with farm and garden products in their season, that are the results of their own toil." Furthermore "ornamental work" should be encouraged when "accompanied by something useful made by the same pupil."[287]

In the report of Superintendent von Coelln for the period ending in 1881 mention was made of the growing interest in the practical phase, as it was called, of education, which he declared was becoming "stronger and stronger" in order to provide some "substitute for the old apprenticeship". How this demand should be met remained to be answered, but he was certain that a law permitting boards of education to establish schools for the training of boys in mechanical pursuits would do no harm and indeed might result in great good. He made the suggestion that drawing at least should be taught in all schools, and that with special reference to its practical use. Subsequently Superintendent Akers declared that a "practical education" was better comprehended under the caption of "industrial training", and that the demand for this sort of education came through the feeling that the schools were educating away from manual work, thus inducing a loss of respect for the advanced subjects offered in the schools as well as leading to the conclusion that what did not minister to the immediate needs was decidedly impractical.[288]

While definite plans had not yet been matured the first report of the Iowa Commissioner of Labor appeared in 1886, in which the declaration was made that a "far better education" was needed to make a successful laborer than was then offered. That is to say, an education that would better fit him for service was not only desirable but it was demanded. Four reasons were assigned for the change which seemed necessary and desirable in educational facilities: first, competition had become universal; second, manufactories were endless in variety; third, there was a decay in the system of apprenticeship; and fourth, certain land once fertile had become old and impoverished. It was concluded, therefore, that education should include not only head work but hand work as well.

The Commissioner dwelt at length upon this phase of instruction, using the results obtained in the Washington Manual Training School of St. Louis as illustrative of what should be expected. It was shown, furthermore, that experiments were then being conducted in industrial training in the schools of other States as well as in commercial centers where it had been demonstrated that such work could be "joined to the ordinary grammar school work with good effect." With such examples it was declared that "Iowa, with its splendid record upon educational interests, ought not to be behind in this *practical education*", which would "dignify labor" and serve as a means of making a living.[289] The matter relative to such instruction was submitted by the Commissioner in accordance with that provision of the statute creating his office which required that he should report "what progress has been made with schools now in operation for the instruction of students in the mechanic arts and what systems have been found most practical with the details thereof."[290] This last provision was due to an amendment to the original bill as introduced in 1884 indicating, it appears, the interest of certain public men in the adoption of some such form of instruction in the Iowa public schools.

Among other influences affecting the introduction of industrial education in this State the proximity of the National Educational Association meeting at Madison, Wisconsin, in 1884, may be included. Many, if not great numbers, of the leading Iowa teachers were in attendance at that meeting, where the exhibit of this form of work, the actual results of the schools where such experiments had been made, was indicative of its possibilities. While elementary as compared to the more recent collections of this nature, it was sufficient to enlighten the educational leaders in many States. It is significant, indeed, that Superintendent Akers, in a report made subsequent to this meeting, explained his previous attitude toward industrial training and developed more fully the notion of this form of education, declaring his sympathy with the movement while at the same time pointing out the "stubborn problems" which confronted the schools at the outset. He concluded that methods then employed must be modified to meet the conditions which must arise upon the introduction of this practical form of instruction. Nevertheless, it was believed that the public mind was prepared for the change which it was declared should come "without unnecessary delay."

The direct methods suggested by the State Superintendent at this time (in 1885) would lead to the development of the shop department of the State Agricultural College, and to the establishment and equipment of a similar department at the State University. The State should provide also for "at least one great industrial school, where large numbers of young people could receive that training which would fit them for the position of masters or foremen in shops connected with the public schools". Moreover, the law should permit the creation of such

departments in county high schools, for the establishment of which the statute already made provision; while cities and towns of a "specified
population should also be empowered to establish
industrial schools or workshops, to be connected
with and form a part of the school system". With
such an arrangement it was suggested that the
customary classification of pupils would also serve
as a basis for divisions in the new department, while
the daily schedule should be "so adjusted that
classes could pass from one school to the other without friction or interruption."[291] Nor was this mere
theory: the plan had been tested in the schools of
other States, although in centers of large population.[292]

It was not, however, until 1888 that any city of
Iowa undertook to carry out these suggestions
which, it is clear, required no further legislation,
since all necessary authority had been granted in
statutes already in force. The credit of leadership
in this movement, as in many others described in
these pages, belongs to Davenport, which provided
first for a "cooking school" in charge of a special
instructor. Both the science and the art of cooking,
it was declared, were included in the instruction.
The attendance in this instance was optional and
limited to pupils of the ninth grade and above.
During the following year (1889) manual training
for boys was also introduced in a course which provided for work in both wood and metal, with drawing
as an important element. From the beginning this

work was not confined to the high school, since boys of fourteen years and over in other grades were admitted. Although optional, when once selected its pursuit was required for an entire year.[293]

About 1890 instruction in "sewing and baking" was provided by a ladies society of Oskaloosa in conjunction with the public schools. The school board appropriated $200 to aid the work; and the classes in this "industrial school", as it was designated, assembled on Saturday afternoon for a session of two hours. In the same year Des Moines introduced both domestic science and manual training for girls — a course of one year in each — while for boys the instruction covering two years included "drawing, joinery and wood turning." In this instance it was provided that such work might be substituted for indicated subjects in other courses.[294] While it is true that these early introductions of industrial work were mainly for higher grade instruction it is evident that the elementary schools were not excluded. It is proper, therefore, to include some of the details of organization in this chapter.

Iowa City was the third school corporation to establish shop work, its equipment being provided in 1892. In no other place, it appears, were such courses adopted until after the year 1900. Furthermore, of the nearly one hundred fifty schools offering industrial work at present (1914), not more than five were in operation in 1900. Moreover, more than two-thirds of the entire number have established these departments since 1906 — at least twenty of them being organized in 1913. The introduction of manual work for girls is still more recent, inasmuch as out of the total of about one hundred forty-five schools where such training is offered, almost two-thirds have made the necessary provisions since 1910. Indeed, twenty-one schools installed such equipment in 1913.

Likewise, domestic science, while the first form of industrial training to be introduced in the schools of the State, was not adopted to any extent until 1911 or thereafter. In 1911 there were about fifty schools with such departments, but in 1914 there are more than one hundred fifty — forty-four having been organized in 1913. Not more than five schools in the State were teaching domestic science before 1906. Thus the greater part of all activities along these lines is very recent.

Finally, there are the courses in agriculture, which, although the first to be recommended, are yet the last in adoption. Probably one hundred seventy-five schools are presenting (in 1914) such work, varying in quantity from one-half to four years. Of the number mentioned, all but twenty-eight have taken up the work since 1910. Forty-three or more began instruction along this line in 1913; and out of the total nearly half confine the course to one-half year. Actual experimental work in agriculture is carried on by at least twenty-five on plots of ground varying in size from three by ten feet to eight and one-half acres. It is true that this field of operation is as yet confined for the most part to high schools, but in some instances the work is already made available in the subordinate grades. If the history of instruction in agriculture follows that of the other industrial subjects, it will not be limited to advanced students. Moreover, of rural schools no account has been taken in this summary; but in these institutions one may expect to find the most fruitful field in agricultural instruction. It may be added that during the period in which manual training or industrial courses have developed, the instruction for boys has been extended to include pupils ranging from the fourth to the twelfth grades of the public schools; in needlework, from the fifth to the twelfth; and in domestic science, from the sixth to the twelfth. Thus, one may assume that agriculture will not long be maintained as a subject for those above the eighth grade only in the schools of town districts.[295]

It was said in 1903 that "because of prevailing or erroneous ideals and the lack of funds to provide rooms and equipment, only a few schools have established manual training departments." Although it was true that only some half dozen towns had dared to undertake this work there was a general interest in the subject and a "more general awakening" was observed. The statistics quoted above demonstrate the truth of this observation. It seems clear that when it was discovered that a comparatively small sum was sufficient to equip a shop for half a hundred boys the development of the work was very rapid. At the same time, the promotion of this movement by the National Educational Association had in some measure affected the introduction of manual training. The Committee of Twelve on rural schools, of which Henry Sabin was the chairman, had declared in favor of manual training in the country school, although it was recognized as a remote possibility under the existing systems of organization. Furthermore, the State Teachers' Association in 1902 gave its support to the introduction of industrial work when it adopted the report of the educational council in substance as follows: manual training should be introduced into the public schools of Iowa in the form of free-hand and mechanical drawing; cutting, weaving, and folding of paper and straw; basketry and clay modeling; work in cardboard, wood, and metals; designing, bench-work, sewing, cooking; and care of domestic animals and gardening. All of this was recommended for the purpose of investing dull subjects with new life, and of developing an idea of values and a wholesome respect for labor. Moreover, it would make schooling a vital part of life, not simply a preparation for life.[296]

It is probable that the publication of information relative to the details of equipment necessary in carrying on this form of instruction, and possibly also the efforts of certain companies to promote a system of correspondence by which the regular instructor would be enabled to direct manual training, had a hastening effect in ripening the sentiment relative to such courses. Superintendent Barrett, assisted by Mr. A. C. Newell, supervisor of manual

training in the West Des Moines schools, issued
through his biennial report in 1894 carefully prepared instructions as to the introduction as well as
the management of such departments. All of these
influences focused about the time when the greatest
advances were made.[297]   It is true, however, that, as
in many other innovations, a definite period of agitation preceded the adoption of industrial training as a
component part of the public school curriculum.

It was the opinion of the Superintendent of
Public Instruction in 1903 that the greatest obstacle
to the successful introduction of industrial work
would be found in the insufficient supply of qualified
teachers, and that the Commonwealth would be compelled to draw upon other States until a sufficient
number could be prepared. Again, in 1908 the same
observation was made relative to instructors in agriculture, there being no provision by which the State
could meet the demand. It seems clear that these
new features for which the schools were made responsible were in advance of the ability of the districts to provide for their presentation — a situation
apparently not foreseen, or at least not seriously
considered by those who insisted upon their adoption.
Thus the recommendation of Superintendent Akers
in 1885 relative to the preparation of instructors was
decidedly in season, and it would have been well for
the State had it pursued some plan similar to that
suggested by him.

The last investigation and report on this subject
was made by the Better Iowa Schools Commission of

the State Teachers' Association in 1912 through a special committee which concluded to recommend the extension of industrial education in the schools, by giving it a place in all courses of study and including in its presentation "the germs and educative extracts of as many trades and industries as possible". Furthermore, the farmer member of this committee, Mr. Thomas H. Barnes, after a special investigation made a personal recommendation relative to industrial training for the boys and girls of the rural schools. The arrangement proposed would include special supervisors in counties and townships for the work adapted to the two sexes. The supervisors were to work under the county superintendent, while the State was to aid in some manner all such special work. It was declared by Professor E. C. Bishop that the first need of instruction in agriculture was better prepared teachers and a legal requirement that this subject become a part of the qualifications. Moreover, the correlation of the home work, in which more than 14,000 boys and girls were enrolled in 1912, with the school interests was becoming a strong factor in the efficiency not only of the rural but also of the town and village schools of the State.[298]

From these facts one may conclude that the call for what has been designated as "the practical in education" has led to the introduction of several forms of industrial training as a part of the public school curriculum. But the public school authorities have proceeded cautiously in adopting measures to provide such instruction, although when convinced of its practicability they have been ready in many communities to admit the new department. At the same time qualified instructors have been insufficient to meet the demand, thereby producing some delay in instituting such work. It seems certain, however, that the industrial education of the present is but preliminary to a much larger development in the future.

EDUCATIONAL EXHIBITS

NATIONAL and international expositions have provided in increasing proportions for the presentation of material illustrative of the actual work of education. At Vienna in 1873 Iowa had a collection of material from the physical laboratory of the State University, but there seems to have been no effort to represent any other form of instruction in the State. Indeed, it was only the advanced methods in Physics then practiced in the State University that induced Professor Gustavus Hinrichs to carry a hundred or more laboratory notebooks of his students to the European city for display alongside with the work of similar schools of science on the continent.[299]

The later exposition at Paris in 1878 seems not to have attracted the educational interests of the elementary schools in this Commonwealth. But the intervening centennial exhibition at Philadelphia was productive of activity which resulted in a representative exhibit of school work from fifty or more towns of the State. In 1875 Superintendent Abernethy had issued instructions for the preparation of material for this exhibit; and while no such elaborate presentation was made as on later occasions of the same kind, Iowa had creditable mention in the final reports. The exhibition, it was said, was comparatively small and in no way remarkable — all the work being the product of some five hundred classes in the public schools.

The general report of the judges declared that while the "average quality was good, perhaps it will be conceded by all that Davenport acquitted herself best. Her schools presented work of nearly every sort shown by the foremost schools of the large cities of the country. The map-drawing was especially noticeable, both for amount and excellence." It was mentioned also that the exhibit of the Davenport training classes was the only one outside the range of common schools. It was said, further, that Iowa was considered as one of the great States of the West, and why she did not acquit herself better in this portion of the exposition was "for her to say."[300]

There was a somewhat better understanding of the importance of such matters when the exhibit was prepared for the National Educational Association meeting at Madison, Wisconsin, in 1884, and for the New Orleans exposition in 1884–1886. For the latter the material used at Madison was re-collected from the schools to which it had been returned, re-arranged, and put in charge of the department of public instruction. The personal supervision of the exhibit was assigned to Professor Thomas H. Macbride, who was later assisted by Mr. Frank M. Leonard.

The General Assembly had provided $1000 for financing the Madison exhibit on condition that the collection would be returned to the State and thereafter remain the permanent possession of the office of the State Superintendent, in so far as he might indicate a desire for the use of the same.[301] Nevertheless, a double effort in a single year was necessary to prepare for the New Orleans and the Madison exhibits, since the latter meeting was in July while the former was designed to open in December following. It was for the display at New Orleans that a map containing nearly 12,000 dots representing the exact location of every school house in the State was prepared with great care. To make this map accurate and authoritative sectional maps of the several counties were first compiled. This was the work of the State department; while forty towns and cities and at least seven counties, as well as all the State educational institutions, made due preparation. Reporting on the matter Professor Macbride said that "only those who saw and studied the exhibit in place" were prepared to "give an opinion of its excellence"; and he observed that in "comprehensiveness" the exhibit from Iowa was unrivalled.

The New Orleans exposition appears to have been the first instance in which the educational system of the State and all the forces connected therewith were brought together in a material way. Something of every grade of instruction from the kindergarten to the University was presented. The experience gained in the earlier effort at Madison had aided greatly in the preparation of this later collection.[302]

The influence of these general exhibitions was reflected in subsequent local displays in cities and counties, and in their maintenance since then at the annual fairs in many communities. The constantly increasing effort to meet the demands of the great international expositions reveals the pride that the State has had in keeping its place educationally well up among neighboring Commonwealths. As the time approached for the World's Columbian Exposition at Chicago activity among the public schools and higher institutions in preparation therefor was first observed at the State Teachers' Association late in 1890. In the following February the Superintendent of Public Instruction advised the presentation of the matter at all meetings of teachers and wherever people connected with the schools were assembled. Then the plans, so far as formulated, were presented to the General Assembly for consideration. To that body six specific recommendations were made as to the content of the display in 1893: first, a general view of all the educational forces of the State; second, a complete statistical history; third, material equipment; fourth, a financial record; fifth, the means of teacher training; and sixth, a tabulation of results.[303] This was the general plan suggested, although it was well known that developments in preparation would determine many unforeseen provisions.

Owing to the demand of school men for a separate

building devoted to educational interests, and also to the uncertainty in some arrangements, the preparation of the exhibit for the World's Columbian Exposition was delayed so that not more than one year remained to complete it. In order to stimulate effort the Iowa commission, through Mr. J. W. Jarnagin, the member in charge of educational matters, determined to offer a series of prizes to be granted under established rules at a preliminary display which should be held during the session of the State Teachers' Association at Cedar Rapids. Accordingly, provision was made for installing this preliminary display in December, 1892, and for the awards under a competent committee. In passing upon the various collections the committee declared, first of all, that those who had responded to the invitation to participate had shown commendable enterprise, while the collection in general was pronounced as being nearer a real exhibition of actual work than was usual. More, indeed, was presented than the prizes would warrant, since certain cities sent general collections which were not entered in the contest — Sioux City, Iowa City, Oskaloosa, and Cedar Rapids being specified.

In the awards at the Cedar Rapids preliminary display Cedar Falls secured first honors for the best general exhibit from any city or town; while the first prize for the best display from rural schools went to District No. 8 of Nokomis Township in Buena Vista County. Mason City stood second among towns, and District No. 2 of Blue Grass Township in Scott

County stood second among rural schools. Clinton came third in its class, while District No. 5 of Adams Township in Greene County came third among the rural districts. In the four groups of work — written, drawing, apparatus, and photography — the awards were well distributed among the competing schools. For the best individual effort Minnie Shafer of Cedar Falls was granted the first prize; the second prize went to Daisy Heath of Brooklyn; and the third prize to Emma Gulbrauson of District No. 8 of Nokomis Township in Buena Vista County.

Thus the nucleus for the Iowa educational exhibit at Chicago in 1893 was formed. After all this had been done, however, and the inspiration of the movement had begun to have the desired effect, it was somewhat discouraging to the commission to find associations and round tables declaring that under no circumstances would they have anything to do with the exhibit unless a separate building could be secured. For a time uncertainty prevailed everywhere, since the colleges, too, were refusing to have a part in the exhibit until it should be determined whether the exposition would open its gates on the Sabbath. But finally Iowa accepted the two thousand feet allotted in the gallery of the great liberal arts building, where, pushed up against the German Empire, she was soon requested to surrender three hundred feet of her space to that government.

Thirty-five cities and towns contributed to this exhibit at Chicago, while six counties — Poweshiek, Clinton, Marshall, Boone, Hardin, and Greene —

maintained general displays from rural districts. At the conclusion of the exposition the commissioners from France and Germany solicited a part of the Iowa collection for illustrative purposes in the training schools of their respective countries, and the proposed Columbian Museum also applied for a portion. Likewise the Philadelphia Educational Museum and the Bureau of Education at Washington formally requested a donation of a part of the exhibit.[304]

Although different opinions relative to the value of school exhibits were expressed during these years, and views were publicly announced both in condemnation and approval, it is significant that only about ten years after the Columbian Exposition another commission was preparing for even greater things at St. Louis. When it is remembered that the General Assembly in 1884 kindly set aside $1000 to aid in the Madison exhibit — an elementary undertaking — and that the Iowa Commission designated a fund of $8000 for the work to be sent to St. Louis, it seems conclusive that those who found no advantage in such exhibits were not upon the popular side. Furthermore, the part taken in this last great international exposition by more than ninety different colleges, city, town and rural schools indicates anything but disapproval of advertising the best things that may be produced; while the presentation of work from twenty-two county school systems reveals an increasing attention to the concrete in instruction, as well as a disposition to conserve results in various

forms. Many things have conspired to produce this
marked change, not the least, it may be said, being
the introduction of industrial work and the development of the rural school along so-called practical
lines.

In collecting the material for the Louisiana Purchase Exposition a plan similar to that carried out in
1893 was presented, the work being brought together
for temporary display during the meeting of the
State Teachers' Association at Des Moines and
thereafter prepared by the commissioner, Mr. F. J.
Sessions, for transportation and installation. When
thus established it was pronounced by observers as
at least equal to other exhibits where a much larger
fund had been available. In many respects, notably
in the industrial education exhibit, Iowa ranked
among the first.[305]

The local interest which may be awakened by a
collective exhibit of the plainest work preserved
from day to day, for which the law of 1874 had provided, is but an elementary type of that which arises
when larger groups are formed. Then, if there be
added to the elementary product the multiplied
forms of industrial work, which appeal to the multitude, the literary collections, artistic productions,
and individual inventions, one may understand the
cause for the continued interest in and the demand
for a repetition of State, national, and international
educational exhibits.

XXI

ELEMENTARY INSTRUCTION UNDER CHURCH DIRECTION

WITHOUT some reference to the private parochial or sectarian schools a history of education in Iowa would be incomplete. Indeed, the two hundred or more of these institutions, enrolling approximately 20,000 pupils in elementary work, are an important element in the educational equipment of the State. While the data upon which to base a discussion of this phase of education are meagre, a general view may, nevertheless, be presented.

In preceding chapters the early private schools which provided instruction to all children who were able to pay the small tuition fee have been described, but the schools now under consideration have been established for an entirely different purpose. Although it may have been true that the moral and religious training was not neglected in the private schools of the early days, the church has recognized a weakness in this particular in the public school of the present. Accordingly, schools which feature instruction in religious doctrine and morals and which are supported by contributed funds are provided in communities where adherents of a particular belief dwell in sufficient numbers. These schools, it need

297

hardly be said, are located at strategic points and are conducted in some instances during that part of the year when the public school is not in session; and they offer not only academic training but also special instruction in morals and religion. With the State and church wholly separated such schools have been held by some sects to be essential to church and family life. It is therefore to those sections of the State where the followers of certain teachings have settled in considerable numbers that one must turn for types of sectarian schools. Unfortunately no clear and comprehensive record of such schools has been preserved by the State department of education.

In this connection it is observed that the Lutheran denomination is largely represented in Bremer County, but it has established schools in other parts of the State as well — notably in the counties of Crawford, Calhoun, Iowa, and Marshall. Nor is its field limited by these institutions for elementary instruction, for it has also secondary schools and colleges which will be considered elsewhere. The Catholic schools of elementary grade, and one may include also their schools for higher instruction, are most numerous in Dubuque County; indeed, the older established communities along the eastern border of the State as well as Carroll, Chickasaw, Howard, and Pottawattamie counties are centers in which these Catholic schools predominate among the private institutions. Moreover, it is true that the Catholic schools outnumber those of any other organization in the State. Besides these the Evangelical, the Swedish and Norwegian Lutherans, the Friends, and the Hollanders in recent years have established elementary or secondary schools having practically the same end in view. Thus one may find in the same community various kinds of private parochial schools, as for example in Sioux County where several of the groups mentioned are well represented.

The earliest in this field of sectarian education were the Catholics, who established a school at Davenport under Father Pelamourgues, so it is said, as early as 1838; St. Raphael's school, at Dubuque in 1846;[306] St. Matthew's school, at Muscatine in 1852; St. Anthony's school, at Davenport in 1853; St. John's parochial school, at Burlington in 1854, and Holy Trinity, at Richmond in Washington County in 1855. There may have been other church schools during this period, but they do not appear to be reported as such. St. Mary's school was established at Dubuque in 1866, and there were two others located at the same place in the following year. One was opened at Lyons in 1864; another at Independence in 1869; and still others at Fort Atkinson and Spillville in Winneshiek County in 1870. St. James' school at Washington was provided in 1871; another was organized at Clinton in 1878; and another at Marshalltown in 1878. In 1879 the first of such schools was assigned to Le Mars, Plymouth County, and in 1883 to Creston, while Haverhill in Marshall County was selected for another in 1885. Osceola County was entered in 1887. Thus, settlements

have been provided with Catholic schools in the succeeding years until there are very few counties that
have no school under the direction of this church.

It was in 1862 that St. Paul's Academy, which
seems to have been organized for elementary instruction, was established by the Lutherans at
Denver in Bremer County. Within the subsequent
twenty years, however, a number of others of similar
character have been opened in the same county;
while at present there are at least sixteen of these
institutions located in that community. The same
denomination in 1871 founded another parochial
school in Minerva Township in Marshall County,
and two years later one was organized in Iowa Township in Iowa County. About the same time also others were established at Lowden in Cedar County and
at Eldorado in Fayette County. Again, in 1878
Boyden in Sioux County was occupied; and during
the succeeding year Lincoln Township in the same
county supported a Lutheran school.[307] It seems
clear, then, that these two denominations, namely,
the Catholics and Lutherans, are the most active in
the establishment and control of private schools, not
only for elementary but for higher instruction as
well.

The enrollment in these sectarian institutions
varies from six pupils in the smallest reported to
seven hundred or more in the largest. Moreover, in
some instances of the one-teacher schools, of which
there are many, the number assigned to an instructor seems to be exceedingly large. In consideration

of the recorded income of many of these institutions one may conclude that they are managed on a remarkably economical plan as compared with the public schools — although any definite conclusion from such limited data would be questionable.

Among schools of this type may be mentioned those established by the Hollanders, which for a time were maintained at Pella and then abandoned for the public schools, only to be revived in more recent years. Coming to Marion County in 1847, the Hollanders established schools under the laws of the State; and it would appear that an opportunity was then presented for the adoption of a complete organization which might have been controlled by the settlement just as the Amana Colony dominates today in its township. But no effort was made to provide that instruction in religious doctrine which the settlement approved until about 1861 when the first attempt to establish a Christian school was made in the village of Pella. A committee having the matter under consideration reported favorably at that time, and the necessary financial support was thereafter provided until about 1867 when the parochial school was suspended. No further effort was made in this direction until 1903, when a new movement resulted in a provision for the founding of a sectarian institution at Orange City in Sioux County in 1904. In each instance the objects set forth included training in the fundamentals of religious doctrine and instruction in the Dutch language — neither of which could be expected from the public school.

The Christian school at Orange City enrolls about two hundred pupils under four teachers; and another of the same character at Sioux Center provides instruction for one hundred thirty under three teachers. In addition to these the farmers in the vicinity have supported another institution, contributing $500 for that purpose. The Hollanders residing in Richland Township in Mahaska County maintain a school of sixty pupils, all of whom are taught by one teacher. Other schools have been projected by this denomination, more especially in the settlements in northwestern Iowa, and it is interesting to note that at Pella where the school was abandoned in 1867 there is a movement to restore it.[308]

Such schools as are described above have obviously no connection with the public school system. This is not true, however, of the schools at the Amana Colony. Here, it seems, all the opportunity desired for instruction in the traditions and beliefs of the sect is present, and at the same time the schools are organized under county or State supervision. This is made possible through the fact that an entire school township is owned and controlled by the Community of True Inspiration and in the seven independent districts organized under the statutes of the Commonwealth the officers are chosen by members of the Community, taxes are levied upon the property of the Community for school support, and teachers are employed from among the adherents of True Inspiration. Thus, while the law is complied with in all respects there remains a control by which the favored instruction peculiar to one people may be secured without molestation. Moreover, the schools are entitled to participation in the interest upon the permanent fund — although, as is well known, the amount is almost negligible when the entire support of schools is considered.

Not only in the matter of instruction is there peculiar privilege, but in the original and voluntary continuation of schools for fifty-two weeks in the year and six days in the week the Community has provided an example which the State at large might profitably study. Moreover, the divisions of the day into the *Lehrschule,* or the period of intellectual training, the *Spielstunde,* or the play time, and the *Arbeitsschule,* or the period of work in which the industrial features of instruction are predominant, offer many suggestions to the critic of our public school routine. All things, it seems, are adjusted by the administrators of the school unit to promote contentment, while the wished-for result — a child trained in the beliefs of his ancestors — is but a matter of time.

It is said that the yard about one of these Amana schools is truly a "German *Kindergarten* with plenty of green grass, big shade-trees, enticing grape-arbors, and a profusion of flowerbeds." Here the play time of the spring and summer is fully improved, while the work includes the care of the school garden. In the winter season the younger children, both boys and girls, are taught to knit and crochet. "Here the stranger is amazed to learn that five year old Minchen is knitting her second pair of stockings, and that little Wilhelm, brim full of mischief, is knitting his father's hose." And it is pointed out that "the atmosphere about the Amana school is more like that of a large household than of the ordinary school." Yet this is a public school which any child of school age is entitled to attend.

From the authority quoted above one may learn that the teachers of the Amana Community are selected for this particular service and the greater number are "old men — men who have devoted a lifetime to the training of Amana's youth. Some of them have taught so long that their pupils to-day are for the most part the children and even the grandchildren of their former pupils." While there is general supervision by the Great Council of the Community, each master is practically free to pursue his own individual method. The instruction extends to the branches taught in the usual grammar grades of the public school, but in addition there are the daily Bible readings and a study of the catechism. Furthermore, an interesting and suggestive feature is noted in the custom of devoting an hour at definite periods for instruction in the "history of the Community" as well as some account of the leaders in its establishment.[309] The entire organization, indeed, is an interesting study in community life existing in the midst of the distracting influences of a rapidly developing Commonwealth and maintaining its early policies, and at the same time complying with the statutes relative to the establishment of public in-

struction.   Where the entire community approves
many otherwise unpopular features may be permitted as the illustration here presented shows.

In addition, therefore, to the general elementary
school system of the State, organized under statutory requirements, many other schools are providing
instruction for thousands of pupils, and may, indeed,
carry them from the lowest grade of instruction
through the college course under the direction of
sectarian authorities.   Moreover, there are those
who patronize the public schools for the usual sessions and prolong the period of instruction and
supplement it by taking the desired religious training in vacation schools.   There are likewise instances
where the schools, although public, are yet so controlled that they perform the functions of parochial
schools; and, while a part of a State system and
under the present laws subject to State inspection,
they are not conducted on the same plan as other
schools of the county in which they are located.   One
might wish that the moral and religious atmosphere
of the public school was such that all would subscribe
to its management and thus make supplementary
methods unnecessary.

21

PART VI
PROPOSED LEGISLATION

XXII

CONSTRUCTION AND RECONSTRUCTION

FROM the history of school legislation and administration in Iowa it is evident that the enactment of a complete and satisfactory code of school legislation is a most complicated and difficult undertaking. It is therefore not surprising to find that many important recommendations though seriously and earnestly advocated were never written into the statutes of the Commonwealth. Moreover, a summary of these recommendations and other suggestions relative to school legislation will not only contribute to the history of education in Iowa but be of interest and value to the student of educational reform.

As early as 1848 the Superintendent, Thomas H. Benton, Jr., advised the repeal of the laws of 1840 and 1847 and the enactment of a new statute, retaining the fundamental principles of the former but constituting a clear and definite piece of constructive legislation. The new law need not, he said, be more compact, but it should be more explicit. And when enacted no delay should operate to prevent its publicity throughout the State. That his authority might be sufficient to secure observance of the provisions of the statute he recommended that his office be empowered to prepare forms for local use. More-

over, it was his opinion that the compensation of all
school officers should be fixed by law and in no instance be referred to the discretion of other authorities.

That the public had a right to have easy access
to the school laws seems not to have occurred to
legislators, and it is well known that for the greater
part of our history only officers responsible for the
execution of the provisions of the law were provided
with such information. At the same time it was declared by the Superintendent of Public Instruction
in 1849 that every family in the State should have
information relative to school legislation, although
the meagre supply of printed laws would in no sense
permit of such extended distribution. To be sure all
educational legislation previous to 1851 was included
by the code commissioners under one title (XIV), in
accordance with the recommendation of the Superintendent of Public Instruction, and thus the school
laws became available to all to whom the *Code of
1851* was distributed.

But the *Code of 1851* was soon out of date. In
1852 the suggested amendments were indicative of
the school legislation that must soon follow. For
example, it was apparent that since the title to school
lands was often questioned the Secretary of State
should be required to preserve an accurate record of
each patent (this was before the creation of the land
office) ; that district secretaries should be empowered
to assess the property therein without reference to
the county assessment roll, for it was often more

difficult to correct the county assessment transcript than to make the property list entire; that some method of admitting non-resident pupils should be devised; that some provision also should be made which would permit towns or districts to continue schools throughout the year; that a rate bill was desirable (it being pointed out that such a statute was in force in most States that had made much progress in education); that it should be made obligatory for districts to expend their money equally upon the summer and winter terms, it being the practice, it is inferred, for some to invest the whole amount in a winter school; that the duties then performed by the township trustees relative to surveying and plotting the sixteenth section, and also those executed by the prosecuting attorney in collecting delinquent interest, would be discharged as well by the county school fund commissioner; and finally, the school law as a whole should be made more specific.[310]

From 1854 to 1857 there were few direct recommendations relative to educational legislation. Indeed, the only recommendation in 1854 was the modest suggestion that the Superintendent of Public Instruction be authorized to subscribe for a school journal as the official organ of his department. In 1856 there were no recommendations — due, to be sure, to the sitting of the Mann commission. But in 1857 Superintendent Fisher quoted largely from the recommendations of the commission of the previous year, emphasizing especially the provision that

would substitute the district township for the independent districts. Moreover, the hope was expressed
that "we have arrived at a new epoch in our legislation on the subject of education". At the same
time the Superintendent pointed out that a question
relative to the amount that should be raised by taxation was about to be presented to the approaching
General Assembly. As an illustration of the serious-
ness of this problem it was shown that if Iowa kept
pace with Massachusetts not less than $650,000 must
be collected — that is to say, one dollar for each
inhabitant. Since this appeared to be impossible it
was suggested that a compromise be effected by raising the levy from the extremes of one-half and one
and one-half, to not less than one and one-half nor
more than two and one-half mills.

It is noteworthy that influences outside of the
State were used on this occasion to impress the General Assembly with the importance of the situation,
since it was declared that, "the adversity which has
fallen so heavily [in 1857] on the Eastern States,
and so lightly on this, has turned the eyes of many
people to the West. They are watching with anx-
iety, your legislation with regard to education, to
determine whether they will cast their lot in this
State. If your legislation is such as there is every
reason to anticipate that it will be, a great addition
may be expected to our population during the ensuing year."[311]

The first General Assembly which met under the
Constitution of 1857 was much in doubt as to its

authority relative to educational legislation since that instrument located the initiation of such legislation with a new department — the Board of Education. In the dilemma one of two things could be done by the General Assembly: enact no legislation whatever, or pass laws and assume the risk of their being declared unconstitutional in those sections which were not immediately associated with the financial part of the system. No action would mean the postponement or suspension of school organization, since the legislature alone could make appropriations and the Board of Education would hold no session until the following December. It was determined, finally, to enact a general education law, although it was well understood that such legislation would in no way affect the authority of the Board of Education. The act was based upon the principle that "it is the duty of the government to make provision for the education, under its own supervision, of all the youth of the State" and that "sufficient money should be provided, by taxation on the whole property of the State, to accomplish this purpose."[312]

While hesitation was manifested in the General Assembly the people were not inactive. This is indicated in a communication of February, 1858, wherein it was observed, "with deep regret", that there was in the General Assembly a disposition to oppose the enactment of a school law, partly on the ground that it would be unconstitutional and partly because it would be acting discourteously toward the new Board which would thereafter be elected. Such an attitude in the legislature would not satisfy the people who for four years, it was declared, had been demanding a change in the school organization — especially since it was evident to everyone that the interests of the State required such action. While it was agreed that the Constitution did provide for a legislative body which should confine its law-making to the interests of education, it was absurd to think that it was the intention of the constitutional convention to leave all the agencies of popular education without any power to regulate their affairs for a period of sixteen months — the time that would elapse from the adoption of the Constitution to the first session of the Board of Education.

The people, it was affirmed, were insistent in their demand for action and feared to leave the matter of legislation to the Board of Education because the Constitution had put it beyond their power to appropriate any funds to carry their legislation into effect. It was therefore essential that the General Assembly should make some provision during the session of 1858; otherwise the old law must stand for at least two years more — a condition not to be thought of after the long period of agitation for advancement. No legislator could excuse himself, it was declared, should there be a failure at this session to grant that which had been so universally expected from the legislature of 1856–1857. Furthermore, the bill then (February 17, 1858) in the hands of the committee was of such a nature that it would doubtless meet with the approval of the Board of Education, while it would at once set in motion the machinery of the educational system.   The adjustment of its parts, which, it was thought the Constitution imposed upon the Board of Education, could be attended to later; while if the whole matter was devolved upon that body the defect due to lack of authority relative to funds would destroy the whole structure.[313]   That is to say, the Board of Education, in the opinion of some at least, was created to cure defects in legislation only and not to promote fundamental changes.

Following the approval of the law of March 12, 1858, favorable views were expressed as to the legislation, since the best talent of the State had been engaged in perfecting it.   All parties — for it was clear that political interest had coöperated to bring about its enactment — were called upon to support the measure in order that it should not "lose vitality by negligence and inattention."   Again, it was said that the State was about to enter upon a new era educationally under this new statute which, there was reason to believe, was "equal if not superior to that of any other State of the Union."[314]

Not all views were of this character, however, and the observation of Governor Ralph P. Lowe that repeated and radical changes in school laws, although sometimes necessary, were always attended with temporary inconveniences and sometimes with serious injury was shown to be true in this instance. In the year immediately following the enactment of the new system there was a demand for its repeal on account of what was called the "bungling system" provided through the district organization. Some political capital, it appears, was made out of this point in 1859; and it was believed in some parts that the law was a mixture of the plans of Horace Mann and the peculiar notions of Senators Jonathan W. Cattell and J. B. Grinnell.[315] The Board of Education seems to have been forgotten along with its deliberations in December, 1858.

It must be concluded, however, that the radical changes incorporated in the law of 1858 were in its favor since interest was at once aroused — even if only the interest of opposition. It was said, indeed, that up to the time of the adoption of the new Constitution few knew under what school law they were operating; while it was clear that no such attention had ever been paid to the cause of popular education as within the months subsequent to the approval of the new legislation.[316] But the opposition was importuning the General Assembly to restore what was termed the former independence, for it was well understood that the legislature possessed authority to overturn any proposition of the State Board of Education. It was a critical period in educational legislation in Iowa.

Although nearly 8000 officers, who were to be the agents in its execution, were elected under this act, very few had any acquaintance with the provisions of the law previous to their selection. There was naturally some confusion; and numerous questions were submitted to the State Superintendents, as well

as to county superintendents, relative to duties devolving upon subordinates.   The opposition often
encountered in the old districts must be met by those
endeavoring to establish a new organization on
which they personally were not fully informed, and
which it was said was not easily comprehended in all
its parts.   But these were recognized by good people
as temporary; and to relieve the situation the convention of county superintendents was called at Iowa
City in 1858.   The questions submitted to Superintendent M. L. Fisher and answered by him — although the replies are not recorded — seem to have
cleared the atmosphere to some extent, while sundry
amendments were proposed for consideration by the
Board of Education or by the General Assembly.
Among these the very first suggested the abolition
of the subdistrict, since this provision of the statute
had caused more trouble than all others put together.
Such divisions, it was declared, were "uselessly multiplied", certain townships having nine or ten when
four or five would be sufficient.   There was a recommendation, also, that scholarships be established in
every district (township) in the State in order to
provide for trained teachers — a plan to which reference has been made in former chapters.   There
was another suggestion, likewise, that would authorize the establishment of schools for a limited time
for the exclusive training of teachers in counties
unable to sustain a high school.[317]

In the following year, 1859, the Secretary of the
Board of Education, although opposing any change

of importance, recommended some minor corrective amendments to the new statute. Had it not been, he said, for certain difficulties which must be overcome his suggestions would have assumed "an entirely different character." One direct amendment he would have, however, which would fix the salary of the county superintendent by law rather than leave it to the determination of the presidents of the district boards as the statute then provided. County superintendents in their several communications were not, it appears, so conservative as the Secretary in their suggestions relative to the reconstruction of the law. Among the many recommendations the following are common: let the civil township be made the school district with a board of three members, a president, a secretary, and a treasurer, each of whom should be compensated for his services, and let the subdistricts be abolished; there should be an institute held annually in each county at the expense of the same; the county superintendent should not be compelled to visit schools more than once a year, but he should be required to explain the law governing the common school; the county superintendent should control the school fund; subdistricts should be authorized to employ their own teachers and to levy taxes for all purposes. Since nine-tenths of the trouble in some counties grew out of the subdistrict system its abolition was repeatedly recommended. Another would make each subdistrict independent as under the old law. At the same time one leader in educational opinion declared that the law should remain unchanged; while another like-minded educator expressed his admiration for the "main features" of the statute.

To some a permanent law was impossible under the provisions of the Constitution, since the two controlling legislative bodies would not or could not harmonize their actions. Again, that part of the act relative to the apportionment of school money was not just since some other basis than the ages of five to twenty-one must be adopted, for the advantages were not equal under such a method. It was said further that there should not be generally more than four districts in a township and no subdistrict with less than forty to sixty pupils. Another would repeal the whole system and abolish the office of county superintendent. Still others found the system defective in working power through omission of important features. On the other hand just as strong declarations were made as to the positive success of the act. Moreover, it was suggested in this symposium of county superintendents that the district secretary should be required to supervise the schools therein, make monthly visits, examine the records, and see that they were properly kept, while the school month and year should be fixed by statute.[318] Thus, local opinion was expressed through the only channel of communication — the county superintendent — who usually reflected the attitude of his constituents.

It has been shown that in 1859 the Board of Education amended the first law (that of March 12,

1858) without fundamentally changing it, and the
reasons therefor were later presented to the General
Assembly by the Secretary who urgently requested
that body not to interfere with its operation. It was
shown in the communication of the Secretary that
the law of 1858 was accepted by the Board almost
without modification because it had already been in
force for six months, and any radical reconstruction
would have been demoralizing. Moreover, modifications would have but added to the confusion arising
over the decision of the Supreme Court. Finally, it
was felt that a defective statute, if well understood,
would prove of greater advantage than a new one.
At the same time early action by the General Assembly (in 1860) was desirable that the Secretary might
know that there would be no modification before he
proceeded to publish and distribute the school laws.

The General Assembly profited by these suggestions, the only amendments made being those necessary to give vitality to the law — namely, those
providing for the collection or expenditure of money
without which the legislation of the Board would
have been ineffective. It was soon recognized that
the chief trouble in legislating for schools was in the
"peculiar provision of the constitution" whereby
there was required the concurrence of two legislative bodies — the General Assembly and the Board
of Education — which were never in session at the
same time. It was doubtful therefore whether a
perfect understanding would ever be possible.

Furthermore, the people did not comprehend the situation under which these two branches of government were often embarrassed. This, it was asserted, was the chief reason for letting the law stand until the time came when the General Assembly should have a clear field, that is to say, could do all the legislating for schools.

During the period immediately following the enactment of the law of 1858 there was manifested in some sections a disposition to take advantage of subdistricts in the construction of new buildings — a feature of the law which the Board of Education sought without complete success to remedy in 1859. Two distinct features had to be adjusted, namely, the provision for the equalization of taxes among the subdistricts of the township, and that requiring the electors of the township to vote a tax for a subdistrict house. It had become quite common for the voters to refuse to sanction a tax after the majority of districts were accommodated. For instance, a township having seven districts might cheerfully erect buildings in five of them and absolutely refuse to assist the other two. Although such practices were recognized as dishonest they were nevertheless accepted as typical of human nature; and so, it was recommended in 1861 that an amendment should compel such a tax levy, the method proposed being through authority conferred upon the county board of supervisors (recently created) to levy a tax upon a township wherein a subdistrict was demanding improvements.[319] In this there appears the sugges-

22

tion of centralization of authority in the county government to enforce a statutory provision which should be primarily enforceable by a township board of education.

In 1863, after the publication of the amended law of 1862, Secretary Benton observed that many objections previously made seemed to have been removed. It was clear to him, moreover, that the chief difficulty, as he had formerly stated, was in the ''conflict of jurisdiction'' between the Board of Education and the General Assembly. He expressed the opinion, also, that the original intention of those who had proposed a Board of Education had been thwarted in the constitutional convention by ''an injudicious compromise'' and that it was not intended to possess legislative authority. Such an opinion, however, appears not to have been in accordance with what took place in the convention. Indeed, from a careful survey of the debates on the matter, one must conclude that this authority was prominently in view during the entire discussion. It was at this time (in 1863) that the abolition of the Board of Education was advised by Mr. Benton; and in anticipation of a return to the independent district system, which he felt to be certain when the General Assembly came into full control, he recommended a special act providing for the transition from the township district to the independent system. It is noteworthy that Secretary Benton distinguished between a general education act and one that might be adopted to designate the details of procedure in passing from one form of organization to another — the first a permanent and the second a temporary statute.

The prevention of errors in legislation was a feature of the recommendation of the Secretary; and in his final report in 1863 he pointed out the consequences of a custom that, although common, should be avoided, namely, "the practice of selecting certain sections from a variety of old laws, and associating them together in a new one." Confusion had often arisen, he affirmed, from this practice, the language of the statutes being frequently ambiguous. Indeed, too little care was exercised in expressing the law and many misconstructions of the school law of 1858 might be traced to this fault. A law should not be amended by changing it in part through a new act which did not specify clearly the section of the law affected. Indeed, it would be far better to repeal the law or section and enact an entirely new statute. No legislation was advised — with the exceptions noted above — since it was considered unwise to make any changes at the time when the attention of the people was so occupied with the exciting interests of war. Furthermore, the system was working well and no cause for immediate action existed.[320]

In the consolidation of the several school acts (in 1862), and in the minor amendments incorporated therein, the recommendations of the Secretary of the Board of Education were generally adopted without modification. The respect with which these recommendations were treated is indicative of the confidence placed in his knowledge of the needs of the

State, as well as of the acknowledgment on the part of legislators that acquaintance with the problems confronting the administration would be of greater value in proposing amendments than petitions from constituents. Mr. Benton had observed the inequities arising under the system of levying school taxes, and had noted the fact that some restrictions were necessary in communities having but few settlers. It was well known, he observed, that some counties contained but one or two townships in which large areas frequently were taxed for the construction of school houses in a distant corner of the district. Indeed, cases were reported (in 1862), and one was specified, where "a tax was levied on land situated over twenty miles" from the proposed school building, while there were other instances in which expensive houses had been erected so far from settlements that the people were unable to take advantage of them for school purposes. To remedy this "abuse of power" some legislation, therefore, was desirable, since the statute then provided that certain lands might be taxed again and again for the construction of buildings which in no way served their possessors.[321]

As a concession to those advocating the independent district, the school law was so amended in 1864 that the subdistrict might levy a special tax on property therein for the support of a term beyond the limit required by law or even that ordered by the township board of directors. There were two reasons, it appears, for this action: first, it was held by

some that no authority permitted boards to extend
the term beyond the legal requirement of six
months; and second, the needs or desires of some
communities in the same township varied. At the
same time, another amendment prohibited the compensation of directors out of the school fund, for,
although the statute made no provision for such
payments, it appears to have been the custom in
some sections to allow directors either a fixed amount
or a per diem for their services. This is to say,
there was no uniform practice since some were paid
as indicated, while the majority, it seems, served
without compensation. It was the duty of the subdirector then to make the annual report to the county
superintendent — a function which, in the opinion
of the Superintendent of Public Instruction, should
be performed by the township district secretary
as it finally came to be through subsequent legislation. A third amendment of this session required
the county treasurer to keep a separate account of
the school house fund where a subdistrict built its
own house; while a fourth involved new provisions
already mentioned in connection with the functions
of the county superintendent.[322]

It was quite generally agreed at this time in the
history of the schools that some more satisfactory
method of securing the required information relative to the district organization, and all local data
essential to a correct summary by county and State
officers, must be adopted. It was recommended,
therefore, in 1865 that all school officers be paid, and

furthermore that they be compelled to perform the
functions imposed upon them. It was not uncommon for the reports of the county superintendent
to be made up from information obtained by indirect methods rather than by the processes which the
law contemplated. It had been observed in certain
instances that officers, who, under the law, should
be responsible were compensated much more liberally than the county superintendent who was forced
to perform his duties or be counted delinquent by
the Superintendent of Public Instruction. Thus,
among the recommendations for improvement some
would provide for a deputy county superintendent
in counties containing eighty or more districts and
also for a more adequate salary for the county
superintendent.

It was further suggested that a uniform system
of grading teachers be adopted throughout the State
under the inspection of the Superintendent of Public
Instruction, while a penalty should be enforced for
employing any person not possessing a license.
Again, a fine of five dollars per day should be imposed upon all teachers presuming to teach without
legal authority. Furthermore, all teachers should
have free instruction in methods of teaching four
weeks each year, and all holding low grade certificates should be compelled to attend the county institute. A school year, too, should consist of ten
months instruction, for five months of which all
pupils should be compelled to attend; the State
should appropriate fifty dollars for the beginning of

a library in each subdistrict, the latter being required to add ten dollars annually or to lose the whole amount; the Board of Examiners should be required to hold sessions in every congressional district; the office of Assistant State Superintendent should be created, which should have full control over county institutes; a limit should be fixed as to the size of the subdistrict, or there should be a return to the independent system, for under the latter form the small district would die out; text-books should be uniform throughout the State; all large schools should be graded while monthly examinations should be abolished, since it was thought that once a quarter was often enough; and finally private schools supplying teachers and promoting the educational interests of the State should be encouraged, at least by so much as to exempt their property from taxation.

There were many other proposed amendments — of which indeed there seemed to have been no limit — some practicable and others visionary. It was pointed out by a county superintendent that compensating directors in the hope of securing better observance of functions would not prove satisfactory. He therefore proposed a statute requiring the township board to appoint a competent man to have charge of all the schools of the township, to examine all teachers therein, and to make all necessary reports directly to the State Superintendent, to visit and supervise the schools, in short to make the township an independent educational unit. It is noticeable that this was in some particulars a proposition to restore the provisions of the law of 1840, and since it came from Jones County the Monticello Township organization may have grown out of this suggestion. At the same time there were those who deemed the school law radically wrong in that too many individuals were concerned in its administration. It was on this occasion that George B. Dennison, superintendent of Muscatine County, repeated a recommendation that he had made to the Board of Education in 1858 relative to the election of the county superintendent by a convention of school officers who should prescribe his duties and fix his salary. Again, a plan of supervision proposed by Rev. Simon Barrows, superintendent of Polk County, would abolish the office of county superintendent and provide for some thirty departments or districts containing from one to four counties according to population. Therein the people should elect a commissioner or inspector to hold office for four years, the same to be regarded as a State officer and be paid from the treasury while his functions should include the examination of teachers, the holding of institutes, lecturing, and supervising the schools of his district. To hold such a position, furthermore, no one should be eligible until he had qualified before the Board of Examiners, it being thought that men of such a type would be induced by the power and honor conferred to accept the office. Another proposition looking toward centralization would make the building of all school houses, except possibly in cities, a function of the State, the cost to be assessed

by the Commonwealth upon the locality interested.[323]
From these illustrative recommendations one may
conclude that the school law was not yet fully up to
the expectations of many persons who were vitally
interested in educational progress.

The majority, however, would not recommend
any radical change in the law as originally provided,
since frequent changes were regarded as detrimental — especially in legislation that touched so
many interests as that affecting education. The advancement in the ten years from 1858 to 1868 was
indicative of the gradual establishment of the law in
the estimation of the people, and the only need for
the present was the removal of defects as they were
pointed out. At the same time it was declared by
some that the less the law was subjected to "legislative tinkering" the better.

MORE LEGISLATION ADVISED

ABOUT 1870 there were evidences of a demand for a
more business-like conduct of school affairs. For
instance, it was shown that the financial rewards of
the teacher were often less than they appeared to be,
since it was not uncommon for them to be paid in
orders which must be discounted or held until the
district secured the necessary funds. It was to correct this injustice that an amendment was proposed
which would require the monthly payment of teachers and likewise the paying over of district funds by
the county treasurer at the end of the same period.
It does not appear, however, that the promoters of
these changes were successful before the legislature.

There was, moreover, a disposition to look with
favor upon a smaller number in the constitution of
boards, both in independent and township districts.
For example, the suggestion was made that three
members — a president, a secretary and a treasurer,
who should be compensated for their services and be
held responsible for specific functions — should compose the board for all forms of districts. Another
proposition would establish a compensated township
board of six members, two being elected each year
according to the system then current in Pennsyl-

vania. It seems clear that at this time board members were often excused for neglect of duty on the plea that they were not allowed any compensation.[324]

In 1873 reference was again made to the fact that the school law had remained practically unchanged since 1858. Although the great number of recommendations relative to certain phases of the system had been published through the office of the Superintendent of Public Instruction, few of them seemed to have been taken seriously. It is interesting to observe that while the compulsory attendance law was not openly proposed until about 1872, it was foreseen sometime before that it would become a factor in subsequent legislation, and that while the school treasurer is still (in 1914) an officer of the district it was declared in 1873 that the office should be abolished and the functions thereafter performed by the county treasurer. There was, however, some legislation in 1872 which, according to the view of Superintendent Abernethy, would create serious disturbance, namely, that providing for the formation of rural independent districts. Two causes were assigned for the enactment of this law: first, the removal of the objectional features of the township system which was representative of territory in its organization rather than of population; and second, the restoration to the people of the district of the entire control over their schools.

It was the opinion of the State Superintendent that "material changes ought not to be made without due deliberation", but there were in 1875 some

amendments that seemed desirable. Officers should
be held to a stricter accountability in handling funds;
or it would be more satisfactory for the county
treasurer to disburse funds directly to those holding
claims against the several districts. Some action
should be taken also to prevent further misapplica-
tion of the school revenue. Again, he would provide
more efficient supervision for the ungraded schools;
and he endorsed the recommendations of the State
Teachers' Association relative to the creation of a
Board of Examiners, as well as the addition of
elementary physics, drawing, or vocal music to the
required list of subjects in the examination of
teachers. It may be said that a recommendation of
two years before would require a knowledge of the
Constitution and civil government of Iowa — a provision as reasonable, it would appear, as that mentioned above, but which seems not to have been so
considered. Further suggestions in 1875 would
amend the law relative to county institutes with a
view to increasing their usefulness, especially by
relieving teachers of a part of the expense "attending their management". County high schools should
be adequately provided for also, their special function being "to afford industrial education, and instruction in the higher branches and in teaching."
And finally, the school year should be so defined as
to make the annual return of school statistics more
satisfactory.[325]

The Fifteenth General Assembly (in 1874)
authorized the Superintendent of Public Instruction

to issue and distribute to school officers 20,000 copies
of the school laws then in force. It appears, however, that it required a subsequent issue of 12,000
more, under orders from the next Assembly, before
the local officers were all supplied. But no provision
was made for the distribution to any citizen, notwithstanding the fact that he might be willing to pay for
the same for his own enlightenment.

Through the biennial reports of county superintendents a great variety of possible legislation, much
of which has or will become a part of the laws of the
State, has been proposed. The fact that these recommendations were repeated year after year
suggests the customary procedure in securing legislation, that is, there was a period of agitation before
attention could be sufficiently drawn to a matter to
secure its serious consideration by the public authorities. For example, as early as 1877 a law to compel
attendance upon some normal school previous to
teaching was suggested. Yet this proposition was
not seriously considered until 1913, and then, under
a commission report. In the same year State uniformity in examinations was recommended; and it
was held important that no one should be permitted
to teach longer than one year upon a second class
certificate, and but eight months upon a third class
certificate, thereby forecasting the provisional certificate of recent legislation. The large number of
officers provided for under the statutes was declared
to be unfortunate; while it was thought that the
recently established independent districts should be

wholly abolished, the township as a single district being substituted therefor. Furthermore, all towns of less than three hundred population should be included in the township district with a board of six members elected at large.. Once more, too, the feasibility of abolishing the numerous treasurers and requiring the county treasurer to disburse all funds was shown to be not only a more safe, but also a more accurate and economical method of the administration of school funds. Indeed, this change would prove to be of greater convenience to all concerned, while saving several hundred dollars in salaries to petty officers.[326]

Since there had been no general systematic revision of the school law since the adoption of the fundamental act of March 12, 1858, it was pointed out in 1879 that ''our school laws have been amended, changed, altered and modified, until they are very difficult to interpret.'' To remedy this condition the Superintendent of Public Instruction proposed to codify and rearrange the laws without further expense than the necessary clerk hire. But no authority had been granted by the previous Assembly by which the department could even publish the laws, and it was currently reported that nearly all districts were without copies of the statutes by which they were governed. That this situation might be relieved it was proposed to authorize boards of education to purchase the statutes by appropriations from the contingent fund, provided the State could not meet the expense of publication, since it was essential that some such provision be made in order that local officers might have some means of informing themselves.

As predicted some years before, a bill providing for compulsory attendance passed the House of Representatives in 1878 but failed to secure sufficient support in the Senate. It was not recommended, however, by the Superintendent of Public Instruction, for he was quite certain that such a statute could not be enforced. Furthermore, he believed that other methods would prove more acceptable and that the desired ends could be obtained through a personal investigation of children whose education was neglected. The General Assembly, however, did succeed in passing one law relative to the organization of boards which proved exceedingly annoying, namely, that by which the president in town boards of six directors was prohibited from voting. Intended to prevent deadlocks, it had resulted in preventing the organization of boards for long periods owing to the fact that no one would accept the office of president and thus be disfranchised as a member. To change this situation, and yet avoid the difficulty which the statute sought to correct, it was proposed to restore the vote of the president and permit the secretary to cast a ballot in case of a tie.[327]

Superintendent von Coelln declared in 1881 that he had purposely refrained from recommending legislation that would involve any change in the organic law. Nevertheless, the great need of general and systematic revision and reconstruction of the

statutes was again emphasized since they had become
so "thoroughly obscured" that it was difficult to
"unravel them." It was observed further that,
while the law originally provided for the district
township, such modifications had occurred that in
1881 approximately one-fourth of the rural schools
were included under independent district management. Therefore, the often-repeated proposition to
make the township the unit was again presented.
At all events let there be one township treasurer for
all independent districts, who should be appointed
by the township trustees or county board of supervisors with a compensation determined by statute.
Moreover, let him be required not only to receive and
disburse all money for the districts included within
the township but also to visit the schools therein,
and to coöperate with the county superintendents
and school boards in the classification and inspection
of schools.[328]   In short, it appears that the office
should develop into that of a township supervisor,
while the chief reason for its creation was declared
to be financial. Nor was there any suggestion of a
suitable selection for supervisory duties other than
in the possible judgment of the appointing authority.
It will be remembered that there had been other
recommendations relative to such supervision and
some instances of its actual practice in this State.

The "unwise and ruinous system" of independent districts continued to be the theme about which
many other minor subjects centered in the official
reports of school officers for many years subsequent

to the passing of the unfortunate statute which authorized their organization. In 1885 the question seemed as conspicuous as ever, since it was observed that confusion was continually arising over boundaries as the State became more fully settled. No provision existed, it was declared, for the adjustment of differences which arose when subdistricts which had been a part of a district township were attached to another having independent districts. Another difficulty experienced in independent city and town districts, and which the legislature had attempted to remedy, existed in the equal number on the board which often resulted in "ties". It was therefore proposed to provide for a president to be elected outside the board of six members, but who should have no vote except in the case of an equal division. It was inquired, too, whether there was any reason in having a term of three years for board members in independent districts and but one in the district township. Why, it was asked, should there be any distinction?

That the controversy over the introduction and change of text-books might be forever settled, Superintendent Akers made the direct recommendation in 1885 that the district purchase and loan such supplies, the contingent fund being employed for this purpose. It was further advised by others that the three funds — teachers, school house, and contingent — be consolidated and known thereafter as "school fund benefits". To these recommendations may be added the following: the establishment of a district

23

graded library; the requirement that all schools be
closed during the normal institute; permission to
teachers to attend conventions without loss of pay;
a county training school for teachers which the State
should aid in the beginning by the appropriation of
$1000; uniformity in the financial year and other
required records; the distribution of the interest on
the permanent fund on the basis of attendance rather
than upon enumeration; the course of instruction in
normal institutes should be established by law and
should include instruction relative to teachers contracts, bonds of secretaries and treasurers, term
reports and official records; and finally, all completed
registers and records of the several districts should
be deposited with the county superintendent ''for
safe keeping''.[329]

As the law stood in 1887 the reports submitted to
the succeeding General Assembly contained no data
more recent than October, 1886 — that is to say, almost an entire year of events most nearly related to
the time of the session could not be included. It was
therefore recommended that the statistical year be
changed to remedy this condition. It appears that
the suggestion was accepted by the Twenty-second
General Assembly and the year so changed that subsequent biennial reports would include information
relative to the preceding year. While this was vital
to an understanding of current matters it was declared at the same time that the ''crying evil'' of the
school system existed mainly in the disjointed relation of school officials. That this might be remedied

it was proposed to provide a county board of education constituted of representatives from each district. Or, by another plan this county board would consist of the presidents of the various boards only, with power to adopt courses of study, rules and regulations to govern the schools of the county, and possibly text-books. A board of this character, it was said, would create no additional expense — always a very great argument in favor of an educational institution.[330]

From 1880 to 1888 the Superintendent of Public Instruction had been authorized to arrange the school laws with amendments, notes, rulings, forms, and decisions as might in his opinion be of value to school officers, and to distribute the same every four years. Furthermore, cloth-bound volumes should be put into the hands of each county superintendent in sufficient numbers to supply the school officers of their respective counties, while other copies in paper covers should be provided for the public through the county auditor at a fixed price. In 1888, however, the "paper bound" portion of this act was repealed. But under such legislation no one except school officers could obtain copies of the school laws — a situation that produced considerable complaint in the following year because persons preparing for the teachers examination were unable to provide themselves with the statutes upon which they might be examined.

It was recommended by Superintendent Sabin in 1889 that the provision relative to the publication and distribution of the school statutes be not only restored but that when bound they should include "the constitution, and an outline of the civil government of the State". Subsequently (in 1892) 40,000 copies of the laws were issued and distributed to district officers, but at the same time no provision was made whereby the expectant teacher, or one already employed, could obtain a copy except through a loan from those officially entitled to benefit by the distribution. It was considered, indeed, as "glaringly inconsistent", in the opinion of Superintendent Knoepfler, for the State to establish a qualification for a certificate and then provide no opportunity for meeting it. It was not demanded that the State should distribute these laws without charge, but it was thought that any individual citizen should be given the opportunity to purchase them at cost. It was not, however, until 1898 that the county auditor was authorized to sell the school statutes in paper binding at the uniform price of twenty cents.[331] Thus, another decade was required to secure action on what seemed a reasonable request.

That greater stability and a more certain maturity of plans might obtain, Superintendent Sabin in 1889 repeated the suggestions previously made, that the provisions for perpetuating the independent district board be applied to the district township. It was proposed further that the entire township board should be required to approve the appointment of teachers; while to qualify for service as a member one should be able "to speak, read, and write the

English language with reasonable facility.'' But the improvement of the rural schools through the employment of better teachers, closer supervision, and more suitable equipment patterned after the best obtainable was held by the same authority to be the legislation most needed. Although the school system as a unit must be duly considered, that which was apparently the most neglected could not be permitted to remain in such a condition.

The revision of the laws under the direction of a commission was urged again in 1893, when it was suggested that the members of such a body should include not less than two educators — one of whom should be the Superintendent of Public Instruction, or one who had but recently held that office — and competent legal talent. It was pointed out that the acquaintance with the school system and with the problems connected with its administration would qualify the Superintendent for expert service in this capacity.[332]

It was in 1895 that Mr. A. H. Davison of the eighth representative district presented the claims of the State to an educational system which, from a survey of the statutes governing it, he declared, did not appear to exist. That is to say, since the management of educational matters rested largely with local boards without centralization of authority, it was evident that much remained to be done before one could assert that this was really a system of public instruction. His recommendations, therefore, relative to the reconstruction of the school laws —

which he observed had been urged for fifteen years
by the heads of the State department — would provide a central board of education to control all the
educational agencies of the State. But that conservative action might mark all deliberations, it was
proposed that a joint commission from the two
houses of the legislature should arrange a comprehensive measure as a substitute for Title XII of the
Code of 1873. Every General Assembly, it was said,
had among its members a number of experienced
educators who could do such work, and they should
be assisted by other competent men in studying the
details of other school systems as well as local conditions. This advisory body should include ''not
only school men, but men of affairs'', for it was a
''notorious fact that those who have only such views
of education as they acquire in the school room are
unfit for so comprehensive a work.''

In this scheme of reorganization it was advised
that the next General Assembly (in 1896) should
provide for some institution within each county for
teacher training. The bill before the previous legislature, which had proposed a training school of sixteen weeks annually in each county, was commended
as a worthy measure; while another plan presented
at this time would establish a permanent normal
school instead of the sixteen weeks training. To
such an institution the graduates from the township
high school — also a part of the proposed arrangement — should be admitted not only for the purposes
of instruction in methods and management but also

for preparation in English, the sciences, drawing, and elementary mechanics, so that the teacher in the rural school might be fitted to "construct simple apparatus for illustrations of school room work". Such schools, it was pointed out, need not be equipped with expensive buildings; but the faculty should be of a high order. With such an institution in every county the necessity for more than two or three State normals for advanced training would disappear. Furthermore, the county institute would be enabled to devote its energies to work of a professional character; and indeed, it should be retained as an inspirational institution which, under the control of the proposed State Board of Education, could be "led in new lines" as circumstances might suggest.

With the establishment of the township central high school there should be incorporated a provision for "township superintendence"— by which, it was declared, the "farmers' school" would be made much more efficient. It was suggested further that "all public schools should be required to use a course of study authorized by the department" with the privilege, however, of adding other branches upon a vote of the district electors. It was observed also that many schools were crippled because they undertook work out of proportion to their abilities, with the result that habits of superficial study were "established for life." With the adoption of the township as the district unit, the abolition of the office of sub-director, and the establishment of an annual term

for which teachers should be employed it was asserted that the evils resulting from the short period
of contracts and lack of permanence in teaching
positions would be largely overcome. Then, too, the
centralization made possible through a township
school would enable the authorities to maintain more
extensive libraries which, while distributed from
house to house in the subdistricts, would yet form a
unit in organization. Finally, the law should prohibit the construction of any school house the plan
for which had not been first approved by the State
department. There should be no "patchwork legislation", but a comprehensive rearrangement by
which a system complete in its details should be
made effective in this State.[333]

These views expressed in 1895 were supported in
1897 when Superintendent Sabin commented upon
the evils associated with the "constant tendency to
amend and patch" the school law by successive legislatures, until "it was almost impossible to interpret
it." He therefore urged the Twenty-seventh General Assembly not to interfere with the provisions of
the *Code of 1897* but to permit a fair trial thereof.
It would, he believed, be a great advantage to the
interests of education if some years should pass before any change was made. Nevertheless, the next
biennial report contained recommendations that
would make rather radical changes in the statutes
governing schools, for Superintendent Barrett
enumerated no less than nineteen specific items
which he considered worthy of legislation. With

few exceptions, however, these were but restatements
of old problems presented from time to time and
already mentioned in these chapters. Again, in 1901
the same authority declared that legislation which
would keep pace with economic changes must provide laws different from those which were suitable
when schools were first established. It was only
necessary to consider, for example, that when there
were no industries affecting the unreasonable employment of children no laws relative thereto were
necessary, but under different conditions favorable
legislation was absolutely essential. Certain statutes likewise were not up to date, and so new ones
should be substituted.

Two years later (in 1903), in his final report,
Superintendent Barrett submitted among many recommendations, the following: the term of the Superintendent of Public Instruction should be extended
to four years with a salary fixed by law at not less
than $4000; there should be appropriated to each
county for institutes not less than $200, instead of
$50, thus relieving teachers from the support of
institutes for which they were paying $50,000, while
county agricultural societies were receiving from the
State nearly $20,000 and the militia nearly $60,000
during the same period; and the requirements relative to examinations should be revised if men and
women were to be retained as teachers for any extended period, for every obstacle to professional
recognition should be removed, while State-wide opportunity to engage in such employment ought to be

provided. It was clearly inconsistent for the compensation of county superintendents to be inversely as their labor — for under the statute they were required to pay their own traveling expenses; and so, the more they traveled to supervise the schools of their county the greater the expense.

There were other amendments which seemed desirable, and some entirely new legislation was proposed at this time. One recommendation is especially noteworthy in that it appears neither to have been suggested before nor since in this Commonwealth, nor up to the present time to have been adopted in more than three or four States. It had in view the employment of the State department to meet the demands frequently made by school authorities for qualified teachers and to aid teachers in securing positions. That is to say, the bringing together of the employer and the employee should be made a State function under the direction of some competent individual attached to the office of the Superintendent of Public Instruction. It was declared that the expenditure of $6,000,000 annually in the salaries of teachers would justify such supervision over their employment. Since teachers agencies were engaged in this very important business there appeared to be no valid reason why the State should not exercise a control through the agencies it already possessed. It was expressly stated, however, that such a suggestion was made solely for the advantage of the contracting parties and not as against teachers agencies in general. If it should be asserted that the State could not bear the expense, a fee of one dollar might be collected for the service to teachers. Any balance above the actual cost of the service should be turned into the treasury of the State.[334] Thus, it appears, the legislature was confronted with new problems or with a reiteration of old ones at every session.

After many years of agitation the General Assembly finally acceded to the recommendation relative to the appointment of a commission "to rearrange, revise and codify the existing laws relating to the public schools, and to recommend additional needed legislation." While some of the results of the work of this commission have already been mentioned it may be pointed out in this connection that its recommendations were more revolutionary than any theretofore proposed. Indeed, one cause for the defeat of the unified measure which was proposed by the commission lay in the nature of the proposed changes. It is certain that the three members, to each of whom definite problems were assigned, sought the best type of organization and consulted the best authority thereon before submitting their conclusions for the joint approval of the commission. Moreover, the most important phases of their report were passed upon by leading educators, by boards of education, and citizens generally, so that there might be a consensus of opinion previous to formulating a bill. Not only through correspondence but also through personal consultation and attendance upon the sessions of conventions and sessions of other commissions was the best information obtainable brought to the use of this commission.

When the report was finally submitted to the Thirty-third General Assembly, as the law required, it contained the following principal recommendations which were new to the legislation of this Commonwealth: the county unit of organization with a county board of education of three members, who should control the educational officers of the county, aided by a local board of three trustees in the school township which, under ordinary conditions, should correspond in boundaries with the civil township; the election of the county or a district superintendent by this county board; the creation of a State board of education; the classification of districts according to population; the substitution of the county treasurer for the school treasurers of the county; the abolition of the teachers' written contract; provision for a State supervisor of schools with the necessary assistants; and many minor changes to secure the effective application of the revised statutes.

All of these principles were incorporated in one bill which, perhaps because of that fact, failed to meet with the approval of the General Assembly. It may be noted, however, that while this report was submitted in November, it was not available for distribution, on account of the delay in printing, until the session of the legislature was well under way, and thus its favorable consideration was greatly handicapped. Not only was the bill rejected but measures proposed in committee as substitutes for certain provisions never went any farther. Since there was not sufficient time for full deliberation, it was recommended that the commission be continued with a larger membership and for a longer period.[335] Although at the time of presentation the recommendations of the commission may have seemed in certain respects revolutionary some of their suggestions have since been followed, in substance at least, and it is highly probable that subsequent legislation will enact a large part of the original bill. Governor Carroll observed in his inaugural address in 1909 that the report of the commission would require careful consideration since it involved some "wide departures" from the law then in force. These, he thought, should neither commend nor condemn the report but be productive rather of more careful consideration. Personally he was favorably impressed with the proposed changes, and with the fact that there was need of a reconstruction of the school code. The importance of the work of the commission, therefore, could not be overestimated.[336]

In the preparation of their report the commission obtained opinions from more than fifty county and city superintendents and college men, among which appear the following: there should be eight months in the legal school year; a minimum wage law; compulsory attendance on county institutes; unlimited renewal of certificates after a certain minimum of experience; the office of school treasurer should be

abolished, and the three funds reduced to two; more
definite authority of the school over outside matters
that affect it; the closing of small schools and consolidation of districts; the clear codification of the
laws, with no theory or radical changes introduced;
State aid to high schools doing a definite amount of
work in agriculture, manual training, domestic
science, and pedagogy; the retention of the election
of county superintendent by the people; the removal
of the office of county superintendent from the influence of politics, and the requirement that this
officer possess at least a five-year State certificate; a
provision for more definite rural supervision; a more
effective enforcement of the truancy law; county
uniformity in text-books under the direction of a
board composed of the county superintendent and
two teachers; the privilege of contracting with teachers for more than one year; a revision of the law
relative to instruction in stimulants and narcotics;
the coördination of institutions in some definite way;
the inspection, under State authority, of all schools;
more judicious classification of colleges on some
basis other than dollars-and-cents and size; a county
unit of organization with a board endowed with
power to manage all rural schools; a legal status for
the city superintendent; a recognition of the contract
which was often broken without penalty; the sys-
tematizing of the law without attempting too much;
a civil township unit of organization; the abolition
of the institute fee; the enlargement of the State
Board of Examiners to seven members; the require-

ment of high school facilities for rural districts;
some required amount of training before being admitted to teachers' examinations, the same to be
offered in all secondary schools; more thoroughness
required in the work of the grades; the classification
of school corporations; the establishment of a standard for high school teachers; and the compulsory
attendance of school officers upon conventions called
by the county superintendent, with provision for
expenses and a per diem.[337] Thus the commissioners
were confronted with a variety of suggestions, some
of which they were able to follow either wholly or
partially in the bill submitted.

The final report of Superintendent Riggs reiter-
ated some of the above recommendations without
undertaking to include many thereof. First, he
would provide for some simple and efficient form of
rural school organization and control, thus eliminat-
ing the three forms which were then authorized by
law. This recommendation seemed to imply a preference for the independent township district as
provided for in Section 2752 of the *Code of 1897*.
Second, he believed there should be a county board
of education having well defined functions. Third,
the office of school treasurer should be abolished —
which appears to have been a recommendation made
so frequently that it has come to be a standing
problem for every legislature. Fourth, the small
school should be temporarily closed. Fifth, there
should be a high school within reasonable reach of
every district school which pupils might attend

at district expense. Sixth, he concurred in the recommendation of his predecessor relative to his own
office, namely, the extension of the term to four years
and the increase of compensation to $4000. Further-
more, the Superintendent of Public Instruction
should be appointed by the Governor or the State
Board of Education, a change he declared which
would be in harmony with policies then adopted in
not less than fifteen States. Seventh, there should
be amendments removing certain restrictions upon
the tax levy, and securing greater safety for the
health of pupils; while the institute registration and
other fees levied upon teachers to the amount of
$68,000 should be abolished.[338]

It was in the early sixties that the State Teachers' Association supported, through contributions
from individuals and their meagre treasury, a State
agent heretofore mentioned in the chapter on institutes. This practice was abandoned when funds
failed. It was, moreover, in harmony with precedent
that the Association in 1911 set aside $2000 from its
increasing resources for the perfectly plain purpose
of bringing to the front certain reforms in the educational policies of the State. With a commission
serving without pay a full investigation of conditions
was undertaken with the aim of being thoroughly
informed relative to needed legislation. In the com-
position of this body the interests of ''farming, business, household duties, and professional life'' were
to be represented for the purpose, it appears, of
having the sanction of these social elements for what-

ever might be submitted. In arriving at conclusions the subcommittees made extensive investigation of the following: school administration in Iowa (State county, and district); rural schools; graded schools; high schools; industrial education; State aid; the school as a community center; and facilities for training teachers. Having summarized these separate reports the commission presented their findings to the State Association in 1912, in which at least twenty-three distinct recommendations for enactment into law were made.

While it is well known that some of the most important suggestions became laws under the skillful leadership of the legislative committee appointed by the Association, the general scope of the reorganization proposed may be briefly presented as follows: there should be voluntary consolidation of the rural schools with a minimum district area of sixteen sections, with State aid for a certain period; the encouragement of rural high schools which should offer courses of study adapted to the community; an increase in the amount of aid already granted to high schools offering normal training; four additional normal schools should be established within the coming five years; at least twelve weeks training should be required of every applicant for a certificate; the normal institute should be abolished and short sessions inspirational in nature be substituted, with compulsory attendance and no loss of pay; there should be an increase in the powers of the State department by providing inspectors and an official

24

force sufficient to reach all grades of instruction; the office of county superintendent should be made equal in importance to any other county office, with raised standards of qualification, and a term of four years, while both that and the office of Superintendent of Public Instruction should become non-partisan whether elective or appointive; the county superintendent should enforce the truancy law; the township should be the unit of the district organization; all school officers should be required to meet in annual convention with compensation for attendance; provision should be made for a reorganization of that which is designated the county board of education; abolition of the office of school treasurer and the substitution of the county treasurer therefor, with the requirement that all school funds draw interest as other county funds; and provision should be made for the holding of all school elections on the same day in March and likewise the organization of all boards at the same time. There were also recommendations providing for the extension of industrial instruction; for the safe-guarding of school elections; for the privilege of contracting to teach for more than one year; for the use of but two funds instead of three, namely, the school house and a general fund; and finally for the recodification of the school laws.[339]

From the foregoing paragraphs it appears that in the field of school legislation there remains but little to be recommended although there is still much to be enacted. It would seem to be hardly possible to mention any subject which is known in educational legislation in any part of the country that has not at some time been proposed in this Commonwealth. To develop a school code which would be inclusive and conservative, offering in a single statute explicit, complete, and definite powers, duties, rights, and remedies, is a problem difficult of attack and still more difficult of solution. Here as elsewhere the reformer must patiently wait upon the processes of gradual evolution.

APPENDICES

APPENDIX A

A COMPARISON OF THE MICHIGAN LAW OF 1838 AND THE IOWA LAW OF 1840

THE school law of Michigan of 1838 and the statute enacted in 1840 in the Territory of Iowa are presented below in parallel columns. With the exception of Sections 21 and 22 there is no variation in the order in which the subject is treated. There are slight changes only in some provisions — for example, the change in the school census age of from five to seventeen to from five to twenty-one. Thus, as is pointed out in the text (Vol. I, p. 9) one could not mistake the source of the Iowa act. Particular attention is called to the sections which mention a Superintendent of Public Instruction and for which the Iowa Legislative Assembly made no provision until a year later. One may notice further some provisions which seem to have been retained throughout subsequent legislation.

THE MICHIGAN STATUTE

Sec. 1. Whenever any school district shall be formed in any township by the board of school inspectors, it shall be the duty of said board to deliver a notice in writing describing the boundaries of said district, and the time and place of the first meeting, to a taxable inhabitant of such district.

Sec. 2. It shall be the duty of such inhabitant to notify every

THE IOWA STATUTE

Sec. 1. Whenever any school district shall be formed in any township by the board of school inspectors, it shall be the duty of said board to deliver a notice in writing describing the boundaries of said district, and the time and place of the first meeting, to a taxable inhabitant of such district.

Sec. 2. It shall be the duty of such inhabitant to notify every

359

qualified voter of such district, either personally or by leaving a written notice at his place of residence, of the time and place of said meeting, at least six days before said meeting.

Sec. 3. Whenever such inhabitant shall neglect or refuse to serve notice as required, he shall forfeit to the district, for the use of its library, the sum of ten dollars, to be recovered in an action of debt by the assessor, when said district shall be organized, before any court of competent jurisdiction.

Sec. 4. The qualified voters, when assembled pursuant to such previous notice, and also at each annual meeting, shall choose a moderator, director and assessor.

Sec. 5. Every white male inhabitant of the age of twenty-one years, residing in such district, liable to pay a school district tax, shall be entitled to vote at any district meeting.

Sec. 6. In case the inhabitants of a district fail to organize the same, or if any district after formation shall be dissolved, such notice shall be renewed in the manner prescribed in the first two sections of this chapter.

Sec. 7. Whenever, from whatever cause, any district shall become destitute of the three officers provided for in this act for the period of six months, or whenever any district shall neg-

qualified voter of such district, either personally or by leaving a written notice at his place of residence, of the time and place of said meeting, at least six days before said meeting.

Sec. 3. Whenever such inhabitant shall neglect or refuse to serve notice as required, he shall forfeit to the district, for the use of its library, the sum of ten dollars, to be recovered in an action of debt by the assessor, when said district shall be organized, before any court of competent jurisdiction.

Sec. 4. The qualified voters, when assembled, pursuant to such previous notice, and also at each annual meeting, shall choose a moderator, director and assessor.

Sec. 5. Every white male inhabitant of the age of twenty-one years, residing in such district, liable to pay a school district tax, shall be entitled to vote at any district meeting.

Sec. 6. In case the inhabitants of a district fail to organize the same, or if any district, after formation, shall be dissolved, such notice shall be renewed in the manner prescribed in the first two sections of this act.

Sec. 7. Whenever from whatever cause any district shall become destitute of the three officers provided for in this act for the period of six months, or whenever any district shall neglect or lect or refuse to hold two successive annual meetings, it shall be taken and held to be dissolved.

Sec. 8. Special meetings may be called by the district board, or by any one of them, on the written request of three legal voters of the district, by giving the required previous notice; but in all such cases the object of the meeting shall be clearly stated in said notice.

Sec. 9. All notices for district meetings, except such as are provided for in the first two sections of this chapter, whether annual or special, shall set forth the day and hour and place of meeting, and be given at least six days previous to such meeting, by being posted up in the most public place in the district.

Sec. 10. The annual meeting of each school district shall be on the first Monday of October.

Sec. 11. Each school district organized under this act, shall be a body corporate, by the name and style of ''school district number   , of the township of   , in the county of   and state of Michigan;'' and in that name capable of suing and being sued, and of holding such real and personal estate as is authorized to be purchased by the provisions of this act, and of selling the same.

Sec. 12. Whenever any suit shall be brought against any

refuse to hold two successive annual meetings, it shall be taken and held to be dissolved.

Sec. 8. Special meetings may be called by the district board, or by any one of them, on the written request of three legal voters of the district, by giving the required previous notice; but in all such cases the object of meeting shall be clearly stated in said notice.

Sec. 9. All notices for district meetings, except such as are provided for in the first two sections of this act, whether annual or special, shall set forth the day and hour and place of meeting, and be given at least six days previous to such meeting, by being posted up in the most public place in the district.

Sec. 10. The annual meeting of each school district shall be on the first Monday of October.

Sec. 11. Each school district organized under this act, shall be a body corporate by the name and style of ''school district number   , of the township of   , in the county of   , and territory of Iowa,'' and in that name capable of suing and being sued, and of holding such real and personal estate as is authorized to be purchased by the provisions of this act, and of selling the same.

Sec. 12. Whenever any suit shall be brought against any

school district, the process shall be by summons, a copy of which shall be left with the assessor of said district at least ten days previous to the return day thereof.

Sec. 13. Whenever lawfully assembled, the qualified voters in each district shall have power,

First. To adjourn from time to time, as may be necessary.

Second. To designate a site for a school-house, and to change the same by a vote of two-thirds at any regular meeting: Provided, That when no site can be established by said inhabitants, the inspectors of the township or townships shall determine where the site shall be; and said determination shall be final.

Third. To purchase or lease an appropriate site, and to build, hire or purchase a school-house, and to impose such tax as shall be sufficient for the payment thereof: Provided, That the amount of such tax shall not exceed in any one year the sum of five hundred dollars.

Fourth. To impose, from time to time, such tax as may be required to keep the school-house in repair, and provide for the necessary appendages: Provided, That all expenses for fuel shall be a tax upon the inhabitants sending pupils to school, in proportion to the number of pupils and the time they shall attend school:

school district, the process shall be by summons, a copy of which shall be left with the assessor of said district at least ten days previous to the return day thereof.

Sec. 13. Whenever lawfully assembled, the qualified voters in each district shall have power,

First. To adjourn from time to time as may be necessary.

Second. To designate a site for a school-house, and to change the same by a vote of two-thirds, at any regular meeting: Provided, That when no site can be established by said inhabitants, the inspectors of the township or townships shall determine where the site shall be, and said determination shall be final.

Third. To purchase or lease an appropriate site, and to build, hire or purchase a school-house, and to impose such tax as shall be sufficient for the payment thereof: Provided, That the amount of such tax shall not exceed in any one year the sum of five hundred dollars.

Fourth. To impose from time to time such tax as may be required to keep the school-house in repair, and provide for the necessary appendages: Provided, That all expenses for fuel shall be a tax upon the inhabitants sending pupils to school in proportion to the number of pupils, and the time they shall attend and provided also, that when any district in which a school-house shall have been built, shall within two years thereafter be divided, and there shall be a tax for a school-house raised in the district to which any portion of such aforesaid district shall have been attached, the remaining portion of such district in which the schoolhouse shall have been built, shall refund to the newly formed district that portion of the tax contributed by such portion of the district so set off.

Fifth. To impose a tax sufficient for the purchase of a suitable library case; also, a sum not exceeding ten dollars annually for the purchase of books, to be selected by a vote of the district, or by the district board when so directed.

Sixth. To designate the place where the library shall be kept, and the person by whom it shall be kept; and the superintendent of public instruction shall establish the necessary rules for the regulation of the library.

Seventh. To determine at each annual meeting the length of time, which shall not be less than three months, the school shall be kept; and to fix the amount of money, in addition to its apportionment, which may be raised for the support of its school teachers the ensuing year; the

school: And provided also, That when any district in which a school-house shall have been built, shall, within two years thereafter, be divided, and there shall be a tax for a school-house raised in the districts to which any portion of such aforesaid district shall have been attached, the remaining portion of such district in which the school-house shall have been built, shall refund to the newly formed district that portion of the tax contributed by such portion of the district so set off.

Fifth. To impose a tax sufficient for the purchase of a suitable library case, also a sum not exceeding ten dollars annually, for the purchase of books to be selected by a vote of the district by the district board, when so directed.

Sixth. To designate the place where the library shall be kept, and the person by whom it shall be kept; and the superintendent of public instruction shall establish the necessary rules for the regulation of the library.

Seventh. To determine at each annual meeting, the length of time, which shall not be less than three months, the school shall be kept, and to fix the amount of money, in addition to its apportionment, which may be raised for the support of its school teachers the ensuing year, the sum so voted not to exceed in any one year ninety dollars: Provided, That in case no sum for the support of schools shall be voted at the annual meeting of any district, the director may call a special meeting for the purpose of voting such tax, at which meeting, the district may, by a vote of two-thirds, vote any sum, not exceeding that authorized to be raised at the annual meeting.

Eighth. To order and direct the sale of any site, that may belong to the district, whenever the school-house shall have been removed, on [or] the sale of such other property and buildings, as may belong to the district.

Sec. 14. The moderator, director and assessor, shall hold their respective offices until the annual meeting next following their appointment, and until others are chosen: Provided, They shall not hold their offices beyond the time of a second annual meeting without re-election.

Sec. 15. Every person elected to any one of the above offices, who, without sufficient cause, shall neglect or refuse to serve, shall forfeit to the district for the use of the library the sum of ten dollars, to be recovered in an action of debt, by the assessor, before any court of competent jurisdiction.

Sec. 16. The moderator shall have power, and it shall be his

sum so voted not to exceed in any one year ninety dollars: Provided, That in case no sum for the support of schools shall be voted at the annual meeting of any district, the director may call a special meeting for the purpose of voting such tax; at which meeting the district may, by a vote of two-thirds, vote any sum not exceeding that authorized to be raised at the annual meeting.

Eighth. To order and direct the sale of any site that may belong to the district, whenever the school-house shall have been removed or the sale of such other property and buildings as may belong to the district.

Sec. 14. The moderator, director and assessor shall hold their respective offices until the annual meeting next following their appointment and until others are chosen: Provided They shall not hold their offices beyond the time of a second annual meeting without re-election.

Sec. 15. Every person elected to any one of the above offices who, without sufficient cause, shall neglect or refuse to serve shall forfeit to the district for the use of the library the sum of ten dollars, to be recovered in an action of debt by the assessor before any court of competent jurisdiction.

Sec. 16. The moderator shall have power and it shall be his

duty, to preside at all meetings
of the district, to sign all warrants for the collection of taxes,
and all orders for the payment of
moneys to be disbursed by the
district, and countersign all warrants of the director upon the
township board of inspectors, for
the moneys apportioned to the
district by said board of school
inspectors.

Sec. 17. The assessor shall
have power, and it shall be his
duty,

First. To obtain, within thirty
days of his election, a transcript
of so much of the last assessment roll of the township or
townships as relates to his district, and shall add to such transcript all the property of persons
who may have become residents
since the last assessment roll was
made, and all the property pur-
chases by non-residents since the
making of said roll; said property to be rated according to the
rule of valuation adopted in
making out the township assessment roll: Provided, That no
property shall be twice assessed,
and the said transcript, together
with such additions as shall be
made as aforesaid, shall be the
assessment roll of said district;
and all taxes to be raised in such
district, shall be levied upon the
taxable property thereof, in proportion to such valuation.

Second. To post up, whenever

duty to preside at all meetings of
the district, to sign all warrants
for the collection of taxes and all
orders for payment of moneys to
be disbursed by the district, and
countersign all warrants of the
director upon the township board
of inspectors for the moneys apportioned to the district by said
board of school inspectors.

Sec. 17. The assessor shall
have power and it shall be his
duty,

First. To obtain within thirty
days of his election, a transcript
of so much of the last assessment
roll of the township or townships
as relates to his district, and
shall add to such transcript all
the property of persons who may
have become residents since the
last assessment roll was made,
and all the property purchased by
non-residents since the making of
said roll; said property to be
rated according to the rule of
valuation adopted in making out
the township assessment roll:
Provided, That no property shall
be twice assessed, and the said
transcript, together with such additions as shall be made as aforesaid, shall be the assessment roll
of said district; and all taxes to
be raised in such district shall be
levied upon the taxable property
thereof in proportion to such
valuation.

Second. To post up whenever

any tax shall have been assessed upon the property of his district, in the most frequented and central place, a list of persons taxed, with the amount set opposite their respective names, so far as their names shall be known, and also a description of the property of persons whose names shall be known, and also a description of the property of persons whose names are not known, at least thirty days previous to the same being offered for collection.

Third.   To call a meeting of the district board, in case any person shall complain to him during the above named period, of being taxed beyond his due proportion, who shall examine into the ground of said complaint, and revise, alter or confirm said assessment, as in their judgment justice shall require; and at the end of the time specified, he shall certify the same upon the tax list, and present it to the moderator for his warrant.

Fourth.   It shall be the duty of the assessor to collect all taxes assessed upon the taxable property of his district, and pay them over on the warrant of the moderator; and in case any person shall neglect or refuse to pay such tax when called upon, it shall be the duty of the assessor to collect the same by distress and sale of the goods and chattels of such person, wheresoever

any tax shall have been assessed upon the property of his district, in the most frequented and central place, a list of persons taxed, with the amount set opposite their respective names, so far as their names shall be known, and also a description of the property of persons whose names shall be known, and also a description of property of persons whose names are not known at least thirty days previous to the same being offered for collection.

Third.   To call a meeting of the district board in case any person shall complain to him, during the above named period, of being taxed beyond his due proportion, who shall examine into the ground of said complaint, and reverse, alter or confirm said assessment as, in their judgment, justice shall require, and at the end of the time specified, he shall certify the same upon the tax list, and present it to the moderator for his warrant.

Fourth.   It shall be the duty of the assessor to collect all taxes assessed upon the taxable property of his district, and pay them over on the warrant of the moderator, and in case any person shall neglect or refuse to pay such tax when called upon, it shall be the duty of the assessor to collect the same by distress and sale of the goods and chattels of such person whenever found in said district, having first published such sale for at least ten days, by posting up notice thereof in the most public place in the district; and in the collection of taxes upon lands and tenements, said assessor shall make returns to the treasurer of the county in the same manner as township collectors; and it shall be the duty of the treasurer to sell the lands and tenements for the collection of said school tax, in the same manner as is required for the collection of township and county taxes.

Fifth. It shall also be the duty of the assessor to appear for and in behalf of his district in all suits brought by or against said district, except the case provided for in the nineteenth section of this chapter.

Sec. 18. The director shall have power, and it shall be his duty,

First. To record all the proceedings of the district in a book to be kept for that purpose, and preserve copies of all reports made to the board of school inspectors.

Second. To employ, by and with the advice and consent of the moderator and assessor, or either of them, qualified teachers, and pay them by a draft upon the township board of inspectors, said draft not to exceed the amount due said district on ac-

found in said district, having first published such sale for at least ten days by posting up notice thereof in the most public place in the district; and in the collection of taxes upon lands and tenements said assessor shall make returns to the county collector; and it shall be the duty of the county collector to sell the lands and tenements for the collection of said school tax, in the same manner as is required for the collection of township and county taxes.

Fifth. It shall also be the duty of the assessor to appear for and in behalf of his district in all suits brought by or against said district, except the case provided for in the nineteenth section of this act.

Sec. 18. The director shall have power and it shall be his duty,

First. To record all the proceedings of the district in a book to be kept for that purpose, and preserve copies of all reports made to the board of school inspectors.

Second. To employ by and with the advice and consent of the moderator and assessor, or either of them, qualified teachers, and pay them by a draft upon the township board of inspectors, said draft not to exceed the amount due said district on account of the apportionment of the board of school inspectors.

Third. Whenever the apportionment shall not be sufficient to pay for the services of any such teachers, it shall be the duty of the director to call a meeting of the district board for the purpose of levying the balance upon the taxable property of the district, the amount so levied not to exceed the sum voted by the district at its annual meeting: and in case said sum so voted, together with the apportionment, shall be found insufficient the deficit shall be assessed upon the parents or guardians of the children in proportion to the length of time they shall severally have attended school during the term or terms when such deficiency shall have arisen.

Fourth. Within ten days of the time of the annual meeting, the director shall take the census of his district, by registering the names of all belonging to it, between the ages of five and seventeen years inclusive.

Fifth. A copy of this list he shall furnish to each and every teacher employed within the district, and require every such teacher carefully to note the time of attendance of each and every scholar, and to make a return of the same to the director.

Sixth. It shall be the duty of the director to provide the neces-

count of the apportionment of the board of school inspectors.

Third. Whenever the apportionment shall not be sufficient to pay for the services of any such teachers, it shall be the duty of the director to call a meeting of the district board for the purpose of levying the balance upon the taxable property of the district, the amount so levied not to exceed the sum voted by the district at its annual meeting; and in case said sum so voted, together with the apportionment, shall be found insufficient the deficit shall be assessed upon the parents or guardians of the children in proportion to the length of time they shall severally have attended school during the term or terms when such deficiency shall have arisen.

Fourth. Within ten days of the time of the annual meeting, the director shall take the census of his district by registering the names of all belonging to it between the ages of five and twenty-one years inclusive.

Fifth. A copy of this list he shall give to each and every teacher employed within the district, and require every such teacher carefully to note the time of attendance of each and every scholar, and to make a return of the same to the director.

Sixth. It shall be the duty of the director to provide the necessary appendages for the school-house, and keep the same in good condition and repair, during the time of school, and an accurate account of all expenses incurred.

Seventh. He shall present said account to the district board, to be assessed and collected in the manner hereinbefore prescribed.

Eighth. It shall be his duty to give the prescribed notice of the annual district meeting, and all such special meetings as shall be called for in accordance with the provisions of this chapter.

Ninth. At the end of the year, the school director shall report to the township board of inspectors at the office of the township clerk,

First. The whole number of children between the ages of five and seventeen;

Second. The number attending school under five and over seventeen;

Third. Whole number that have attended school during the year;

Fourth. Length of time a school has been kept by a qualified teacher;

Fifth. Amount of money received from the board of school inspectors;

Sixth. Amount received for library;

Seventh. Amount of money raised in the district;

Eighth. Purposes for which it was raised; and

sary appendages for the school-house, and keep the same in good condition and repair during the time of school, and an accurate account of all expenses incurred.

Seventh. He shall present said account to the district board to be assessed and collected in the manner hereinbefore prescribed.

Eighth. It shall be his duty to give the prescribed notice of the annual district meeting, and all such special meetings as shall be called for in accordance with the provisions of this act.

Ninth. At the end of the year the school director shall report to the township board of inspectors at the office of the township clerk.

First. The whole number of persons between the ages of five and twenty-one.

Second. The number attending school under five and over twenty-one.

Third. Whole number that have attended school during the year.

Fourth. Length of time a school has been kept by a qualified teacher.

Fifth. Amount of money received from the board of school inspectors.

Sixth. Amount received for library.

Seventh. Amount of money raised in the district.

Eighth. Purposes for which it was raised, and,

25

Ninth. Books used in said school.

Sec. 19. The moderator, director and assessor shall constitute the district board, and they shall have power, and it shall be their duty,

First. To levy and assess upon the taxable property all moneys voted by the district, and the deficit, if any, agreeably to the third provision of the eighteenth section of this chapter, and the sums requisite for the necessary appendages and fuel for the school-house, during the continuance of any school.

Second. To equalize the assessment roll of fractional school districts, formed from different counties, whenever in their judgment the assessment rolls of the townships out of which said district was formed, shall be unequal.

Third. To purchase or lease a site, as designated by the district, for the school-house, in the corporate name thereof; to build, hire or purchase such school-house out of the funds collected for that purpose, and to make sale of any site or property of the district, as directed by the inhabitants thereof, at an annual or special meeting.

Fourth. To divide the public moneys received by the district, for the year into not more than two parts, and to assign and ap-

Ninth. Books used in said school.

Sec. 19. The moderator, director, and assessor shall constitute the district board, and they shall have power and it shall be their duty,

First. To levy and assess upon the taxable property all moneys voted by the district, and the deficit, if any, agreeably to the third provision of the eighteenth section of this act, and the sums requisite for the necessary appendages and fuel for the school house during the continuance of any school.

Second. To equalize the assessment roll of fractional school districts formed from different counties, whenever, in their judgment, the assessment rolls of the townships out of which said district was formed shall be unequal.

Third. To purchase or lease a site as designated by the district for the school-house in the corporate name thereof, to build, hire or purchase such school-house out of the funds collected for that purpose, and to make sale of any site or property of the district as directed by the inhabitants thereof, at an annual or special meeting.

Fourth. To divide the public moneys received by the district for the year in not more than two parts, and to assign and apply

ply one of such portions to each term a school may be kept, in payment of the teachers for services for the same: Provided, That no money shall be paid to any teacher who has not received a certificate, as provided in the twenty-ninth section of this chapter.

Fifth. To require of the assessor a bond, to be given to the district, in double the amount of taxes to be collected in the district, with two sufficient sureties, to be approved by the moderator and director, conditioned for the faithful appropriation of all moneys that may come into his hands by virtue of his office; said bond to be lodged in the hands of the moderator, and in case of a nonfulfilment of the condition thereof, the moderator and director, or either of them, may cause a suit for the penalty of said bond to be commenced in the name of the district, before any court of competent jurisdiction.

Sixth. To present at each annual meeting of the district a report setting forth an accurate account of all moneys received by them, or any of them, during the preceding year, and of the disbursement of the same; which report shall contain the items of such receipts and disbursements, and such report shall be recorded by the director in a distinct book to be provided and kept for that purpose.

one of such portions to each term a school may be kept, in payment of the teachers for services for the same: Provided, That no money shall be paid to any teacher who has not received a certificate as provided in the twenty-ninth section of this act.

Fifth. To require of the assessor a bond to be given to the district in double the amount of taxes to be collected in the district, with two sufficient sureties to be approved by the moderator and director, conditioned for the faithful appropriation of all moneys that come into his hands by virtue of his office: said bond to be lodged in the hands of the moderator; and in case of a nonfulfilment of the condition thereof, the moderator and director, or either of them, may cause a suit for the penalty of said bond to be commenced in the name of the district, before any court of competent jurisdiction.

Sixth. To present at each annual meeting of the district, a report setting forth an accurate account of all moneys received by them or any of them during the preceding year and of the disbursement of the same, which report shall contain the items of such receipts and disbursements, and such report shall be recorded by the director in a distinct book to be provided and kept for that purpose.

Sec. 20. The district board shall have power to fill by appointment any vacancy that shall occur from whatever cause, and it shall be the duty of the board to supply such vacancy within ten days after the time of its occurrence.

Sec. 21. Each member of the district board shall receive such compensation for his services as shall be voted in district meetings.

Sec. 22. Each and every district that shall comply with the fifth provision of the thirteenth section of this chapter, shall be entitled to its proportion of the clear proceeds of all fines collected within the several counties, for any breach of the penal laws; and also its proportion of the equivalent for exemption from military duty, which fines and equivalents shall be paid over by

Sec. 20. The district board shall have power to fill by appointment any vacancy that shall occur, from whatever cause, and it shall be the duty of the board to supply such vacancy within ten days after the time of its occurrence.

Sec. 21. Each and every district that shall comply with the fifth provision of the thirteenth section of this act, shall be entitled to its proportion of the clear proceeds of all fines collected within the several counties for any breach of the penal laws, and also its proportion of the equivalent for exemption from military duty, which fines and equivalent shall be paid over by the several officers collecting the same to the treasurers of their respective counties, to be by them apportioned amongst the several townships in the county according to the number of persons between the ages of five and twenty-one years inclusive.

Sec. 22. Each member of the district board shall receive such compensation for his services as shall be voted in district meetings.

the several officers collecting the same, to the treasurers of their respective counties, to be by them apportioned amongst the several townships in the county, according to the number of children between the ages of five and seventeen years inclusive.

Sec. 23. There shall be chosen at each annual township meeting, three school inspectors, in the same manner as other township officers are chosen, who shall hold their office until others are chosen.

Sec. 24. Said inspectors shall have power, and it shall be their duty,

First. To meet within ten days of their election at the office of the township clerk, who shall be ex-officio clerk of the board, and organize by choosing one of their number chairman, who shall preside at their meetings.

Second. To divide the township into such a number of districts, and to regulate and alter the boundaries of said school districts, as may from time to time be necessary: Provided, no district shall contain more than nine sections.

Third. To describe and number the school districts of their township.

Sec. 23. There shall be chosen at each annual township meeting, three school inspectors in the same manner as other township officers are chosen, who shall hold their office until others are chosen.

Sec. 24. Said inspectors shall have power and it shall be their duty,

First. To meet within ten days of their election at the office of the township clerk, who shall be ex-officio clerk of the board, and organize by choosing one of their number chairman, who shall preside at their meetings.

Second. To divide the township into such a number of districts, and to regulate and alter the boundaries of said school districts, as [may] from time to time be necessary.

Third. To apply for and receive from the county treasurer all moneys appropriated for the primary schools and district libraries in their townships, and from the collector of the township all moneys raised therein for the same purpose, as soon as the same may be due.

Fourth. To apply for and receive from the county treasurer, all moneys appropriated for the primary schools and district libraries in their townships, and from the collector of the township all moneys raised therein for the same purpose, as soon as the same shall be due.

Fifth. To apportion the school and library money received by them on or before the first of March in each year, among the several school districts in their township, in proportion to the number of children in each, between the ages of five and seventeen years, as the same shall be shown by the last annual report of the director of each district: Provided, No school money shall be apportioned to any district, from which a report shall not have been received, nor to any district in which a school shall not have been kept, at least three months during the year immediately preceding, by a qualified teacher, except the first distribution, and provided that no library money shall be apportioned to any district that shall not have complied with the fifth provision of the thirteenth section of this chapter.

Sec. 25. The chairman of the board of inspectors, shall be the treasurer of said board; and it shall be the duty of the inspectors to require of said chairman

Fourth. To describe and number the school districts of their township.

Fifth. To apportion the school and library money received by them, on or before the first day of March in each year, among the several school districts in their township, in proportion to the number of persons in each between the ages of five and twenty-one years, as the same shall be shown by the last annual report of the director of each district: Provided no school money shall be apportioned to any district from which a report shall not have been received, nor to any district in which a school shall not have been kept at least three months during the year immediately preceding by a qualified teacher, except the first distribution: And provided, That no library moneys shall be apportioned to any district that shall not have complied with the fifth provision of the thirteenth section of this act.

Sec. 25. The chairman of the board of inspectors, shall be the treasurer of said board, and it shall be the duty of the inspectors to require of said chairman a bond, to be given to the township in double the amount to be received by him, in two sufficient sureties, to be approved by the township clerk, conditioned for the faithful appropriation of all moneys that may come into his hands by virtue of his office; said bond to be lodged with the township clerk, who is hereby authorized, in case of the non-fulfilment of the condition of said bond, to sue for the penalty thereof, before any court of competent jurisdiction.

Sec. 26. On or before the twentieth day of October of each year, they shall make out and transmit to the county clerk a report, setting forth the whole number of districts in their township, together with the several particulars set forth in the reports of the school directors.

Sec. 27. If any board of school inspectors shall neglect or refuse to make such report by the time set forth in the preceding section, they shall forfeit to the use of the schools of their township the sum of fifty dollars, and the full amount of the money lost by their failure, with interest on the same, to be recovered in an action of debt by the township collector, before any court having competent jurisdiction of the same.

Sec. 28. Whenever it may be

a bond to be given to the township in double the amount to be received by him, in two sufficient sureties to be approved by the township clerk, conditioned for the faithful appropriation of all moneys that may come into his hands by virtue of his office, said bond to be lodged with the township clerk, who is hereby authorized, in case of the non-fulfilment of the condition of said bond, to sue for the penalty thereof before any court of competent jurisdiction.

Sec. 26. On or before the twentieth day of October of each year, they shall make out and transmit to the clerk of the district court a report setting forth the whole number of districts in their township, together with the several particulars set forth in the reports of the school directors.

Sec. 27. If any board of school inspectors shall neglect or refuse to make such report by the time set forth in the preceding section, they shall forfeit to the use of the schools of their township the sum of fifty dollars, and the full amount of the money lost by their failure, with interest on the same, to be recovered in an action of debt by the township collector before any court having competent jurisdiction of the same.

Sec. 28. Whenever it may be

necessary or convenient to form a district from two or more adjoining townships, the inspectors, or a majority of them, from each of such adjoining townships, may form a district, regulate and alter the same; and the director of such district so formed, shall make returns to each township from which said district is formed, specifying in said returns that only which belongs to said township.

Sec. 29. It shall be the duty of the inspectors to examine annually all persons offering themselves as candidates for teaching primary schools in their township, in regard to moral character, learning, and ability to teach school; and if satisfied that such candidates possess the requisite qualifications, they shall deliver to the person so examined a certificate, signed by them, in such form as shall be prescribed by the superintendent of public instruction, which certificate shall be in force one year from the date thereof.

Sec. 30. Whenever the inspectors shall deem it necessary, they may re-examine any teacher of any primary school in their township, and if found wanting in the requisite qualifications, they may annul any certificate given to such teacher, by giving to such person ten days' written notice to that effect, and filing the same

necessary or convenient to form a district from two or more adjoining townships, the inspectors, or a majority of them from each of such adjoining townships, may form a district, regulate and alter the same; and the director of such district so formed shall make returns to each township from which said district is formed, specifying in said returns that only which belongs to said township.

Sec. 29. It shall be the duty of the inspectors to examine annually all persons offering themselves as candidates for teaching primary schools in their township, in regard to moral character, learning and ability to teach school, and if satisfied that such candidates possess the requisite qualifications, they shall deliver to the person so examined a certificate signed by them, in such form as shall be prescribed by the superintendent of public instruction, which certificate shall be in force one year from the date thereof.

Sec. 30. Whenever the inspectors shall deem it necessary, they may re-examine any teacher of any primary school in their township, and if found wanting in the requisite qualifications, they may annul any certificate given to such teacher by giving to such person ten day's written notice to that effect, and filing in the office of the clerk of their township.

Sec. 31. It shall be the duty of the inspectors to visit all such schools in their township, at least twice in each year, as shall be organized according to law, to inquire into their condition, examine the scholars, and give such advice to both teachers and scholars as they shall deem proper.

Sec. 32. In case of the death, or removal, or disability to act of any one of the inspectors, the board shall fill such vacancy by appointment.

Sec. 33. Whenever any district board shall fail to supply any vacancy within the time limited in section twenty, the board of inspectors shall fill the same by appointment.

Sec. 34. The inspectors shall be entitled to receive for their services the sum of one dollar and fifty cents per day, to be audited and paid as the accounts of other township officers are audited and paid.

Sec. 35. Any person elected or appointed school inspector, who shall neglect or refuse, without sufficient cause, to serve as such, shall forfeit to the use of the school fund of his township the sum of twenty-five dollars, to be recovered as prescribed in the twenty-fifth section of this chapter.

Sec. 36. The township clerk

the same in the office of the clerk of their township.

Sec. 31. It shall be the duty of the inspectors to visit all such schools in their township, at least twice in each year, as shall be organized according to law, to inquire into the condition, examine the scholars, and give such advice to both teachers and scholars as they shall deem proper.

Sec. 32. In case of the death, or removal, or disability to act of any one of the inspectors, the board shall fill such vacancy by appointment.

Sec. 33. Whenever any district board shall fail to supply any vacancy within the time limited in section twenty, the board of inspectors shall fill the same by appointment.

Sec. 34. The inspectors shall be entitled to receive for their services the sum of one dollar per day, to be audited and paid as the accounts of other township officers are audited and paid.

Sec. 35. Any person elected or appointed school inspector who shall neglect or refuse, without sufficient cause, to serve as such, shall forfeit to the use of the school fund of his township the sum of twenty-five dollars, to be recovered as prescribed in the twenty-fifth section of this act.

Sec. 36. The township clerk

shall be ex-officio clerk of the board of school inspectors, and shall have power, and it shall be his duty,

First. To attend all meetings of the inspectors, and to prepare, under their direction, all their reports, estimates and apportionments of school moneys, and record the same, and all their proceedings, in a book to be kept for that purpose.

Second. To receive and keep all reports made to the inspectors from the directors of the several school districts, and all the books and papers belonging to the inspectors, and file the same in his office.

Third. To receive all such communications as may be directed to him by the superintendent of public instruction, and dispose of the same in the manner directed therein.

Fourth. To transmit to the clerk of the county all such reports as may be made for such clerk by the inspectors within the time limited in this chapter, and generally to do and execute all such things as belong to his office and may be required of him by the inspectors.

Sec. 37. It shall be the duty of each and every county clerk to receive all such communications as may be directed to him by the superintendent of public instruc-

shall be ex-officio clerk of the board of school inspectors, and shall have power and it shall be his duty,

First. To attend all meetings of the inspectors and to prepare, under their direction, all their reports, estimates and apportionments of school moneys, and record the same and all their proceedings in a book to be kept for that purpose.

Second. To receive and keep all reports made to the inspectors from the directors of the several school districts, and all the books and papers belonging to the inspectors, and file the same in his office.

Third. To receive all such communications as may be directed to him by the superintendent of public instruction, and dispose of the same in the manner directed therein.

Fourth. To transmit to the clerk of the district court all such reports as may be made for such clerk by the inspectors, within the time limited in this act, and generally to do and execute all such things as belong to his office, and may be required of him by the inspectors.

Sec. 37. It shall be the duty of each and every clerk of the district court, to receive all such communications as may be directed to him by the superintendent

tion, and dispose of the same in the manner therein directed.

Sec. 38. It shall be the duty of the clerk of each county, on or before the twentieth of November of every year, to make and transmit to the superintendent of public instruction a report in writing, containing the whole number of townships in his county, distinguishing townships from which the required reports have been made to him by the inspectors of schools, and containing a certified copy of all their reports; and the board of supervisors or commissioners of each county are hereby authorized to allow to the clerk of their counties such compensation as they may deem proper for the services he may perform under and by virtue of the provisions of this chapter.

Sec. 39. Any clerk who shall neglect or refuse to make such report, by the time so limited, shall, for each offence, forfeit the sum of one hundred dollars to the use of the schools of said county, to be recovered in an action of debt, to be commenced forthwith by and in the name of the superintendent of public instruction; and the money so recovered shall, when received by the superintendent, be paid into the treasury of the county, to the credit and for the use of the district or districts

of public instruction, and dispose of the same in the manner therein directed.

Sec. 38. It shall be the duty of each clerk of the district court, on or before the twentieth of November of every year, to make and transmit to the superintendent of public instruction, a report in writing, containing the whole number of townships in his county, distinguishing townships from which the required reports have been made to him by the inspectors of schools, and containing a certified copy of all their reports; and the board of supervisors or commissioners of each county are hereby authorized to allow to the clerk of the district courts such compensation as they may deem proper for the services he may perform under and by virtue of the provisions of this act.

Sec. 39. Any clerk who shall neglect or refuse to make such report by the time so limited, shall, for each offence, forfeit the sum of one hundred dollars, to the use of the schools of said county, to be recovered in an action of debt to be commenced forthwith by and in the name of the superintendent of public instruction. And the money so recovered shall, when received by the superintendent, be paid into the treasury of the county, to the credit and for the use of the dis-

which may suffer from such neglect of the clerk, and the sum
may be drawn out by the proper
authority of said district or districts.

Sec. 40. The moneys to be
hereafter distributed annually for
the support of primary schools,
shall be payable on the first Monday of January in each year, on
the warrant of the auditor general, to the treasurers of the several counties.

Sec. 41. The treasurers of the
counties shall apply for and receive such moneys as are apportioned to their respective counties, when the same shall become
due.

Sec. 42. The treasurer of each
county, when he shall receive such
moneys, shall give notice in writing to the chairman or clerk of
the board of school inspectors of
each township in his county, of
the amount of school and library
moneys apportioned to such township, and shall hold the same,
subject to the order of the inspectors.

Sec. 43. In case any moneys
apportioned to any township shall
not be applied for by such inspectors, the moneys so remaining
shall be added to the moneys next
received by the treasurer for distribution from the superintendent
of public instruction, and in the
same proportion distributed.

Sec. 44. Whenever the clerk of

trict or districts, which may suffer from such neglect of the
clerk; and the sum may be drawn
out by the proper authority of
said district or districts.

Sec. 40. The moneys to be
hereafter distributed annually for
the support of primary schools,
shall be payable on the first Monday of January in each year, on
the warrant of the auditor of
public accounts to the treasurers
of the several counties.

Sec. 41. The treasurers of the
counties shall apply for and receive such moneys as are apportioned to their respective counties
when the same shall become due.

Sec. 42. The treasurer of each
county, when he shall receive such
moneys, shall give notice in writing to the chairman or clerk of
the board of school inspectors of
each township in his county, of
the amount of school and library
moneys apportioned to such township, and shall hold the same subject to the order of the inspectors.

Sec. 43. In case any moneys
apportioned to any township shall
not be applied for by such inspectors, the moneys so remaining
shall be added to the moneys next
received by the treasurer for distribution from the superintendent
of public instruction, and in the
same proportion distributed.

Sec. 44. Whenever the clerk of

any county shall receive from the superintendent notice of the amount of moneys to be disbursed in the several townships in his county, he shall file the same in his office, and within one week transmit a certified copy thereof to the clerk of the board of commissioners, which copy said clerk shall lay before the commissioners at their next annual meeting.

Sec. 45. It shall be the duty of the commissioners at such meeting, to add to the sums of money to be raised in each of the townships of the county, a sum equal to that which shall have been apportioned to such township from the school fund, to be levied and collected in the same manner as other moneys are directed to be raised in the townships.

Sec. 46. The commissioners shall cause and require the collector of each township, by their warrant, to pay such moneys, when collected, to the chairman of the board of school inspectors, in such township, for the use of schools therein.

Sec. 47. Should any township neglect or refuse to elect a board of school inspectors, the collector shall pay the moneys so collected to the county treasurer, to be apportioned among the several townships, as provided in the fortieth section of this chapter.

any county shall receive from the superintendent notice of the amount of money to be disbursed in the several townships in his county, he shall file the same in his office, and within one week transmit a certified copy thereof to the clerk of the board of commissioners, which copy said clerk shall lay before the commissioners at their next regular meeting.

Sec. 45. It shall be the duty of the commissioners, at such meeting, to add to the sums of money to be raised in each of the townships of the county, a sum equal to that which shall have been apportioned to such township from the school fund, to be levied and collected in the same manner as other moneys are directed to be raised in the townships.

Sec. 46. The commissioners shall cause and require the collector of each township by their warrant to pay such moneys, when collected, to the chairman of the board of school inspectors in such township for the use of schools therein.

Sec. 47. Should any township neglect or refuse to elect a board of school inspectors, the collector shall pay the moneys so collected to the county treasurer to be apportioned among the several townships as provided in the fortieth section of this act.

Sec. 48. Each and every officer created by the provisions of this chapter, who shall receive, by virtue of his office, any books, papers or moneys, and shall refuse to deliver the same to his successor in office, or shall wilfully mutilate or destroy the same, or any part thereof, shall be deemed guilty of a misdemeanor, and liable to a fine of not less than fifty dollars, nor more than five hundred, at the discretion of the court.— *Revised Statutes of Michigan*, 1837–1838, pp. 238–249.

Sec. 48. Each and every officer created by the provisions of this act, who shall receive, by virtue of his office, any books, papers, or moneys, and shall refuse to deliver the same to his successor in office, or shall wilfully mutilate or destroy the same, or any part thereof, shall be deemed guilty of a misdemeanor and liable to a fine of not less than fifty dollars nor more than five hundred, at the discretion of the court.

Sec. 49. All acts and parts of acts coming within the purview of this act, are hereby repealed. — *Laws of the Territory of Iowa,* 1839–1840, pp. 101–110.

APPENDIX B

A COMPARISON OF THE UNION SCHOOL LAW OF OHIO OF 1854 AND THE IOWA LAW OF 1857

THE Union school law of Ohio (1854), passed originally, it appears, for the benefit of the cities of Akron and Massillon, was submitted, after minor changes, for adoption by the General Assembly of Iowa early in 1857. But it is believed that none of the members of the Assembly knew the source of the statute, owing to the indirect manner of its presentation. As was said in the text (Vol. I, pp. 36–38), the act possessed features not common to the school legislation of this Commonwealth. The parts in which it underwent changes in the adaptation to Iowa conditions may be seen below.

THE OHIO STATUTE

Sec. I. That any incorporated city or town in this state, or any incorporated town or village, except such city, town or village as is now in whole or part governed as to schools by some special law heretofore passed, containing within the town or village plot, as laid out and recorded, two hundred inhabitants or more, with the territory attached or hereafter to be attached to said city, town or village, for school purposes, may be organized into and established as a single

THE IOWA STATUTE

Sec. 1. That any incorporated city, town or school district in this State, containing two hundred inhabitants or more, with the territory attached, or hereafter to be attached to said city, town or district, for school purposes, may be organized into and established as a single district, in the manner and with the power hereinafter specified.

school district, in the manner and with the powers hereinafter specified, but the provisions of this act shall not apply to any city, town or village, or any part thereof, which is now governed as to schools by any special law.

Sec. II. That in order to such organization, written notices shall be posted up in three or more of the most public places in said contemplated district, signed at least by six resident freeholders of the same, requesting the qualified electors in said district to assemble upon a day, and at some suitable place in said district, to be named in said notices, then and there to vote, by ballot, for or against the adoption of this act, which notices shall be so posted up at least ten days next prior to said meeting.

Sec. III. That the electors assembled at said time and place shall proceed to appoint a chairman, assistant chairman, and clerk, who shall be judges of said election. That the electors in favor of the adoption of this act for said district, shall write upon their ballots ''school law,'' and those opposed thereto, shall write upon their ballots ''no school law,'' the adoption or rejection of this act to be determined by a majority of the votes to be cast in manner aforesaid.

Sec. IV. That in case a majority of votes shall have been

Sec. 2. That in order to such organization, written notices shall be posted up in three or more of the most public places in said contemplated district, signed by at least one-fourth of the voters of said city or town, requesting the qualified electors in said district to assemble upon a day, and at some suitable place in said district, to be named in said notices, then and there to vote by ballot for or against the adoption of this act, which notices shall be so posted up at least ten days prior to said meeting.

Sec. 3. That the electors assembled at said time and place shall proceed to appoint a chairman, assistant chairman and clerk, who shall be the judges of said election. The electors in favor of the adoption of this act for said district, shall have upon their ballots ''For the law;'' and those opposed thereto shall have upon their ballots ''Against the law;'' the adoption or rejection of this act to be determined by a majority of the votes cast in manner aforesaid.

Sec. 4. That in case a majority of votes shall have been

cast for said law, the electors of
said districts shall assemble at
the place last aforesaid, within
twenty days from the time of
the adoption of said act, of
which at least ten days' previous
notice shall be given by said
chairman and clerk, in the manner aforesaid, and shall then
choose by ballot six directors of
the public schools of said district,
two of whom shall serve for one
year, two for two years, and two
for three years; the time that
each shall serve to be designated
on the ballots, and annually
thereafter there shall be chosen
in the same manner two directors,
each of whom shall serve for
three years, and until their successors shall be elected and qualified; such intermediate vacancies
as may occur to be filled by the
acting directors till the next annual election, when such vacancies shall be filled by the electors.

Sec. V.   That said directors,
within ten days after their appointment as aforesaid, shall
meet and organize by choosing
from their number a president,
secretary, and treasurer; that
said treasurer, before he enters
upon the duties of his office, shall
give bond payable to the state of
Ohio, with security to be approved by said board, and to be
by them kept, conditioned for the

cast for said law, the electors of
said district shall assemble at the
place last aforesaid, within twenty days from the time of the
adoption of said act, of which at
least ten days' previous notice
shall be given by said chairman
and clerk, in the manner aforesaid, and shall then choose by
ballot six directors for the public
schools of said district, two of
whom shall serve for one year,
two for two years, and two for
three years; the time that each
shall serve to be designated on
the ballots, and annually on the
second Monday of March thereafter, there shall be chosen in the
same manner, two directors, each
of whom shall serve for three
years and until their successors
are elected and qualified; such
intermediate vacancies as shall
occur, to be filled by the acting
directors till the next annual election, when such vacancies shall be
filled by the electors.

Sec. 5.   That said directors
within two days after their election as aforesaid, shall each,
having taken an oath or affirma-
tion for the faithful performance
of the duties of his office, meet
and organize by choosing from
their number a president, secretary, and treasurer; that said
secretary and treasurer each, before he enters upon the duties of
his office, shall give bond payable

26

faithful discharge of his duties as such treasurer.

Sec. VI. That said directors and their successors in office shall be a body corporate, by the name of the board of education of said city, town or village, and as such, and by such name, shall receive all moneys and other property belonging or accruing to said district, or to said city, town, or village, or any part of the same, for the use or benefit of the public schools therein, and the said board shall be capable of contracting and being contracted with, suing and being sued, pleading and being impleaded, in any court of law or equity, and also shall be capable of receiving any gift, grant, bequest, or devise, made for the use of the public schools in said city, town, or district, and all moneys accruing to said city, town, or district, for school purposes, under any law of this state, shall be paid over to the treasurer of said board of education.

Sec. VII. Said board of education may hold stated meetings at such times and places in said district as they may appoint, four members of said board at all meetings thereof constituting a quorum for business; that special meetings thereof may be called

to the State of Iowa, with security to be approved by said board, and to be kept by the president, conditioned for the faithful discharge of his duties as such officer.

Sec. 6. That said directors, and their successors in office, shall be a body corporate by the name of the board of education of said city or town, and as such and by such name shall receive all monies and other property belonging or accruing to said district or to said city or town, or any part of the same, for the use or benefit of the public schools therein; and the said board shall be capable of contracting and being contracted with, suing and being sued, pleading and being impleaded, in any court of law or equity; and also be capable of receiving any grant, gift, bequest, or devise, made for the use of the public schools of said city, town, or district; and all monies accruing to said city, town, or district, for school purposes, under any law of this State, shall be paid over to the treasurer of said board of education.

Sec. 7. Said board of education may hold stated meetings, at such times and places in said district, as they may appoint, four members of said board at all meetings thereof constituting a quorum for business; and special meetings thereof may be called by the president or by any two members, on giving one day's notice of the time and place of the same, and said board, by resolution, shall direct the payment of all moneys that shall come into the hands of the treasurer, and no money shall be paid out of the treasury except in pursuance of such resolution, and on the written order of the president, countersigned by the secretary.

Sec. VIII. That whenever said board shall deem it necessary to purchase or erect a school house, or school houses for said district, or to purchase sites for the same, they shall call a meeting of the legal voters in said district, by giving at least ten days' notice of the time, and place, and object of said meeting, in some newspaper printed in, and in general circulation in such district, if any such there be, and if there be no such newspaper, then by posting up written or printed notices thereof, at five or more of the most public places in said district, and the president of said board, and in his absence, one of the other directors, shall act as chairman of said meeting, and said meeting may determine by a majority vote upon the erection of a school house or school houses, and the purchase of a site or sites therefor, and the amount of money to be raised for the purpose aforesaid, and the

by the president or by any two members, on giving one day's notice of the time and place of the same, and said board by resolution shall direct the payment of all monies that shall come into the hands of the treasurer, and no money shall be paid out of the treasury except in pursuance of such resolution, and on the written order of the president countersigned by the secretary.

Sec. 8. That whenever said board shall deem it necessary to purchase or erect a school house or school houses for said district, or to purchase sites for the same, they shall call a meeting of the legal voters in said district, by giving at least ten days' notice of the time and place and object of said meeting in some newspaper printed in and of general circulation in such district, or by posting up written or printed notices thereof, at five or more of the most public places in said district; and the president of said board, and in his absence, one of the other of said directors shall act as chairman of said meeting, and said meeting may determine by a majority vote upon the erection of a school house or school houses, and the purchase of a site or sites therefor, and the amount of money to be raised for the purpose aforesaid, and the time or times when the same shall be paid, which monies so voted shall time, or times, when the same shall be paid, which moneys, so voted, shall be thereupon certified by the board of education by its chairman and secretary, to the auditor of the county, and shall be assessed in said district, collected and paid over to the treasurer of said district, in the same manner as the tax hereinafter provided for in the twelfth section of this act.

Sec. IX. It shall be the duty of said board, so soon as the means for that purpose can be provided, to establish in said district an adequate number of primary schools to be so located as best to accommodate the inhabitants thereof, and in which the rudiments of education shall be taught, and it shall be the further duty of said board, to establish in said district, a suitable number of other schools of a higher grade or grades, wherein instruction shall be given in such studies as may not be provided for in the primary schools, the number of schools and also of the different grades thereof, to be determined by said board; and it shall be the further duty of said board to decide what branches shall be taught in each and all of said schools: Provided, that no other language than the English or German, shall be taught therein, except with the concurrence of two-thirds of said board.

be assessed and collected by the secretary of said board, in like manner as taxes for school house purposes are now, or may hereafter be collected under the laws of the State, and, on the order of the president, paid over to the treasurer of the board.

Sec. 9. It shall be the duty of said board as soon as the means for that purpose can be provided, to establish in said district an adequate number of primary schools to be so located as best to accommodate the inhabitants thereof, and in which the rudiments of education shall be taught; and it shall be the further duty of said board to establish in said district a suitable number of other schools of a higher grade or grades, wherein instruction shall be given in such studies as may not be provided for in the primary schools; the number of schools and also of the different grades thereof, to be determined by said board; and it shall be the further duty of said board to decide what branches shall be taught in each and all of said schools: Provided, That no other language than the English shall be taught therein, except with the concurrence of two-thirds of said board.

Sec. X. Admission to said schools shall be gratuitous to the children, wards, and apprentices of all actual residents in said district, who may be entitled to the privileges of the public schools, under the general laws of this state: Provided, that said board shall have power to admit to said schools other pupils, upon such terms, or upon the payment of such tuition, as they may prescribe.

Sec. XI. Said board shall have power to make all necessary regulations for said schools, to prescribe and enforce rules for the admission of pupils into the same, not inconsistent with the preceding section, and the examination that pupils must pass preparatory to admission into the schools of higher grades than the primary; to subdivide said school district, if they shall think proper; to select sites for school houses; to superintend the building of the same, and to pay therefor, their appurtenances, furniture and apparatus; to borrow money for the erection of school houses upon a majority vote of said district therefor, and to incur all other expenses of said school system, and pay the same from the public moneys of said district.

Sec. XII. It shall be the duty of said board to keep said schools

Sec. 10. Admission to said schools shall be granted to the children, wards and apprentices of all actual residents in said district who may be entitled to the privileges of the public schools under the general laws of this State, subject to the provisions of section 13 of this act: Provided, That said board shall have power to admit to said schools other pupils, upon such terms, or upon the payment of such tuition as they may prescribe.

Sec. 11. Said board shall have power to make all necessary regulations for said schools, to prescribe and enforce rules for the admission of pupils into the same, not inconsistent with the preceding section, and the examination that pupils must pass preparatory to admission into the schools of higher grades than the primary; to subdivide said school district if they shall think proper, to select sites for school houses, to superintend the building of the same, and to pay therefor, and for their appurtenances, furniture and apparatus; to borrow money for the erection of school houses, upon a majority vote of said district therefor, and to incur all other expenses of said school system, and pay the same from the public monies of said district.

Sec. 12. It shall be the duty of said board to keep said schools in operation not less than thirty-six, nor more than forty-four weeks of each year, to determine the amount of the annual tax to be raised for the purpose aforesaid, including all the necessary expenses of said schools, except for the erection of school houses and the purchase of sites; and on or before the first day of July, of each year, to make known the amount of such tax to the auditor of the county in which said district is situate; and thereupon it shall be the duty of said auditor to assess the same upon the taxable property of the said district as the same appears on the grand list in his office, and the said tax shall be collected by the county treasurer, in the same manner, and at the same time, with the state and county taxes, and when collected shall be paid over to the treasurer of said board: (a) Provided, however, that the tax to be assessed under this section shall not exceed four mills on the dollar upon the taxable property of said district, as the same appears upon the grand list; provided further, that in case the amount so authorized to be raised, together with the other school moneys of said district, shall be insufficient to support said schools for the portion of the year mentioned in this section, that said board of education

in operation not less than thirty, nor more than forty-four weeks in each year, to determine the amount of the annual tax to be raised for the purposes aforesaid, including all the necessary expenses of said school, except for the erection of school houses and the purchase of sites; and on or before the first day of September in each year, the secretary of said board shall obtain a transcript of the last assessment roll of the county, and shall add thereto any taxable property in said district, therein omitted, having himself assessed the value thereof, and shall collect said tax in such manner as is now or may hereafter be prescribed for the collection of other school district tax: Provided, That it shall be the duty of the secretary to return to the treasurer of the county, on or before the fifteenth day of November in each year, a transcript from said district assessment, containing the description of each parcel of real estate on which the said taxes remain due and unpaid, with the amount of tax against the same, and thereupon it shall be the duty of said treasurer to collect said taxes as county any [and] State taxes; and all such taxes as shall remain due and unpaid after the 15th day of November, shall draw interest from and after said may require such sum as may be necessary to support the same for the residue of said time, to be charged at the discretion of said board upon the tuition of the pupils attending such schools: Provided, however, that the children of indigent parents, or orphans, who are unable to pay such charges, shall not be excluded from said schools for the non-payment of the same; and it shall be the further duty of said board to keep an accurate account of their proceedings, and of their receipts and disbursements for school purposes, and at the annual meeting for the choice of directors in said district to make report of such receipts, and the sources from which the same were derived, and of said disbursements, and the objects to which the same were applied, and they shall also make report at the same time of such other matters relating to said schools as they may deem the interests of the same to require.

Sec. XIII. That said board of education, within twenty days after their election, shall appoint three competent persons, citizens of said district, to serve as school examiners of the public schools therein, one to serve for one year, one for two years, and one for three years, from the time of their appointment, and until their successors shall be appointed,

date at the same rate as delinquent county and State taxes.

Sec. 13. The tax provided for in the preceding section shall in no case exceed five mills on the dollar upon the taxable property of said district in any one year, and in case the amount so authorized to be raised, together with the other school monies of said district, shall be insufficient to support such schools for the portion of the year mentioned in the and annually thereafter said board shall appoint one examiner to serve for three years, and till his successor is appointed and qualified; and said board shall fill all vacancies that may occur from death, removal, or otherwise. Said examiners, or any two of them, shall examine any persons that may apply for that purpose with the intention of becoming teachers in any of the schools in said district, and if they find the applicant, in their opinion, qualified to teach in any of said schools, and to govern the same, and of good moral character, they shall give said applicant a certificate naming the branches in which the holder of said certificate was found qualified to teach, and no person shall be permitted to teach in said schools without such certificate — and said examiners may, in all cases, when two of their number concur, have power to annul such certificate, and when so annulled, the person holding the same shall be discharged as a teacher of said schools; said examiners shall also separately, or otherwise, together with said board of education, or any of them, or such person as they may appoint, or invite, visit said schools as often as once in every term, and observe the discipline, mode of teaching, progress of the pupils, and such other matters as they

12th section of this act, said board of education may require such sum as may be necessary to support the same for the residue of said time, to be charged at the discretion of said board, upon the tuition of the pupils attending such schools: Provided, however, that the children of indigent parents or orphans who are unable to pay such charges, shall not be excluded from said schools for the non-payment of the same.

may deem of interest, and make such suggestions and report thereupon to said board as they may think proper, which report may be published at the discretion of said board.

Sec. XIV. Upon the adoption of this act in the manner herein provided by any city, town, village, or district, all laws now in force therein, inconsistent herewith, are hereby repealed.

Sec. XV. That said board of education or the treasurer thereof, shall have power to collect any charge or account for tuition, in the same manner as the treasurer of any common school district in this state, is now or may hereafter be authorized to collect any such charge or account.— Swan's *Revised Statutes of Ohio*, 1854, pp. 858–861.

Sec. 14. It shall be the duty of said board of education to keep an accurate account of their proceedings, and of their receipts and disbursements for school purposes, and at the annual meeting for the choice of directors in said district, to make report of such receipts, and the sources from which the same were derived, and of said disbursements, and the objects to which the same were applied; and they shall also make report at the same time of such other matters relating to said schools as they may deem the interests of the same to require.

Sec. 15. That said board of education, within twenty days of their election, shall appoint three competent persons, citizens of said district, to serve as school examiners of the public schools therein, each of whom shall be sworn or affirmed to the faithful discharge of the duties of his office, one to serve for one year, one for two years, and one for three years from the time of their appointment and until their successors shall be appointed; and annually thereafter said board shall appoint one examiner, to serve for three years, and till his

successor is appointed and qualified, and said board shall fill all
vacancies that may occur from
death, removal, or otherwise.
Said examiners or any two of
them, shall examine any person
that may apply for that purpose,
with the intention of becoming
teachers in any of the schools in
said district, and if they find the
applicant in their opinion, qualified to teach in any of said
schools, and to govern the same,
and of good moral character,
they shall give said applicant a
certificate naming the branches in
which the holder of said certificate was found qualified to teach,
and no person shall be permitted
to teach in said schools without
such certificate; and said examiners may in all cases, when two
of their number concur, have
power to annul such certificate,
and when so annulled, the person
holding the same shall be discharged as a teacher of said
schools; said examiners shall also
separately or otherwise, together
with said board of education, or
any of them, or such person as
they may appoint, or invite, visit
said schools as often as once in
each school month, and observe
the description, mode of teaching,
progress of the pupils, and such
other matters as they deem of
interest, and make suggestions,
and report thereupon to said
board as they may think proper,

which report may be published at
the discretion of said board.

Sec. 16. That said board of
education, or the secretary thereof, shall have power to collect any
charge or account for tuition, in
the same manner as the secretary
of any common school district in
this State, is now, or may hereafter be authorized to collect any
such charge or account.

Sec. 17. That upon the adoption of this act, in the manner
herein provided, by any city,
town or district, such adoption
shall not affect the debts due to
or from said district, or any contract with said district existing
at the time of such adoption.

Sec. 18. All laws and parts of
laws relating to schools, which
conflict with the provisions of
this act, shall be so construed as
not to interfere with the provisions of this act.

Sec. 19. This act shall be in
force and take effect from and
after its publication according to
law.

Approved January 28, 1857.

Laws of Iowa, 1856–1857, pp.
234–240.

APPENDIX C
CHRONOLOGICAL LIST OF MEETINGS OF THE IOWA STATE TEACHERS' ASSOCIATION

	PLACE	PRESIDENT	LOCATED THEN
1854	Muscatine	John A. Parvin	Muscatine
	Iowa City		
1855	No meeting was held this year.		
1856	Muscatine	James L. Enos	Cedar Rapids
	Iowa City		
1857	Dubuque	D. Franklin Wells	Iowa State University
	Iowa City		
1858	Davenport	Christopher C. Nestlerode	Principal Union School, Tipton
1859	Washington	Frederick Humphrey	Cedar Rapids
1860	Tipton	D. Franklin Wells	Iowa State University
1861	Muscatine	Abram S. Kissell	City Superintendent, Davenport
1862	Mt. Pleasant	Christopher C. Nestlerode	City Superintendent, Tipton
1863	Grinnell	M. K. Cross	Tipton
1864	Dubuque	Henry K. Edson	Denmark Academy
1865	Oskaloosa	Oran Faville	Superintendent Public Instruction
1866	Cedar Rapids	Leonard F. Parker	Iowa College
1867	Des Moines	Moses M. Ingalls	Muscatine
1868	Keokuk	Theodore S. Parvin	Iowa State University
1869	Marshalltown	William M. Brooks	Tabor College
1870	Waterloo	Jonathan Piper	City Superintendent, Manchester
1871	Council Bluffs	Samuel J. Buck	Iowa College
1872	Davenport	Stephen N. Fellows	Iowa State University
1873	Iowa City	L. M. Hastings	City Superintendent, Ottumwa
1874	Des Moines	Allen Armstrong	City Superintendent, Council Bluffs

	PLACE	PRESIDENT	LOCATED THEN
1875	Burlington	James H. Thompson	City Superintendent, Des Moines
1876	Grinnell	C. P. Rogers	City Superintendent, Marshalltown
1877	Cedar Rapids	Phoebe W. Sudlow	City Superintendent, Davenport
1878	Marshalltown	Henry Sabin	City Superintendent, Clinton
1879	Independence	William J. Shoup	Principal Lincoln School, Dubuque
1880	Des Moines	Robert G. Saunderson	City Superintendent, Burlington
1881	Oskaloosa	Samuel Calvin	Iowa State University
1882	Cedar Falls	R. A. Harkness	Parsons College
1883	Des Moines	L. L. Klinefelter	County Superintendent, Cerro Gordo County
1884	Des Moines	Homer H. Seerley	City Superintendent, Oskaloosa
1885	Des Moines	William F. King	President Cornell College
1886	Des Moines	Moses W. Bartlett	Iowa State Normal School
1887	Cedar Rapids	L. T. Weld	City Superintendent, Nevada
1888	Des Moines	Josiah L. Pickard	President Iowa State University
1889	Des Moines	Lottie E. Granger	County Superintendent, Page County
1890	Des Moines	James McNaughton	City Superintendent, Council Bluffs
1891	Des Moines	Hamline H. Freer	Cornell College
1892	Cedar Rapids	Theodore H. Hacker	County Superintendent, Franklin County
1893	Des Moines	Frank B. Cooper	City Superintendent, Des Moines
1894	Des Moines	William M. Beardshear	President Iowa Agricultural College
1895	Des Moines	Richard C. Barrett	County Superintendent, Mitchell County
1896	Des Moines	William Wilcox	City Superintendent, Atlantic
1897	Des Moines	A. B. Warner	City Superintendent, Missouri Valley
1898	Des Moines	Amos N. Currier	Acting President, State University

	PLACE	PRESIDENT	LOCATED THEN
1899	Des Moines	Freeman H. Bloodgood	County Superintendent, Fayette County
1900	Des Moines	W. O. Riddell	Principal High School, West Des Moines
1901	Des Moines	Albion W. Stuart	City Superintendent, Ottumwa
1902	Des Moines	Charles E. Shelton	President, Simpson College
1903	Des Moines	Finley M. Witter	County Superintendent, Muscatine County
1904	Des Moines	D. Sands Wright	State Normal School
1905	Des Moines	Joseph J. McConnell	City Superintendent, Cedar Rapids
1906	Des Moines	J. H. T. Main	President Iowa College
1907	Des Moines	F. E. Lark	County Superintendent, Monona County
1908	Des Moines	Abbie S. Abbott	Principal High School, Cedar Rapids
1909	Des Moines	E. J. H. Beard	City Superintendent, Newton
1910	Des Moines	Hill M. Bell	President Drake University
1911	Des Moines	Fred Mahannah	Inspector of Normal Training in High Schools
1912	Des Moines	Alice Dilley	High School Principal, Osceola
1913	Des Moines	J. H. Beveridge	City Superintendent, Council Bluffs
1914	Des Moines	John E. Stout	Cornell College

NOTES AND REFERENCES

NOTES AND REFERENCES

CHAPTER I

[1] *Laws of the Territory of Iowa,* 1838–1839, p. 180.

[2] *Laws of the Territory of Iowa,* 1839–1840, p. 108; see also Appendix A in this volume. Inspectors in Iowa were allowed one dollar a day for their services, whereas in Michigan the compensation was one dollar and a half.

[3] *Laws of Iowa,* 1846–1847, p. 128; *Laws of Iowa,* 1848–1849, p. 106.

The "financial necessity" was the chief reason it seems for the change in management. Indeed, the use of such a term as "supervision" in relation to any division less than the State was not then admitted.

[4] *Laws of the Territory of Iowa,* 1839–1840, p. 101; *Laws of the Territory of Iowa,* 1840–1841, p. 37; *Laws of Michigan* (Revised Statutes), 1838, p. 238.

The Superintendent of Public Instruction was allowed a compensation of $250 annually.

[5] *Laws of the Territory of Iowa,* 1841–1842, p. 93.

[6] *Journal of the Council,* 1841–1842, Appendix, p. 278.

[7] *Journal of the Council,* 1841–1842, Appendix, p. 291; *Laws of the Territory of Iowa,* 1841–1842, p. 93.

The clerk of the boards of county commissioners became thereafter the means of communication between the counties and the legislatures.

CHAPTER II

[8] *Laws of Iowa,* 1846–1847, pp. 121–133. The Superintendent would be chosen on the first Monday in April, 1847, according to Section 24 of this act, since that was the "next annual election".

[9] See Brigham's *James Harlan,* Chs. V, VI; also 1 Greene (Iowa)

68. The adverse decision of the court was made on the ground that the publication of a statute in newspapers without the direct authority of the General Assembly was not sufficient to make it effective under the Constitution. The law had been distributed by the Secretary of State throughout the Commonwealth and was well known to the people who believed it to be in force and who therefore had acted in accordance therewith.— See Art. III, Sec. 27 of the Constitution of 1846.

10 See Brigham's *James Harlan*, pp. 58–63.

11 *Journal of the Senate*, 1848–1849, pp. 302–304, 309–321.

12 *Laws of Iowa*, 1848–1849, pp. 95, 96. The Constitution did not permit the Governor to receive a larger annual salary than $1000 for the first ten years of statehood.

13 *Laws of Iowa*, 1848–1849, p. 151. See chapters on school funds in Vol. I of this work.

A minor act during this session required the Superintendent to certify to the Auditor of State the fact that certain dumb or blind persons were entitled to aid from the State in securing an education. These facts were to form a part of his report to the General Assembly. — *Laws of Iowa*, 1848–1849, p. 148.

14 *Statutes of the State of Iowa Relating to Common Schools Including Forms, Regulations, and Instructions*, 1849, pp. 3, 4, 87–103.

15 *Statutes of the State of Iowa Relating to Common Schools Including Forms, Regulations, and Instructions*, 1849, pp. 104–112. There was no school journal then published in Iowa; but Mr. J. L. Enos, later identified with *The Iowa Instructor*, was publishing *The Northwestern Educator* at Chicago, this being among the journals recommended.

16 *Laws of Iowa*, 1849, p. 93; *Laws of Iowa*, 1851, pp. 175, 179, 228.

17 *Report of the Superintendent of Public Instruction* in the *Journal of the Senate*, 1850–1851, Appendix, pp. 124, 125.

Mr. D. Franklin Wells was placed in charge of the new building in District No. 1, Bloomington Township, when its building was completed, and it was furnished under his direction.— *Annual Report*, District No. 1, Bloomington Township, 1854, p. 4.

Superintendent Benton recommended that at least two copies

of Barnard's *School Architecture* be placed in the hands of school fund commissioners for the use of the districts in the county.

[18] *Report of the Superintendent of Public Instruction* in the *Journal of the Senate,* 1850–1851, Appendix, p. 171. It has been said that the "creation of this office with a slight change of name was deduced from the Prussian system."

[19] *Report of the Superintendent of Public Instruction* in the *Journal of the Senate,* 1852–1853, Appendix, pp. 109, 110.

The term "regular" is essential here, for a supplementary report was issued later by Superintendent Benton and submitted during the administration of his successor.

[20] *Report of the Superintendent of Public Instruction* in the *Journal of the Senate,* 1854–1855, Appendix, pp. 143, 144, 160–163.

The *Code of 1851* provided that the election of the Superintendent should occur in April, 1851, and triennially thereafter, so that Thomas H. Benton, Jr., served six years beginning with 1848.— *Code of 1851,* p. 170.

The average wage for men teachers in 1854 was less than $20 and for women less than $10 per month, the lowest being $12 and $6.70 respectively, according to reports of that date.

[21] *Report of the Superintendent of Public Instruction,* pp. 14–16, in the *Iowa Legislative Documents,* 1857.

[22] *Journal of the Board of Education,* First Session, pp. 31, 32; *Acts, Resolutions and Forms, Adopted by the Board of Education,* First Session, p. 25.

CHAPTER III

[23] *Laws of Iowa,* 1858, p. 76.

[24] *Journal of the Board of Education,* First Session, pp. 69, 70; *Acts, Resolutions and Forms, Adopted by the Board of Education,* First Session, pp. 25–30.

The compensation of the State Superintendent had been fixed at $1500 with a contingent fund not to exceed $250. The Board of Education, however, increased the contingent allowance for the secretary to $750.

[25] *Report of the Secretary of the Board of Education,* 1859, pp. 3–11, 15, 16; *Acts, Resolutions and Forms, Adopted by the Board of*

Education, First Session, p. 24.   The report for 1859 here cited is not a part of the bound volume of the *Journal of the Board of Education.*

26 *Report of the Secretary of the Board of Education,* 1861, in the *Journal of the Board of Education,* pp. 8, 10–13, 16, 22, 23.

27 *Report of Thomas H. Benton,* pp. 3, 6, 7, in the *Iowa Legislative Documents,* 1864, Vol. I.

28 *Report of the Acting Secretary of the Board of Education,* pp. 26–34, in the *Iowa Legislative Documents,* 1864, Vol. I.   Mr. H. A. Wiltse submitted an outlined course of study in six grades which he deemed suitable for adoption in all the rural schools.

29 *Report of the Secretary of the Board of Education,* pp. 5–25, in the *Iowa Legislative Documents,* 1864, Vol. I.

Thomas H. Benton, Jr., had then served ten years as the head of the school system — six as Superintendent from 1848 to 1854, and four as Secretary of the Board of Education from 1858 to 1862.

30 *Laws of Iowa,* 1864, p. 53; *Report of the Superintendent of Public Instruction,* p. 9, in the *Iowa Legislative Documents,* 1868, Vol. I.

Mr. Faville had acquired a noteworthy reputation in his campaign for Lieutenant Governor in the fall of 1857.   The papers of the State commented on the fact that while he was addressing the German voters in Dubuque he spoke in their own tongue, thereby making a "marked impression on that class of our citizens."   He was everywhere spoken of as a "gentleman of high moral worth and ability" as well as "a statesman of a pure and lofty type".— *The Iowa Citizen* (Des Moines), Vol. II, No. 34, Oct. 7, 1857.

31 *Report of the Superintendent of Public Instruction,* pp. 14, 22, 23–25, 26, 28, in the *Iowa Legislative Documents,* 1866, Vol. I.

32 *Report of the Superintendent of Public Instruction,* pp. 16–28, 36–55, in the *Iowa Legislative Documents,* 1868, Vol. I.

It was probably Mr. Jerome Allen who chronicled the death of Mr. D. Franklin Wells and who prepared for the *Iowa School Journal* (of which Mr. Wells was the editor-in-chief) the sketch of his life.— *Iowa School Journal,* Vol. X, p. 86.

At the age of nineteen Mr. Wells began teaching a small school in New York, at a compensation of $12 per month in money.   He "boarded around", as was the custom in that day.   After a second term taught in New Jersey, he entered the Albany Normal School, graduating in 1852. It was fresh from his student life that he came to the schools of Muscatine which he served three years, leaving them for the State University of Iowa, then but recently organized. When the Normal Department of the State University was temporarily abandoned in 1866 he was chosen as State Agent of the State Teachers' Association, and it was from this position that he was called by appointment to the office of Superintendent of Public Instruction. Elected by the people in 1868, he had entered upon his duties when death halted him at his home in Iowa City.

[33] *Report of the Superintendent of Public Instruction*, pp. 24, 28–34, 35, 36, in the *Iowa Legislative Documents*, 1870, Vol. I.

Mr. A. S. Kissell commenced his educational work in Iowa in 1858 as principal of the grammar school in Davenport. Within the same year, when the districts of that city were consolidated, he became city superintendent — the first position of such a character in Iowa — where he remained for six years. It was he who organized the training school at Davenport and placed over it a teacher from the Oswego, New York, Normal School. He served also as county superintendent of Scott County from May, 1858, to October, 1859. Appointed as Superintendent of Public Instruction, he was later elected to the same office, not only for the unexpired term but also for the subsequent two years. His educational work was completed in Iowa, for on removing to another State he engaged in mercantile pursuits until his death in 1888.— *Report of the Superintendent of Public Instruction*, pp. 17, 18, in the *Iowa Legislative Documents*, 1890, Vol. II.

Governor Merrill said that Mr. Kissell was appointed by him to the office without his (Kissell's) solicitation and against his protest. The Governor insisted on making the appointment because he believed that Mr. Kissell was possessed of a degree of enthusiasm rarely excelled. In accepting the place Mr. Kissell surrendered a position which offered a compensation double that of the office of State Superintendent.

[34] *School Law Decisions*, 1884, pp. 63, 64; *Laws of Iowa*, 1868, p. 157; *Revision of 1860*, p. 98.

[35] *Laws of Iowa*, 1868, p. 224.

[36] *Report of the Superintendent of Public Instruction*, p. 141, in the *Iowa Legislative Documents*, 1872, Vol. I; Shambaugh's *Messages and Proclamations of the Governors of Iowa*, Vol. III, p. 270.

37 *Report of the Superintendent of Public Instruction*, pp. 17–119, in the *Iowa Legislative Documents*, 1872, Vol. I.

CHAPTER IV

38 *Report of the Superintendent of Public Instruction*, pp. 40–46, 58, 59, 74, 164, 184, in the *Iowa Legislative Documents*, 1874, Vol. I.

39 *Report of the Superintendent of Public Instruction*, pp. 14–50, in the *Iowa Legislative Documents*, 1876, Vol. I. Each State had been invited by the department of superintendence of the National Educational Association to prepare a history of its educational system for the centennial exhibition at Philadelphia in 1876. Perhaps this influenced the preparation of the material as submitted in this report.

40 *Report of the Superintendent of Public Instruction*, pp. 47–51, in the *Iowa Legislative Documents*, 1878, Vol. I; the same, p. 59, in the *Iowa Legislative Documents*, 1880, Vol. III; the same, pp. 30, 31, in the *Iowa Legislative Documents*, 1882, Vol. II.

Mr. Carl W. von Coelln was trained in the University of Bonn, where he was a classmate of Carl Schurz. Coming to America in 1855 he was employed on a dairy farm in Ohio, during which time he acquired the English language. He came to Des Moines in 1861 and there taught for six months in the public schools. Later he established an academy in Dubuque County, and soon after was engaged as teacher of mathematics in Iowa College. Still later he taught in Missouri and served as principal of the west side schools in Waterloo, from which place he was chosen Superintendent of Public Instruction. His last work was that of editor of the *Henry County Times.— Midland Schools*, Vol. XXVII, p. 265.

41 *Report of the Superintendent of Public Instruction*, pp. 29, 44, in the *Iowa Legislative Documents*, 1884, Vol. II; the same, pp. 8, 52, 87, 100, in the *Iowa Legislative Documents*, 1886, Vol. V; the same, p. 10, in the *Iowa Legislative Documents*, 1888, Vol. II.

Mr. John W. Akers was elected Superintendent of Public Instruction while city superintendent of the Cedar Rapids schools. He had previously been in charge of the Vinton schools and also those of Waterloo. Since his retirement from the office of State Superintendent he has been identified with the Chicago schools.

42 *Report of the Superintendent of Public Instruction*, pp. 52, 82,

in the *Iowa Legislative Documents,* 1890, Vol. II; the same, pp. 21, 22, in the *Iowa Legislative Documents,* 1892, Vol. II; the same, pp. 157, 160, in the *Iowa Legislative Documents,* 1896, Vol. II; the same, pp. 112–117, 158, in the *Iowa Legislative Documents,* 1898, Vol. II.

The *Iowa Educational Directory,* now so essential to every school man, was inaugurated by Superintendent Henry Sabin in 1894. The publication of papers on current topics, begun by Superintendent Akers, was extended by Mr. Sabin.

On the occasion of his final address before the State Teachers' Association in 1898 the most sincere attitude of respect and even affection was evidenced when Superintendent Sabin came forward to introduce Dr. W. T. Harris, who had once been his pupil. And again when he set out for his home on the distant Pacific coast in September, 1913, there was a feeling of the deepest regret among the school men who knew him personally. The best twenty-five years of his life were given to the schools of Iowa.

See *Midland Schools,* Vol. XII, p. 141, and also Vol. XXVIII, p. 36.

The services of Mr. Ira C. Kling as Deputy Superintendent of Public Instruction are noteworthy. For eight years he was with Superintendent Henry Sabin, who said of him: "Fifteen years' service in this office has given him a knowledge of the school laws unsurpassed by any man in Iowa. . . . For purity of design and honesty of purpose, his official record is without spot or blemish. In the revision of the school law he was often in consultation with the committees and was mainly instrumental in securing some of the most important changes. . . . He has been to me a wise adviser, an able, loyal assistant, and a faithful friend."— *Report of the Superintendent of Public Instruction,* p. 144, in the *Iowa Legislative Documents,* 1898, Vol. II.

[43] *Report of the Superintendent of Public Instruction,* pp. 118, 119, 129, 130, in the *Iowa Legislative Documents,* 1894, Vol. II.

Mr. John B. Knoepfler had been in charge of the schools of Fayette, West Union, and Lansing, Iowa. After the expiration of his term in the State office he returned to Lansing, but was called later to the State Teachers' College as head of the Department of Modern Languages.—See *The Iowa Normal Monthly,* Vol. XV, p. 255.

[44] *Report of the Superintendent of Public Instruction,* pp. 25, 26, in the *Iowa Legislative Documents,* 1900, Vol. II; the same, p. 27, in

the *Iowa Legislative Documents,* 1902, Vol. III; the same, p. xxii, in the *Iowa Legislative Documents,* 1904, Vol. IV.

Mr. Richard C. Barrett was for twelve years county superintendent in Mitchell County, and after his six years of service in the State office was appointed to the department of civics in the State College of Agriculture and Mechanic Arts at Ames. At the time of his death in 1909 he had held this position for five years. Mr. A. C. Ross, his deputy, was among those who had aided in establishing the graded schools in the Commonwealth.

45 *Report of the Superintendent of Public Instruction,* Pt. I, pp. 16, 66, in the *Iowa Legislative Documents,* 1906, Vol. V; the same, pp. 15, 50–65, in the *Iowa Legislative Documents,* 1907, Vol. I; the same, pp. 40–45, in the *Iowa Legislative Documents,* 1909, Vol. I; the same, Pt. I, pp. 18–35, in the *Iowa Legislative Documents,* 1911, Vol. I.

Mr. John F. Riggs was formerly county superintendent of Henry County, city superintendent of the Mt. Pleasant schools, and when elected to the State office was superintendent of the schools at Sigourney.

46 *Report of the Superintendent of Public Instruction,* pp. 31, 32, in the *Iowa Legislative Documents,* 1913, Vol. III; *Laws of Iowa,* 1913, pp. 88–90.

The act of 1913 extends the term of the Superintendent of Public Instruction to July 1, 1915, when the first appointee to this office will assume his duties.

The present Superintendent, Mr. A. M. Deyoe, was elected to this office from Hancock County while serving his third term as county superintendent.

CHAPTER V

47 *Laws of Iowa,* 1858, p. 72; *Acts, Resolutions and Forms, Adopted by the Board of Education,* First Session, p. 20.

Before the law of March 12, 1858, had been declared unconstitutional William Y. Lovell, county superintendent of Dubuque County, issued a full report which included the required data from every township. This is probably the first report of the kind in the State.

48 *Laws of Iowa,* 1858, pp. 72–75; *Acts, Resolutions and Forms, Adopted by the Board of Education,* First Session, pp. 21–23.

As originally provided in the bill the county would have been required to pay the traveling expenses of the county superintendent to meetings called by the Secretary of the Board of Education. But the people, it was feared, would be opposed to such an expense.

[49] *The Voice of Iowa*, Vol. III, pp. 50, 74. In commenting on this convention Superintendent Fisher observed that the attendance was remarkable since there was no railroad east or west beyond Iowa City or Cedar Rapids, and none north and south. Superintendents were there from the ''Missouri line, and the confines of Minnesota, from the banks of the Mississippi, and from those of the Missouri.''

[50] *Report of the Superintendent of Public Instruction*, p. 21, in the *Iowa Legislative Documents*, 1859–1860.

[51] *Report of the Secretary of the Board of Education*, 1859, pp. 4–14.

[52] *The Iowa Instructor*, Vol. I, pp. 115, 154.

[53] *The Iowa Instructor*, Vol. I, pp. 378, 379.
The compensation permitted under the act of the State Board of Education in 1859 might not, under ordinary conditions, exceed $28 annually — two dollars a day for holding about fourteen examinations. For a special examination a fee of one dollar might be collected, but these charges were uncertain.

[54] *Report of the Secretary of the Board of Education*, 1861, in the *Journal of the Board*, pp. 14, 15.
While this agitation was prominent in Iowa, neighboring States were concerned with similar problems. In Illinois, for example, the Superintendent of Public Instruction declared that the want of supervision in the State was very great, pervading ''its whole framework, from the central department at Springfield, to the smallest and remotest district in the State.'' It was his belief that the remedy lay ''in the plan of *county superintendencies* — the committal of the educational interests of each county to the direct supervision of one person'' who should devote his entire time to that work.— From a *Review of the Report of Newton Bateman* by Dr. J. Maynard in *The Iowa Instructor*, Vol. II, p. 248.

It was about this time that Wisconsin provided that each county should elect one superintendent of schools; while those counties having 25,000 population might elect two superintendents at the discretion of the board of county supervisors. Moreover, any county which contained two senatorial districts must elect two superintendents. The salary was to be determined by the county board, but a minimum of $600 was established for counties of 15,000, with a minimum of $400 for all above 8000. Any sum above this, however, was permitted.— *Wisconsin Journal of Education* quoted in *The Iowa Instructor*, Vol. II, p. 316.

55 *Laws of Iowa*, 1862, p. 218.

56 *Laws of Iowa*, 1864, p. 117.

57 *Laws of Iowa*, 1866, pp. 159, 161.

58 *The Iowa Instructor*, Vol. II, p. 371. Mr. T. S. Parvin of Johnson County, Mr. James McClung of Cedar County, and Mr. Amos Dean of Benton County composed this committee.

59 *The Iowa Instructor and School Journal*, Vol. V, p. 110.

60 *The Iowa Instructor and School Journal*, Vol. VIII, p. 31.

61 *The Iowa School Journal*, Vol. X, pp. 263–270. Two members of this committee, Superintendent L. M. Hastings, then of Ottumwa, and Mr. W. A. Willis, then principal of the West Des Moines high school, are now residents of Iowa City, the latter being actively engaged as proprietor of the Iowa City Academy.

62 *The Iowa School Journal*, Vol. XI, pp. 216–221. A request was made at this time that the next convention be called at the same time and place as the meeting of the State Teachers' Association. In the same year (1870) a district meeting of county superintendents was called at Manchester to cover a program outlined for four days.

63 *Report of the Superintendent of Public Instruction*, p. 42, in the *Iowa Legislative Documents*, 1870, Vol. I; see also 17 Iowa 228.

64 *Laws of Iowa*, 1870, pp. 31, 98, 140, 165; *Laws of Iowa* (General), 1872, p. 118.

65 *Report of the Superintendent of Public Instruction*, pp. 31, 32, in the *Iowa Legislative Documents*, 1872, Vol. I.

66 *Report of the Superintendent of Public Instruction*, pp. 55, 57, 58, in the *Iowa Legislative Documents*, 1872, Vol. I.

67 *Report of the Superintendent of Public Instruction*, pp. 41, 42, 101, in the *Iowa Legislative Documents*, 1874, Vol. I.

CHAPTER VI

[68] *Journal of the House,* 1872, pp. 179, 180.

[69] *The Iowa School Journal,* Vol. XIII, pp. 190–193.

[70] *Report of the Superintendent of Public Instruction,* pp. 129, 130, in the *Iowa Legislative Documents,* 1876, Vol. I. The report of the committee on school legislation is quoted in full.

[71] *Journal of the House,* 1878, p. 197; *The Iowa Normal Monthly,* Vol. II, pp. 111–113; Bowman's *The Administration of Iowa* in the Columbia University *Studies in History, Economics and Public Law,* p. 51.

The republican convention in Johnson County recommended that nominees for office do all in their power to secure the abolition of the office of county superintendent. At the same time, however, the convention nominated a man for the office.— *The Iowa Normal Monthly,* Vol. III, p. 54.

[72] 52 Iowa 111; *The Iowa Normal Monthly,* Vol. III, p. 15.

[73] *The Iowa Normal Monthly,* Vol. VII, p. 25, Vol. IX, pp. 19–23. In December following Mr. J. S. Shoup made a report on a course of study for rural schools before the section of county superintendents at the State Teachers' Association.— *Proceedings of the Iowa State Teachers' Association,* Vol. XXXI, p. 186.

[74] *Report of the Superintendent of Public Instruction,* p. 76, in the *Iowa Legislative Documents,* 1888, Vol. II.

[75] *Report of the Superintendent of Public Instruction,* p. 129, in the *Iowa Legislative Documents,* 1888, Vol. II.

[76] *Report of the Superintendent of Public Instruction,* p. 23, in the *Iowa Legislative Documents,* 1892, Vol. II; the same, pp. 159, 160, in the *Iowa Legislative Documents,* 1896, Vol. II; *The Iowa Normal Monthly,* Vol. XVII, p. 406.

Wisconsin, Indiana, Pennsylvania, and New Jersey were cited by Superintendent Sabin.

A resolution of the State Teachers' Association in 1861 had declared for a non-partisan in the office of county superintendent. He should be a practical and experienced teacher, and the only question should concern his fitness for the place.— *The Iowa Instructor,* Vol. II, p. 370.

[77] *Report of the Superintendent of Public Instruction*, pp. 24, 25, in the *Iowa Legislative Documents*, 1892, Vol. II; *Journal of the House*, 1892, pp. 47, 101, 307, 308, 737.

[78] *Report of the Superintendent of Public Instruction*, pp. 18, 19, 26, 27, in the *Iowa Legislative Documents*, 1900, Vol. II.

President Homer H. Seerley and County Superintendent B. P. Holst pointed out the influences that were interfering with effective service in the county superintendency.— *The Iowa Normal Monthly*, Vol. XXI, pp. 132, 192.

[79] *Report of the Superintendent of Public Instruction*, p. 112, in the *Iowa Legislative Documents*, 1898, Vol. II.

It was in 1876 that legislation provided that no one should be deprived of the office of county superintendent or of any other school office on account of sex.— *Laws of Iowa*, 1876, p. 126.

[80] *Laws of Iowa*, 1874, p. 45; *Laws of Iowa*, 1876, p. 126; *Laws of Iowa*, 1878, p. 36; *Laws of Iowa*, 1882, pp. 23, 42; *Laws of Iowa*, 1900, p. 84.

[81] *Laws of Iowa*, 1898, p. 50; *Laws of Iowa*, 1902, p. 76; *Laws of Iowa*, 1906, p. 87; *Laws of Iowa*, 1913, pp. 94, 95.

The first application of the new method of selecting the county superintendent appears to have been in the case of filling a vacancy in Buena Vista County. In this instance Mr. H. C. Moeller was appointed by the convention of school board presidents, although he was not a resident of the county — thus demonstrating the principle for which the law stands, namely, the professionalizing of the county superintendency.

CHAPTER VII

[82] *Acts, Resolutions and Forms, Adopted by the Board of Education*, First Session, pp. 15, 34. This action seems to have been in part a response to a petition from Mr. A. S. Kissell of Davenport who advised legislation to permit the employment of a city superintendent.

[83] *Report of the Directors of Public Schools*, District No. 1, Bloomington Township, Muscatine, Iowa, 1856, p. 9; *The Iowa Instructor*, Vol. III, p. 349; *The Iowa Citizen* (Des Moines), Vol. II, No. 44, Dec. 16, 1857; *Report of the Secretary of the Board of Education*, Dubuque, 1858, pp. 14, 15, 16.

[84] *Rules and Regulations, Common Schools of Iowa City*, 1865, pp. 2–4.

[85] *The Iowa Instructor and School Journal*, Vol. VI, pp. 350, 351, 383, Vol. VIII, p. 249; *The Iowa School Journal*, Vol. X, p. 377.
Mr. W. E. Crosby was Secretary of the National Educational Association at its meeting in Trenton, New Jersey, in 1869.

[86] *Muscatine City Schools*, 1870–1871, p. 2; *Rules and Regulations Independent District*, Clinton, 1870, p. 23.

[87] *Report of the Superintendent of Public Instruction*, p. 124, in the *Iowa Legislative Documents*, 1896, Vol. II; *The Iowa Normal Monthly*, Vol. XVIII, p. 90, Vol. XX, pp. 73, 87, 93, 207.
In this connection it is impossible to make more than the briefest reference to these deserving men.

[88] *Report of the Superintendent of Public Instruction*, p. 23, in the *Iowa Legislative Documents*, 1900, Vol. II; Oldt's *History of Dubuque County*, pp. 917, 923; *The Iowa School Journal*, Vol. XII, p. 224.

[89] *The Iowa Normal Monthly*, Vol. XII, p. 217; *Report of the Superintendent of Public Instruction*, pp. 151, 152, in the *Iowa Legislative Documents*, 1892, Vol. II.

[90] *Proceedings of the Iowa State Teachers' Association*, 1876, p. 83; *The Iowa Normal Monthly*, Vol. XII, p. 220.

[91] *Report of the Superintendent of Public Instruction*, p. lxxxvi, in the *Iowa Legislative Documents*, 1904, Vol. IV.

[92] *Report of the Superintendent of Public Instruction*, p. 63, in the *Iowa Legislative Documents*, 1884, Vol. II. The reference is to a paper upon *City Supervision* by President Homer H. Seerley.

CHAPTER VIII

[93] *Constitutional Debates*, 1857, Vol. I, pp. 39, 40, 78. The resolution which brought the matter before the convention was introduced by Mr. Edward Johnstone of Lee County.

[94] *Constitutional Debates*, 1857, Vol. II, pp. 726, 727, 728, 756. Mr. J. C. Hall who supported the amendment was a delegate from Des Moines County.

[95] *Constitutional Debates*, 1857, Vol. II, p. 729. The true reason for the failure of the Mann commission bill in 1857 was declared to have been, not the incompetency of the General Assembly, but rather because it did not discriminate between white and colored youths.

[96] *Constitutional Debates*, 1857, Vol. II, p. 745; Shambaugh's *Messages and Proclamations of the Governors of Iowa*, Vol. II, pp. 45, 46.

[97] *Constitutional Debates*, 1857, Vol. II, p. 749.

[98] *Constitutional Debates*, 1857, Vol. II, p. 753.

[99] *Constitutional Debates*, 1857, Vol. II, p. 757.

[100] *Constitutional Debates*, 1857, Vol. II, p. 843. This amendment by substitution was introduced by Mr. Rufus L. B. Clark of Henry County, a native of Connecticut. Such a board as he proposed exists in Connecticut and the provisions relative thereto have been in force since 1849.

The question of taxation for public education brought forth an amendment to exclude the property of colored persons from such levies, inasmuch as, in the opinion of some delegates, it would be admitting that this State was not exclusively for "white men".

[101] *Constitutional Debates*, 1857, Vol. II, pp. 767, 934, 945. It was fortunate that the Board of Education had for its first "constitutional president" Oran Faville, the first Lieutenant Governor, since no one was better qualified for such an important position.

[102] *Constitutional Debates*, 1857, Vol. II, p. 944; *Constitution of Iowa*, Art. IX, Sec. 8.

[103] *Constitutional Debates*, 1857, Vol. II, pp. 949, 1030.

[104] *Constitutional Debates*, 1857, Vol. II, pp. 957, 1029; *Constitution of Iowa*, Art. IX, Pt. I.

About the word "youths" much bitter discussion ensued, for by the insertion of the term the provision would admit "blacks" as well as "whites" to school privileges.

CHAPTER IX

[105] *Journal of the Board of Education*, First Session, p. 3; *The Iowa Citizen* (Des Moines), Vol. III, No. 43, Dec. 8, 1858; Bowman's

The Administration of Iowa in the Columbia University *Studies in History, Economics and Public Law,* p. 31.

MEMBERS OF THE STATE BOARD OF EDUCATION

DISTRICT	TERM	NAME	LOCATION
First	Four years	Charles Mason	Burlington, Des Moines Co.
Second	Four years	T. B. Perry	Albia, Monroe County
Third	Two years	George P. Kimball	Clarinda, Page County
Fourth	Four years	D. E. Brainard	Magnolia, Harrison County
Fifth	Four years	Dan Mills	New Jefferson, Greene Co.
Sixth	Two years	Samuel F. Cooper	Grinnell, Poweshiek Co.
Seventh	Two years	Thomas H. Canfield	Bellevue, Jackson County
Eighth	Four years	Frank M. Connelly	Marengo, Iowa County
Ninth	Two years	O. H. P. Roszelle	Independence, Buchanan Co.
Tenth	Four years	A. B. F. Hildreth	St. Charles, Floyd County
Eleventh	Two years	Isaac J. Mitchell	Boonsboro, Boone County
Ex Officio		Gov. R. P. Lowe	Keokuk, Lee County
President		Lieut. Gov. Oran Faville	Mitchell, Mitchell County

— From *The Literary Advertiser and Public School Advocate,* Vol. I, No. 2, p. 3; *Journal of the Board of Education,* p. 7.

Six members therefore served during the entire active history of the board, inasmuch as they drew the four year term. Of the other five only one, Mr. S. F. Cooper, was reëlected.

106 7 Iowa 262. This case came up from the lower court in Dubuque County, where in a suit of the *District Township of the City of Dubuque vs. The City of Dubuque* the matter was decided in favor of the plaintiff. This decision was reversed in the higher tribunal.

107 *Acts, Resolutions and Forms, Adopted by the Board of Education,* First Session, p. 4. Judge John F. Dillon, of the seventh district, urged the passage of this act early in the session.

108 *The Iowa Citizen* (Des Moines), Vol. III, No. 44, Dec. 15, 1858. Mr. T. B. Perry consistently maintained the attitude that the people should have large powers in regulating school affairs, not only in district and local matters but also in the selection of State officers. It was he who contended for the retention of the office of Superintendent of Public Instruction and stoutly maintained the superiority of the independent district.

109 *The Iowa Citizen* (Des Moines), Vol. III, No. 45, Dec. 22, 1858.

110 *Journal of the Board of Education*, First Session, p. 19; *The Iowa Citizen* (Des Moines), Vol. III, No. 45, Dec. 22, 1858.

The constitutional debates were cited as containing evidence that it was not the intention to limit the authority of the Board so as to exclude the Agricultural College.

111 *Acts, Resolutions and Forms, Adopted by the Board of Education*, First Session, pp. 39, 40.

Mr. J. B. Grinnell was chairman of the committee which drafted the educational law of March 12, 1858. There was doubt, he wrote later, as to the authority of the General Assembly to legislate on the subject. Nevertheless, some action was deemed imperative since matters were such that the Superintendent of Public Instruction had received 1400 letters in reference to provisions of former acts in a single year. And, although there may have been some question as to jurisdiction, the General Assembly had prepared the basis for future action by the Board and had provided funds to carry out its legislation. While the courts had decreed that such authority did not rest with the General Assembly it would be a simple matter to correct the error by reënactment.— From a letter appearing originally in the *Montezuma Republican*, but summarized in *The Iowa Citizen* (Des Moines), Vol. III, No. 45, Dec. 22, 1858.

112 *The Iowa Citizen* (Des Moines), Vol. III, Nos. 45, 46, Dec. 22, 29, 1858; *Acts, Resolutions and Forms, Adopted by the Board of Education*, First Session, p. 8.

113 *The Iowa Citizen* (Des Moines), Vol. IV, No. 45, Dec. 21, 1859. It is probable that the ''Black man'' referred to was a protégé of John Brown.

114 *The Iowa Citizen* (Des Moines), Vol. IV, No. 42, Nov. 30, 1859.

115 *Laws of Iowa*, 1858, p. 340; Shambaugh's *Messages and Proclamations of the Governors of Iowa*, Vol. II, pp. 141, 143, 230, 359, 360.

116 *The Iowa State Register*, Vol. V, No. 3, March 14, 1860. Reference was made in this editorial to the fact that Judge Hall had supposed himself immortalized by this feature of the new Constitution.

117 *The Iowa State Register*, Vol. VI, No. 46, Dec. 25, 1861.

118 *The Iowa State Register*, Vol. VI, No. 44, Dec. 11, 1861, p. 2.

[119] *The Iowa State Register,* Vol. VI, No. 45, Dec. 18, 1861. The founders of Guttenberg came to this country in a government vessel in company with Kossuth as refugees following the Hungarian War.

[120] *The Iowa State Register,* Vol. VI, No. 45, Dec. 18, 1861; *School Laws of Iowa,* 1864, p. 25. Samuel J. Kirkwood, Philip Viele, and D. W. Ellis composed the committee which submitted this bill. It was unanimously adopted.— *Journal of the Board of Education,* Third Session, p. 38.

[121] Shambaugh's *Messages and Proclamations of the Governors of Iowa,* Vol. III, pp. 7, 8.

[122] *The Iowa Instructor and School Journal,* Vol. V, pp. 182, 215; *School Laws of Iowa,* 1864, p. 31.

Only one member of this Board survives, and he is consistently maintaining his attitude on the questions presented to the Board in its deliberations, as may be seen from the following letter addressed to the writer under date of January 28, 1914:

"Yours of 26th inst. is duly received. I was a member of the State Board of Education as you have stated. According to my best information, I am the only surviving member of that old board. The others have all passed away. As you have a copy of the Journal before you, you can understand what were the various measures proposed, and how they were disposed of.

"That grand and good old man, Judge Charles Mason of Burlington, and I, were closely associated in our views of the various questions that arose during the most important contests. The Horace Mann System of township district schools arose, and was presented by warm advocates. But Judge Mason and I opposed the plan, and insisted upon the independent district system, which has finally prevailed.

"I am still opposed to the township district system, and consider it not so practical as the independent district system.

"If there is anything further that you may wish to inquire about, please inform me, and I shall gladly respond as fully as I may be able. I assure you I am very glad to have heard from you.

Respectfully,

T. B. Perry"

CHAPTER X

123 *School Laws of Iowa*, 1864, p. 26; *Report of the Secretary of the State Board of Education*, p. 16, in the *Iowa Legislative Documents*, 1861–1862, Vol. I.

124 *The Iowa Instructor*, Vol. III, pp. 319, 320. The announcement of these resolutions was signed by Anson Hart, the ex officio Secretary of the Board of Trustees of the University.

125 *The Iowa Instructor and School Journal*, Vol. V, pp. 196–198. These certificates being perpetual were equivalent in duration to the diploma granted under laws governing the second State Board of Examiners.

126 *The Iowa School Journal*, Vol. XIV, No. 5, p. 188.

127 *The Iowa Instructor and School Journal*, Vol. V, p. 183.

128 *The Iowa Instructor and School Journal*, Vol. VI, p. 26.

129 *Report of the Superintendent of Public Instruction*, p. 47, in the *Iowa Legislative Documents*, 1868, Vol. I.

130 *The Iowa School Journal*, Vol. XIV, No. 5, p. 188.

131 *Report of the Superintendent of Public Instruction*, p. 127, in the *Iowa Legislative Documents*, 1876, Vol. I.

132 From the proceedings of the State Teachers' Association in 1874 as set forth in the *Report of the Superintendent of Public Instruction*, p. 129, in the *Iowa Legislative Documents*, 1876, Vol. I.

133 *Journal of the Senate*, 1876, pp. 356, 454. For a copy of this bill see *Report of the Superintendent of Public Instruction*, p. 7, in the *Iowa Legislative Documents*, 1878, Vol. I.

134 Shambaugh's *Messages and Proclamations of the Governors of Iowa*, Vol. IV, p. 330.

135 *Report of the Superintendent of Public Instruction*, p. 88, in the *Iowa Legislative Documents*, 1880, Vol. III.

136 *The Iowa Normal Monthly*, Vol. V, pp. 148, 266, 267; *Laws of Iowa*, 1882, pp. 153, 154.

137 *The Iowa Normal Monthly*, Vol. VI, p. 105.

138 *Report of the Superintendent of Public Instruction*, pp. 47, 48, in the *Iowa Legislative Documents*, 1884, Vol. II.

The system of examinations which Iowa had endured for years was set forth by Mr. A. B. Warner in 1884. He explained to some extent the reasons why so few came up for State licenses, finding in the long list of subjects not common to the schools an obstacle that would not soon be overcome. Then, the practice of limiting county certificates in validity not only to one jurisdiction but also in time, and a refusal to recognize in any way the diplomas from high schools, State institutions, and colleges was entirely inconsistent.—See *The Iowa Normal Monthly*, Vol. VII, p. 423.

[139] Shambaugh's *Messages and Proclamations of the Governors of Iowa*, Vol. V, p. 267; *Laws of Iowa*, 1890, p. 35.

[140] *Code of 1897*, p. 908; *Laws of Iowa*, 1900, pp. 74, 83.

[141] *Report of the Superintendent of Public Instruction*, p. 51, in the *Iowa Legislative Documents*, 1896, Vol. II.

[142] *Laws of Iowa*, 1902, p. 71; *Laws of Iowa*, 1906, p. 87; *Laws of Iowa*, 1907, p. 148; *Report of the Superintendent of Public Instruction*, pp. 23–27, 142, in the *Iowa Legislative Documents*, 1906, Vol. V.

[143] *Midland Schools*, Vol. XXII, p. 143. This includes a review of one year under the new certificate law by Superintendent John F. Riggs.

[144] *Report of the Superintendent of Public Instruction*, pp. 25, 27, in the *Iowa Legislative Documents*, 1909, Vol. I.

[145] *Report of the Superintendent of Public Instruction*, p. 47, in the *Iowa Legislative Documents*, 1911, Vol. I.

[146] *Report of the Superintendent of Public Instruction*, p. 117, in the *Iowa Legislative Documents*, 1909, Vol. I.

CHAPTER XI

[147] From a letter by Dr. J. L. Pickard, dated March 19, 1913.

[148] *Report of the Superintendent of Public Instruction* in the *Journal of the Senate*, 1850–1851, Appendix, pp. 144, 145, 146. The "National Convention of the friends of Public Education" in which Thomas H. Benton, Jr., of Iowa had a prominent part, met in Philadelphia in 1849. The next year the "American Association for the advancement of Education" was permanently organized.

[149] *Catalogue of the Teachers' Institute*, Tipton, Iowa, 1856, pp.

4–8. Since the institute adopted a resolution to the effect that this was the first of its kind, in the absence of evidence to the contrary, it may be concluded that those of an earlier day were different in management.

150 *Report of the Superintendent of Public Instruction*, p. 20, in the *Iowa Legislative Documents*, 1857.

151 *Report of the Commissioners of Revision of the School Laws*, 1856, p. 196.

152 *Laws of Iowa*, 1858, p. 78; *Acts, Resolutions and Forms, Adopted by the Board of Education*, 1858, p. 29.

153 *Report of the Secretary of the Board of Education*, 1859, pp. 18, 19.

154 *Educational Laws of Iowa, State Board of Education*, p. 33; *Revision of 1860*, p. 358; *Journal of the Board of Education*, Second Session, 1859, p. 46.

155 *Report of the Secretary of the Board of Education*, pp. 17, 19, 55, in the *Iowa Legislative Documents*, 1861–1862; *School Laws of Iowa*, 1864, p. 25.

156 *The Iowa State Register*, Vol. VI, No. 4, March 6, 1861, No. 8, April 3, 1861.

A private school conducted by Mr. E. D. Hawes was postponed because of the institute being held in the rooms which the school was to occupy.

157 *The Iowa Instructor*, Vol. I, p. 387, Vol. II, pp. 27, 152, 153.

The county institutes each to be held one week and scheduled for 1861 were as follows:

COUNTY	PLACE	TIME OF BEGINNING
Lee	Keokuk	March 25th, 1861
Des Moines	Burlington	April 1, 1861
Louisa	Wapello	April 8, 1861
Muscatine	Muscatine	April 15, 1861
Scott	Davenport	April 22, 1861
Clinton	De Witt	April 29, 1861
Jackson	Bellevue	May 6, 1861
Dubuque	Dubuque	May 13, 1861
Clayton	Garnavillo	May 20, 1861

County	Place	Time of Beginning
Allamakee	**Waukon**	May 27, 1861
Winneshiek	Decorah	June 3, 1861
Fayette	West Union	June 10, 1861
Buchanan	Independence	June 17, 1861
Delaware	Delhi	June 24, 1861
Jones	Anamosa	July 1, 1861
Linn	Marion	July 8, 1861
Cedar	Tipton	July 15, 1861
Johnson	Iowa City	July 22, 1861
Washington	Washington	July 29, 1861
Henry	Mount Pleasant	August 5, 1861
Van Buren	Keosauqua	August 12, 1861
Jefferson	Fairfield	August 19, 1861
Keokuk	Sigourney	August 26, 1861
Iowa	Marengo	September 2, 1861
Benton	Vinton	September 9, 1861
Black Hawk	Waterloo	September 16, 1861
Bremer	Waverly	September 23, 1861
Chickasaw	Bradford	September 30, 1861
Floyd	St. Charles City	October 7, 1861
Hardin	Eldora	October 14, 1861
Marshall	Marshall	October 21, 1861
Tama	Toledo	October 28, 1861
Poweshiek	Montezuma	November 4, 1861
Jasper	Newton	November 11, 1861
Marion	Knoxville	November 18, 1861
Mahaska	Oskaloosa	November 25, 1861
Wapello	Ottumwa	December 2, 1861
Davis	Bloomfield	December 9, 1861
Appanoose	Centerville	December 16, 1861
Monroe	Albia	December 23, 1861

(Signed) Thomas H. Benton, Jr.
Secretary of the Board of Education.
Copied from *The Iowa Instructor*, Vol. II, p. 153.

[158] *The Iowa Instructor*, Vol. III, pp. 61, 93; *Keokuk County News*, November 8, 1861, cited in *The Iowa Instructor*.
The county institutes each to be held one week and scheduled for

1861–1862 were as follows, the place being assumed as announced in 1861:

COUNTY	PLACE	TIME OF BEGINNING
Des Moines	Burlington	October 14, 1861
Lee	Keokuk	October 21, 1861
Davis	Bloomfield	October 28, 1861
Appanoose	Centerville	November 4, 1861
Clarke	————	November 11, 1861
Lucas	————	November 18, 1861
Monroe	Albia	November 25, 1861
Wapello	Ottumwa	December 2, 1861
Jefferson	Fairfield	December 9, 1861
Henry	Mount Pleasant	December 16, 1861
Louisa	Wapello	December 23, 1861
Washington	Washington	December 30, 1861
Keokuk	Sigourney	January 6, 1862
Mahaska	Oskaloosa	January 13, 1862
Poweshiek	Montezuma	January 20, 1862
Iowa	Marengo	January 27, 1862
Johnson	Iowa City	February 3, 1862
Cedar	Tipton	February 10, 1862
Scott	Davenport	February 17, 1862
Clinton	De Witt	February 24, 1862
Jackson	Bellevue	March 2, 1862
Jones	Anamosa	March 10, 1862
Linn	Marion	March 17, 1862
Benton	Vinton	March 24, 1862
Tama	Toledo	March 31, 1862
Marshall	Marshall	April 7, 1862
Hardin	Eldora	April 14, 1862
Grundy	————	April 21, 1862
Black Hawk	Waterloo	April 28, 1862
Buchanan	Independence	May 5, 1862
Delaware	Delhi	May 12, 1862
Dubuque	Dubuque	May 19, 1862
Clayton	Garnavillo	May 26, 1862
Fayette	West Union	June 2, 1862
Bremer	Waverly	June 9, 1862
Butler	————	June 16, 1862

County	Place	Time of Beginning
Franklin	————	June 23, 1862
Cerro Gordo	————	June 30, 1862
Floyd	St. Charles City	July 7, 1862
Chickasaw	Bradford	July 14, 1862
Winneshiek	Decorah	July 21, 1862
Allamakee	Waukon	July 29, 1862
Howard	————	August 4, 1862
Mitchell	————	August 11, 1862

A. S. Kissell,
D. F. Wells,
M. K. Cross,　　} Executive Committee.
S. F. Cooper,
E. Y. Lane,

The Iowa Instructor, Vol. III, p. 61.

159 *The Iowa Instructor and School Journal*, Vol. V, p. 3. Other agents were appointed to succeed Moses Ingalls — Mr. A. S. Kissell, Mr. Jonathan Piper, and Mr. D. F. Wells serving at different periods in this capacity.

160 *Report of the Secretary of the Board of Education*, pp. 17–21, 43, in the *Iowa Legislative Documents*, 1864, Vol. I.

161 *Report of the Superintendent of Public Instruction*, pp. 27, 35, 37, in the *Iowa Legislative Documents*, 1868, Vol. I; *Laws of Iowa*, 1864, p. 55; *The Iowa Normal Monthly*, Vol. XII, p. 389.

It was not until 1866 that the State department began to preserve a record of institute attendance.

162 *The Iowa Instructor and School Journal*, Vol. VIII, pp. 118, 119, 157, 251, Vol. IX, p. 54.

There were but thirty-seven teachers' institutes held in Ohio in 1866, this being the largest number since their establishment in 1854, although it was said that the State made liberal provision for their support.— *The Iowa Instructor and School Journal*, Vol. VIII, p. 252.

163 *The Iowa Instructor and School Journal*, Vol. IX, pp. 155–156.

164 *The Iowa Instructor and School Journal*, Vol. X, p. 57.

165 *Report of the Superintendent of Public Instruction*, p. 73, in the *Iowa Legislative Documents*, 1870, Vol. I.

Some of the opposition to institutes was produced by that provision of the law permitting the payment to teachers who attended while schools were in session. It would cease, it was said, if teachers bore all the expense.

166 *Report of the Superintendent of Public Instruction*, pp. 53, 153, in the *Iowa Legislative Documents*, 1872, Vol. I.

There were institutes in 1871 conducted entirely by teachers themselves, as was the practice in those first established.

167 *Report of the Superintendent of Public Instruction*, pp. 162, 168, 175, 186, in the *Iowa Legislative Documents*, 1872, Vol. I.

168 *Report of the Superintendent of Public Instruction*, pp. 193, 206, 208, 212, 213, 214, 215, in the *Iowa Legislative Documents*, 1872, Vol. I.

169 *Report of the Superintendent of Public Instruction*, p. 141, in the *Iowa Legislative Documents*, 1874, Vol. I.

170 *Report of the Superintendent of Public Instruction*, pp. 93, 96, 122, in the *Iowa Legislative Documents*, 1874, Vol. I.

CHAPTER XII

171 *Laws of Iowa* (Public), 1874, p. 45. The normal institute under voluntary support was in evidence previous to this time — not less than fifteen from four to eight weeks in duration being held in, 1873.

172 *Report of the Superintendent of Public Instruction*, p. 130, in the *Iowa Legislative Documents*, 1876, Vol. I. The resolutions adopted by the State Teachers' Association in 1875 are included in this report.

173 *The Iowa Normal Monthly*, Vol. I, p. 227; *Report of the Superintendent of Public Instruction*, pp. 8–10, in the *Iowa Legislative Documents*, 1878, Vol. I.

174 *Minutes of the Faculty of the State University of Iowa*, Vol. I, pp. 457, 471; *The Iowa Normal Monthly*, Vol. II, pp. 23–25.

175 *The Iowa Normal Monthly*, Vol. II, p. 232, Vol. III, pp. 204, 205.

176 *Proceedings of the State Teachers' Association* in *The Iowa Normal Monthly*, Vol. IV, p. 211.

The committee appointed to compile a course of study met at

Cedar Rapids in the following March during a terrific snow storm which prevented the presence of one of the members, Mr. Jacob Wernli of Le Mars.

Dubuque County had operated under a four years' course for institutes a year previous to the State movement.

[177] *Report of the Superintendent of Public Instruction*, pp. 88, 95, 97, 99, in the *Iowa Legislative Documents*, 1886, Vol. V.

[178] *Report of the Superintendent of Public Instruction*, pp. 25, 27, in the *Iowa Legislative Documents*, 1888, Vol. II.

[179] *Report of the Superintendent of Public Instruction*, p. 165, in the *Iowa Legislative Documents*, 1888, Vol. II; *The Iowa Normal Monthly*, Vol. X, p. 61.

The convention at Washington was held in the spring of 1872. During the summer a four weeks normal institute was conducted at the same place. In 1873 Superintendent Abernethy called a convention of county superintendents at this place to observe the methods employed, and as a result there was formulated a bill for normal institutes which became a law in 1874. It is probable the State Normal Institute was also projected here.

[180] *Report of the Superintendent of Public Instruction*, p. 66, in the *Iowa Legislative Documents*, 1890, Vol. II; the same, pp. 51, 52, in the *Iowa Legislative Documents*, 1892, Vol. II; the same, pp. 28–31, in the *Iowa Legislative Documents*, 1896, Vol. II.

[181] *Report of the Superintendent of Public Instruction*, pp. 141, 142, in the *Iowa Legislative Documents*, 1898, Vol. II.

By a provision of the *Code of 1897* no school could remain in session during an institute meeting without permission from the county superintendent.— *Code of 1897*, p. 941.

[182] *The Iowa Normal Monthly*, Vol. XXII, p. 318, Vol. XXIV, p. 57. To provide a course for those completing the established four years of institute work, Cherokee County in 1896 added a fifth or professional year. Woodbury County had a similar arrangement.

[183] *Report of the Better Iowa Schools Commission*, 1912, pp. 53, 64; *Laws of Iowa*, 1913, pp. 246–248.

[184] See *Midland Schools*, Vol. XXII, p. 205. Mr. James C. Gilchrist, the first principal of the State Normal School, and Mr. A. S. Welch, the first president of the State Agricultural College, both men

of experience in the normal schools of Pennsylvania and Michigan, were conspicuous leaders in institute work in 1869. They did not hesitate to announce their availability through the only educational journal in the State.

CHAPTER XIII

185 Barnard's *Journal of Education,* Vol. I, p. 3.

186 *The Voice of Iowa,* Vol. II, p. 30.

187 *The Voice of Iowa,* Vol. II, pp. 120–125.

188 Parker's *Higher Education in Iowa,* Bureau of Education Circular of Information No. 6, 1893, pp. 186, 187.

189 *Constitutional Debates,* 1857, Vol. II, p. 727. See also the chapters in this volume on the State Board of Education.

190 *The Voice of Iowa,* Vol. I, p. 121, Vol. II, pp. 8–13, Vol. I, p. 156, Vol. II, p. 29. The last two citations are to pages containing phonetic type — a style which provided a character for every sound. It is not probable that these pages could be reproduced at this time.

The Phonetic Association was an active organization in Iowa for several years, keeping lecturers in the field to promote the movement for the introduction of the system in the public schools.

191 *The Voice of Iowa,* Vol. II, pp. 112–117. The first annual meeting of the Iowa Phonetic Association was held at the conclusion of the meeting of the State Teachers' Association which was held at the same place (Iowa City). Mr. J. H. Sanders, the agent of the Phonetic Association, had been in the field since April 1, 1858, and declared now that a large majority of the teachers had assured him that the system would be introduced ''as soon as the necessary schoolbooks could be obtained''— that is to say, books in phonetic type.— *The Voice of Iowa,* Vol. II, p. 109.

192 *The Voice of Iowa,* Vol. III, pp. 33–43. The treasurer's report for the first three years was first submitted at this meeting in the following form:

''There has been received in the Treasury, from memberships, since June 15th, 1856, $34.00.

"Paid out on vote of the Association, Aug. 14th, 1856,

C. Child's bill	$4.00
For Printing Programme	6.00
" " cards	2.00
" Janitor's Bill	9.00
Total	$21.00

G. B. DENISON
Treasurer"

Davenport, Sept. 8, 1858.

193 *The Iowa Instructor,* Vol. I, pp. 4–16.

194 *The Iowa Instructor,* Vol. I, pp. 317, 370.

195 *The Iowa Instructor,* Vol. I, p. 378. The globes and maps used by Dr. Reynolds are still preserved by Mrs. Gilbert R. Irish, whose father purchased them from the widow of Dr. Reynolds. These include a terrestrial and a celestial globe.

196 *The Iowa Instructor,* Vol. I, pp. 371–377. Iowa had five representatives at the National Teachers' Association which met at Buffalo, New York, in 1860, namely, Miss Eliza A. Worline (Mrs. S. W. Rathbun of Marion, Iowa), Mary J. A. Gillaspie, and Mr. C. C. Nestlerode, all from Tipton, and Dr. William Reynolds and Mr. D. F. Wells of Iowa City. The two ladies mentioned were the only ones present "from the North-West".— *The Iowa Instructor,* Vol. I, p. 387.

197 *The Iowa Instructor,* Vol. II, pp. 27, 282, 283, 317, 345, 362–378. According to the report of the treasurer the expenses of the Association in 1858 were $15.85, and in 1860 they were $16.40, the balance on hand, $28.00, being the same for both years.

198 *The Iowa Instructor,* Vol. III, pp. 366–379, 382. Mr. Charles K. Adams of Michigan, being present on this occasion, was invited to become an honorary member of the Association. While the number of delegates present was not officially recorded it was reported as two hundred.

199 *The Iowa Instructor and School Journal,* Vol. V, pp. 1–14. These journals were united in 1862.

200 *The Iowa Instructor and School Journal,* Vol. VI, pp. 1–13.

201 *The Iowa Instructor and School Journal,* Vol. VI, p. 330.

202 *The Iowa Instructor and School Journal,* Vol. VII, pp. 1–9.

203 *The Iowa Instructor and School Journal,* Vol. VIII, pp. 8–19, 27.

CHAPTER XIV

204 *The Iowa Instructor and School Journal,* Vol. VIII, pp. 52, 53.

205 *Report of the Superintendent of Public Instruction,* pp. 50–52, in the *Iowa Legislative Documents,* 1868, Vol. II.

The Mississippi & Missouri (or Rock Island) Railroad reached the city limits of Des Moines on August 30, 1867, and trains were running early in September, but too late to accommodate the members of the State Association.

206 *The Iowa School Journal,* Vol. X, pp. 1–11.

207 *Proceedings of the Iowa State Teachers' Association,* 1869, p. 4. The proceedings of this session were published by Hanford & Holt of Vinton.

208 *Proceedings of the Iowa State Teachers' Association,* 1869, pp. 6, 7, 12.

209 *The Iowa School Journal,* Vol. XI, pp. 356–383. Mr. W. E. Crosby, then superintendent of the Davenport schools and formerly secretary of the National Association, had presented an invitation to that body previous to the meeting in Waterloo, and so this was but an endorsement of his action.

210 See *Report of the Superintendent of Public Instruction,* pp. 114–117, in the *Iowa Legislative Documents,* 1872, Vol. I.

211 *The Iowa School Journal,* Vol. XII, pp. 407–414.

212 *The Iowa School Journal,* Vol. XIV, pp. 41–49. The committee appointed to collect material for a history of education in Iowa advertised for ''full and minute information'' under six specified heads: (1) school legislation; (2) on the period preceding free schools; (3) each high school, training school, or normal school; (4) the academies, colleges, and universities of Iowa, ''living and dead''; (5) county institutes; and (6) the early history of the State Teachers' Association, the records previous to 1869 having been lost.— *The Iowa School Journal,* Vol. XIV, p. 95.

It was said in 1873 that this committee had gathered a large amount of material.

213 *Report of the Superintendent of Public Instruction*, pp. 72–74, in the *Iowa Legislative Documents*, 1874, Vol. I.

214 *Report of the Superintendent of Public Instruction*, pp. 128–130, in the *Iowa Legislative Documents*, 1876, Vol. I.

215 *Proceedings of the Iowa State Teachers' Association*, 1876, pp. 3–9, 17, 69.

216 *Proceedings of the Iowa State Teachers' Association*, 1876, pp. 29, 55, 62, 68.

The committee on the ''History of Education in Iowa'', which now consisted only of Professor Leonard F. Parker, the chairman, made a final report in 1876. Originally appointed in 1872, Mr. Jonathan Piper and Mr. C. C. Nestlerode were the other members, but for the three years thereafter the chairman alone was continued. The methods employed were outlined and it was recommended that the material collected be placed in the hands of the librarian of the State University.— *Proceedings of the Iowa State Teachers' Association*, 1876, p. 72.

217 *The Iowa Normal Monthly*, Vol. I, pp. 146, 173, 182, 183, 206, 209, 215.

218 *The Iowa Normal Monthly*, Vol. II, pp. 177, 200, 212, 220, 239. The enrollment at Marshalltown in 1878 was reported as 204. In the previous year it had been 160; in 1876 it was 179; in 1875 it was 146; in 1874 it was 101; in 1873 it was 93; in 1872 it was 80; and in 1871, at the meeting in Council Bluffs, it was 131.

219 *The Iowa Normal Monthly*, Vol. III, pp. 11, 13.

220 *The Iowa Normal Monthly*, Vol. III, pp. 127, 172, 225.

221 *The Iowa Normal Monthly*, Vol. IV, pp. 150, 175, 207.

222 *The Iowa Normal Monthly*, Vol. V, pp. 154, 189, 222.

The Southwestern Association comprising the territory in twenty-five counties met at Red Oak in the summer of 1880 in order not to conflict with the State meeting. As early as 1881 its members recommended that the organization be made permanent.

223 *The Iowa Normal Monthly*, Vol. VI, pp. 146, 147, 192, 193, 199, 208, 252.

CHAPTER XV

224 *The Iowa Normal Monthly*, Vol. VII, pp. 221–223, 315. During the session of 1883, Mr. T. S. Parvin suggested that the executive committee make an effort to obtain the history of education in Iowa from 1834 to 1844.

225 *The Iowa Normal Monthly*, Vol. VIII, pp. 211, 269, 277. For a full report of this session see the January, February, and March numbers of Vol. VIII of *The Iowa Normal Monthly*.

226 *The Iowa Normal Monthly*, Vol. IX, pp. 215, 216.

227 *Proceedings of the Iowa State Teachers' Association*, 1886, pp. 6, 9, 10; *The Iowa Normal Monthly*, Vol. X, p. 232.

Miss E. J. Hyndman of Epworth Seminary was the only woman honored with a place among the speakers of 1886.

228 *Proceedings of the Iowa State Teachers' Association*, 1887, pp. 13, 15, 17; *The Iowa Normal Monthly*, Vol. XI, p. 265.

The names of the women appearing in 1887 were as follows: Lou M. Wilson, city superintendent in West Des Moines; Anna E. McGovern, State Normal School; Mrs. A. E. Thomas, Drake University; Mrs. A. N. Filson, superintendent in Cedar County; Mrs. L. G. Murdock, superintendent in Wapello County; Lottie E. Granger, superintendent in Page County; Mrs. C. B. Webster of Winterset; and Lizzie K. Matthews of Des Moines.

229 *Proceedings of the Iowa State Teachers' Association*, 1888, pp. 14, 15; *Report of the Superintendent of Public Instruction*, p. 89, in the *Iowa Legislative Documents*, 1892, Vol. II.

230 *Proceedings of the Iowa State Teachers' Association*, 1889, pp. 7, 16.

231 *Proceedings of the Iowa State Teachers' Association*, 1890, pp. 2, 16.

232 *Proceedings of the Iowa State Teachers' Association*, 1891, pp. 40, 55, 189.

233 *Proceedings of the Iowa State Teachers' Association*, 1892, pp. 12, 13, 64.

234 *Proceedings of the Iowa State Teachers' Association*, 1893, pp. 102, 103; *Laws of Iowa*, 1894, p. 88.

As early as 1866 the General Assembly had been requested to provide for the publication of the proceedings of the Association. In the published proceedings of 1893 one may find the call for and the minutes of the first session, that of May, 1854, in Muscatine. These papers were discovered in 1888.

235 *Proceedings of the Iowa State Teachers' Association*, 1895, pp. 6, 8, 1896, p. 5.

Special papers relative to ''Fifty Years of Education in Iowa'' were presented at this meeting by some who had been connected with the former reminiscent program at Cedar Rapids.— See *Proceedings of the Iowa State Teachers' Association*, 1896, pp. 84–108.

236 *Proceedings of the Iowa State Teachers' Association*, 1897, pp. 7, 16.

237 *The Iowa Normal Monthly*, Vol. XXII, pp. 282, 283; *Proceedings of the Iowa State Teachers' Association*, 1898, pp. 61, 83, 106, 107.

238 *Proceedings of the Iowa State Teachers' Association*, 1899, pp. 4, 91, 128; *The Iowa Normal Monthly*, Vol. XXIII, pp. 270–275.

239 *Proceedings of the Iowa State Teachers' Association*, 1900, p. 9.

240 *Proceedings of the Iowa State Teachers' Association*, 1900, pp. 5, 7; 1901, pp. 3, 4, 6, 7.

241 *Proceedings of the Iowa State Teachers' Association*, 1902, pp. 6, 8, 11; 1903, p. 8.

242 *Proceedings of the Iowa State Teachers' Association*, 1904, pp. 20–75. The papers of this anniversary occasion form a part of the published proceedings, and one must consult them for details.

243 *Proceedings of the Iowa State Teachers' Association*, 1905, pp. 7, 49; *The Iowa Normal Monthly*, Vol. XXIX, p. 315.

244 *Proceedings of the Iowa State Teachers' Association*, 1906, pp. 5, 6; *The Iowa Normal Monthly*, Vol. XXXI, pp. 103, 319, 460.

245 *Proceedings of the Iowa State Teachers' Association*, 1908, p. 10; 1909, p. 18; 1910, pp. 17, 20, 122; *Midland Schools*, Vol. 26, p. 117.

246 *Midland Schools*, Vol. 26, pp. 107, 108, 110; *Proceedings of the Iowa State Teachers' Association*, 1912, pp. 26, 27; see also the *Report of the Better Iowa Schools Commission*, 1912.

For a chronological list of the meetings of the State Teachers' Association see Appendix C.

CHAPTER XVI

247 *The Voice of Iowa*, Vol. I, pp. 148–151; *The Iowa Instructor*, Vol. II, p. 188.

248 *The Iowa Normal Monthly*, Vol. XI, pp. 175, 423, Vol. XII, pp. 71, 161.

249 *The Iowa Normal Monthly*, Vol. XIII, pp. 174, 176, 177, 252, 320. It is not expedient to follow these different institutions to their dissolution, although it is possible to do so.

250 *The Iowa Normal Monthly*, Vol. XVII, p. 458, Vol. XVIII, p. 124.

251 *The Iowa Normal Monthly*, Vol. XVIII, pp. 310, 311.

252 *The Iowa Normal Monthly*, Vol. XVIII, pp. 362, 426, 441, 469, Vol. XIX, pp. 230, 442.

253 *The Iowa Normal Monthly*, Vol. XXXIII, p. 167. Among those appearing before the district associations during these years mention may be made of the following: Superintendent Henry Sabin and his successors in office, President Homer H. Seerley, Governor Leslie M. Shaw, Jonathan Piper, Col. Francis W. Parker, William Hawley Smith, President J. R. Kirk, Ira W. Howerth, Arnold Tompkins, S. Y. Gillan, E. Benjamin Andrews, Jessie L. Gaynor, George E. Vincent, M. V. O'Shea, Robert McIntyre, Charles Emory Smith, Benjamin Terry, Albert E. Winship, Orville T. Bright, Jane Addams, William A. Quayle, and many citizens of the localities in which the meetings were held.

254 *Report of the Superintendent of Public Instruction*, p. 46, in the *Iowa Legislative Documents*, 1896, Vol. II.

CHAPTER XVII

255 *The Iowa Journal of Education*, Vol. II, No. 8, p. 189; *Report of the Superintendent of Public Instruction*, p. 131, in the *Iowa Legislative Documents*, 1876, Vol. I.

Copies of the journal may be found in the Dubuque City Library. The one mentioned above is bound with a miscellaneous collection of catalogs in the library of The State Historical Society of Iowa.

[256] *Journal of the Senate,* 1854, Appendix, p. 159.

[257] *The Voice of Iowa,* Vol. I, p. 2.

[258] *Laws of Iowa,* 1858, p. 107.

[259] *The Voice of Iowa,* Vol. I, p. 90. This offer of Mr. Stevens, a Des Moines banker, was made through President R. Weiser of Central College of Iowa.

[260] *The Voice of Iowa,* Vol. I, pp. 115, 134. Mr. J. L. Enos, the editor of *The Voice of Iowa,* had been the publisher of the *Progressive Era* in 1854 — a publication known later as the *Cedar Valley Times.* Subsequently Mr. Enos established the *Cedar Valley Farmer,* which it appears was abandoned for *The Voice of Iowa.*

[261] *The Iowa Instructor and School Journal,* Vol. V, pp. 1, 2; *The Iowa Instructor,* Vol. III, p. 381.

[262] *Journal of the State Board of Education,* Second Session, pp. 49, 52.

[263] *Laws of Iowa,* 1864, p. 54. The small paper of Mr. Samuel Storrs Howe was printed at the job office of William Crum at No. 10, Iowa Avenue, Iowa City, first in four pages and later in eight. It was sold at three cents a number, or twelve numbers for twenty-five cents.— See *The Literary Advertiser and Public School Advocate,* Vol. I, No. 2, p. 1.

[264] *The Iowa School Journal,* Vol. X, p. 28.

[265] *The Iowa School Journal,* Vol. XI, p. 21.

[266] *The Iowa Normal Monthly,* Vol. I, p. 1. W. J. Shoup continued in editorial charge of this journal until 1884, when owing to ill health he disposed of his interests. Mr. G. W. Jones succeeded as editor and James A. Edwards as business manager — the latter remaining with the publication as business manager or editor until his death in 1912.

[267] *The Iowa Normal Monthly,* Vol. IX, pp. 463, 464.

[268] *The Iowa Normal Monthly,* Vol. XVII, p. 88.

[269] *Report of the Superintendent of Public Instruction,* pp. 102, 103, in the *Iowa Legislative Documents,* 1896, Vol. II.

29

CHAPTER XVIII

270 *Laws of Iowa*, 1839–1840, p. 103; *Journal of the Council*, 1841–1842, Appendix, pp. 281, 282. See also Appendix A in this volume.

In 1841, District No. 1 of Denmark Township in Lee County voted $13.21 for a library, while District No. 4 appropriated $5 for the same purpose.

271 *Journal of the Constitutional Convention*, 1846, p. xxi.

272 *Report of the Superintendent of Public Instruction*, pp. 69, 91, 96, in the *Iowa Legislative Documents*, 1878, Vol. I; the same, p. 84, in the *Iowa Legislative Documents*, 1880, Vol. III.

273 *The Iowa Normal Monthly*, Vol. VII, pp. 388, 390; *Report of the Superintendent of Public Instruction*, p. 86, in the *Iowa Legislative Documents*, 1884, Vol. II.

274 *Report of the Superintendent of Public Instruction*, pp. 138, 209, in the *Iowa Legislative Documents*, 1892, Vol. II; the same, p. 104, in the *Iowa Legislative Documents*, 1898, Vol. II.

275 *Report of the Superintendent of Public Instruction*, pp. 81, 90, in the *Iowa Legislative Documents*, 1900, Vol. II; *Code of 1897*, Sec. 2783.

Not less than 400 districts had taken advantage of the Code provisions previous to 1900.

276 *Laws of Iowa*, 1900, pp. 83, 87.

277 *Report of the Superintendent of Public Instruction*, pp. 287, 322, 324, 326, 344, in the *Iowa Legislative Documents*, 1902, Vol. III; see also *Midland Schools*, Vol. XIX, p. 82.

278 *The Iowa Normal Monthly*, Vol. VIII, p. 278.

279 *Report of the Superintendent of Public Instruction*, p. 204, in the *Iowa Legislative Documents*, 1896, Vol. II.

280 *Report of the Superintendent of Public Instruction*, p. 205, in the *Iowa Legislative Documents*, 1896, Vol. II.

281 *Midland Schools*, Vol. XX, p. 37; *Report of the Superintendent of Public Instruction*, pp. 29, 50, in the *Iowa Legislative Documents*, 1911, Vol. I.

It was not until 1907 that the National Education Association provided for a library section in its programs.

CHAPTER XIX

[282] Cooley's *Michigan: A History of Governments*, p. 307.

The first vocational school on Iowa soil was established under the authority of the government of the United States in 1835 in accordance with the Indian treaty of 1832. It was for the purpose of instructing the children of the Winnebagoes in "reading, arithmetic, gardening, agriculture, carding, spinning, weaving and sewing" and such other branches as the president of the United States might recommend. It was located on the Yellow River in what is now Fairview Township, Allamakee County, and was in charge of Rev. David Lowry, assisted by Colonel Thomas as farmer and two women instructors.— A. M. May in *The Register and Leader*, April 16, 1913, p. 6; also Kappler's *Indian Affairs — Laws and Treaties*, Vol. II, p. 346.

[283] Shambaugh's *Messages and Proclamations of the Governors of Iowa*, Vol. I, pp. 403, 404; *Constitution of 1846*, Art. X.

There is extant a press item that in 1843 twelve congregational clergymen proposed to establish in Buchanan County a manual labor college, and purchased therefor the water rights at a certain point on the Wapsipinicon River that a mill might become a part of the equipment in connection with other industrial appliances. This refers, doubtless, to the "Iowa Band" of congregational ministers who came to Iowa in 1843.— *The Miners Express* (Dubuque), Dec. 15, 1843, as quoted in *The Iowa Capitol Reporter* (Iowa City), Dec. 23, 1843.

[284] *Western College Advocate* (1858), Vol. III, No. 1, pp. 2, 7. When it was proposed in 1858 to establish an agricultural college in this State it was suggested that Western College, already employing a professor of agriculture and agricultural chemistry, be recognized as possessing the means to teach "both the theory and practice of scientific agriculture".— *Western College Advocate*, Vol. III, No. 1, p. 13.

[285] *The Voice of Iowa*, Vol. II, p. 140–142.

[286] Jones's *The Quakers of Iowa*, Pt. IV, Ch. III.

[287] *Laws of Iowa*, 1874, p. 59. In a paper prepared for the use of the Bureau of Education (1876) Mr. J. Fred Myers of Denison, Iowa, among other important recommendations for improvement in public school efficiency, suggested the establishment of "County Normal and Industrial Colleges" which were to be free to all within the county, and the courses therein were to include many of the features which

have become a part of the instruction in industrial training.— *Report of the Superintendent of Public Instruction*, pp. 41–43, in the *Iowa Legislative Documents*, 1876, Vol. I.

288 *Report of the Superintendent of Public Instruction*, pp. 30, 31, in the *Iowa Legislative Documents*, 1882, Vol. II; the same, p. 21, in the *Iowa Legislative Documents*, 1884, Vol. II.

289 *Report of the Commissioner of Labor*, pp. 67, 71, 80, 87, in the *Iowa Legislative Documents*, 1886, Vol. IV.

290 *Laws of Iowa*, 1884, p. 135.

291 *Report of the Superintendent of Public Instruction*, pp. 137, 138, 140, 141, in the *Iowa Legislative Documents*, 1886, Vol. V.

292 *Report of the Commissioner of Education*, 1882–1883, p. cclxxxvii.

293 *Report of the Superintendent of Public Instruction*, p. 170, in the *Iowa Legislative Documents*, 1892, Vol. II.

In 1890 there were 236 girls enrolled in the Davenport school of domestic science, and 155 boys in the shop work.

294 *Report of the Superintendent of Public Instruction*, pp. 162, 194, in the *Iowa Legislative Documents*, 1892, Vol. II.

295 See *The Iowa Educational Directory*, 1913–1914, pp. 78–80, 85–87, 91–95, 99–101.

296 *Proceedings of the Iowa State Teachers' Association*, 1902–1903, p. 10; *Report of the Superintendent of Public Instruction*, pp. 3, 4, in the *Iowa Legislative Documents*, 1904, Vol. IV.

297 *Report of the Superintendent of Public Instruction*, pp. 6–28, in the *Iowa Legislative Documents*, 1904, Vol. IV.

298 *Report of the Better Iowa Schools Commission*, 1912, pp. 40–49, 65.   The State aid now granted to schools teaching industrial subjects is noted in the chapters which deal with school districts.

CHAPTER XX

299 *The School Laboratory of Physical Science* (Iowa City), 1872, Vol. II, p. 49.

300 *General Report of the Judges of Group XXVIII*, pp. 31, 32, in *Reports and Awards, International Exhibition*, 1876, (Philadelphia)

Vol. VIII. The judges reported further that ''The State, strangely enough, has no normal school belonging to its system, and hence could not be represented by one; but it has a State University in rather a prosperous condition, with a normal department, and a most excellent and flourishing State College of Agriculture and the Mechanic Arts, neither of which made itself known at the Exhibition.''

301 *Laws of Iowa,* 1884, p. 138.

302 *Report of the Commission, World's Industrial and Cotton Centennial,* 1884–1886, pp. 26–28, 41–45. The report contains detailed information relative to the cities, towns, counties, and institutions making this exhibit.

303 *Report of the Superintendent of Public Instruction,* pp. 145–147, in the *Iowa Legislative Documents,* 1892, Vol. II.

304 *Report of the Iowa Columbian Commission,* 1893, pp. 199–208; *Report of the Superintendent of Public Instruction,* pp. 174–180, in the *Iowa Legislative Documents,* 1894, Vol. II.

305 *Report of the Iowa Commission to the Louisiana Purchase Exposition,* 1904, pp. 124–130. The amounts appropriated by some other States for the educational exhibit are as follows: Missouri, $50,000; New York, $35,000; Massachusetts, $20,000; Pennsylvania, Kansas, and Minnesota, each, $10,000. Iowa appropriated $8000, of which $500 was not used for the purpose.

CHAPTER XXI

306 Burns's *The Growth and Development of the Catholic School System in the United States,* pp. 26–29, 89, 148; Oldt's *History of Dubuque County,* p. 932; Downer's *History of Davenport and Scott County,* Vol. I, p. 945; *Annals of Iowa* (1st Series), Vol. I, p. 170.

307 *Report of the Superintendent of Public Instruction,* pp. 82–96, 208–220, in the *Iowa Legislative Documents,* 1913, Vol. III.

308 Van der Zee's *The Hollanders of Iowa,* pp. 266–270.

309 Mrs. Shambaugh's *Amana: The Community of True Inspiration,* pp. 198, 199, 201, 202, 205, 208.

CHAPTER XXII

310 *Journal of the Senate,* 1850–1851, Appendix, pp. 119, 175; 1852–1853, pp. 109–112.

311 *Report of the Superintendent of Public Instruction*, pp. 24, 25, in the *Iowa Legislative Documents*, 1857.

312 *Report of the Superintendent of Public Instruction*, pp. 7, 8, in the *Iowa Legislative Documents*, 1859–1860.

313 *The Iowa Citizen* (Des Moines), Vol. III, No. 1, February 17, 1858.

314 *The Iowa Citizen* (Des Moines), Vol. III, No. 9, April 14, 1858, No. 10, April 21, 1858.

315 Shambaugh's *Messages and Proclamations of the Governors of Iowa*, Vol. II, p. 142; *The Iowa State Journal* (Des Moines), Vol. III, No. 27, August 13, 1859.

316 *The Iowa Instructor*, Vol. I, pp. 27, 28. The collection of the school tax under the new act was enjoined in the independent district of the Tipton Union School. It was dissolved by the district judge, W. E. Miller, but being carried to the Supreme Court was contested there by the district authorities, the result being a decision in their favor in 1861. In the meantime the teachers had no salary, although they continued to fill their respective positions.— *Proceedings of the Second Reunion of the Tipton Union School*, 1887, p. 53; 12 Iowa 409.

317 *Report of the Superintendent of Public Instruction*, pp. 21, 22, 23, in the *Iowa Legislative Documents*, 1859–1860.

318 *Report of the Secretary of the State Board of Education*, 1859, pp. 20, 25–48.

319 *Report of the Secretary of the State Board of Education*, 1861, in the *Journal of the Board*, pp. 8, 9, 10–14.

320 *Report of the Secretary of the State Board of Education*, pp. 3–5, 7, 8, in the *Iowa Legislative Documents*, 1864, Vol. I. References here are to the report of Thomas H. Benton, Jr., there being three separate reports relative to this period.

321 *The Iowa School Journal*, Vol. III, pp. 36, 37.

322 *The Iowa Instructor and School Journal*, Vol. V, pp. 215, 216. An instance illustrating the need of regulating payments to school officers of the township was cited in which they drew $107 for services, while the other expenses connected with maintenance of the school for twenty-eight weeks amounted to but $140.— *Report of the*

Superintendent of Public Instruction, p. 57, in the *Iowa Legislative Documents,* 1864, Vol. I.

323 *Report of the Superintendent of Public Instruction,* pp. 39, 40, 47, 53, 58, 62, 68, 73, 76, in the *Iowa Legislative Documents,* 1866, Vol. I. References here are to abstracts from the reports of county superintendents.

From Sand Creek Township in Union County a resolution was sent up declaring that ''we judge the School Laws of Iowa ought to be modified so as to allow the Board of School Directors to pay for their labor. Also the laws for dividing the School Fund, so the county tax could be divided equally to townships.''— *The Iowa Instructor and School Journal,* Vol. VI, p. 349.

CHAPTER XXIII

324 *Report of the Superintendent of Public Instruction,* pp. 58, 69, in the *Iowa Legislative Documents,* 1870, Vol. I; the same, pp. 152, 171, in the *Iowa Legislative Documents,* 1872, Vol. I.

325 *Report of the Superintendent of Public Instruction,* pp. 33, 119, in the *Iowa Legislative Documents,* 1874, Vol. I; the same, pp. 132, 133, in the *Iowa Legislative Documents,* 1876, Vol. I.

326 *Report of the Superintendent of Public Instruction,* pp. 67, 96, 105, in the *Iowa Legislative Documents,* 1878, Vol. I.

327 *Journal of the House,* 1878, p. 357; *Laws of Iowa,* 1878, p. 100; *Report of the Superintendent of Public Instruction,* pp. 61, 62, in the *Iowa Legislative Documents,* 1880, Vol. III.

328 *Report of the Superintendent of Public Instruction,* pp. 32, 33, 78, in the *Iowa Legislative Documents,* 1882, Vol. II.

329 *Report of the Superintendent of Public Instruction,* pp. 164–166, 168, 170, 172, 173, 174, 176, in the *Iowa Legislative Documents,* 1886, Vol. V.

The contingent fund was created by the State Board of Education in 1859, and has since been maintained as one of the three funds with which treasurers must keep a separate account.

330 *Report of the Superintendent of Public Instruction,* pp. 3, 155, 176, in the *Iowa Legislative Documents,* 1888, Vol. II; *Laws of Iowa,* 1888, p. 114.

331 *Laws of Iowa,* 1880, p. 141, 1888, p. 82; *Report of the Super-*

intendent of Public Instruction, p. 51, in the *Iowa Legislative Documents*, 1890, Vol. II; the same, pp. 136, 137, in the *Iowa Legislative Documents*, 1894, Vol. II; *Laws of Iowa*, 1898, pp. 51, 52.

Under the provisions of the *Code of 1873* the Superintendent might at his discretion publish the school laws after the adjournment of each General Assembly. Such authority had been granted him since 1864.

332 *Report of the Superintendent of Public Instruction*, pp. 55, 56, in the *Iowa Legislative Documents*, 1890, Vol. II; the same, p. 18, in the *Iowa Legislative Documents*, 1892, Vol. II; the same, p. 137, in the *Iowa Legislative Documents*, 1894, Vol. II.

333 *Report of the Superintendent of Public Instruction*, pp. 243–247, in the *Iowa Legislative Documents*, 1896, Vol. II.

The address incorporated in this report was delivered before the school directors' section at the Northwestern Teachers' Association in 1895.— See *The Iowa Normal Monthly*, Vol. XVIII, p. 444.

334 *Report of the Superintendent of Public Instruction*, p. 144, in the *Iowa Legislative Documents*, 1898, Vol. II; the same, pp. 18, 19, in the *Iowa Legislative Documents*, 1900, Vol. II; the same, p. 11, in the *Iowa Legislative Documents*, 1902, Vol. III; the same, pp. lxxviii–lxxxvi, in the *Iowa Legislative Documents*, 1904, Vol. IV.

The States of Massachusetts, Michigan, and Minnesota have adopted provisions of this nature. The Minnesota statute was enacted in 1913.

335 *Laws of Iowa*, 1907, p. 225; *Report of the Educational Commission*, 1908, pp. 73, 74, 76, 77, 84, 85, 90, 93; *Midland Schools*, Vol. XXIII, pp. 163, 227.

This commission was composed of three members: Professor Frederick E. Bolton of the State University, to whom was assigned for investigation the certification of teachers, the State Board of Education, the county superintendency, teachers institutes, and the classifying of schools; Mr. W. H. Baily, who was to investigate the plans for the codification of the laws, the unit of school organization, school officers, and the adoption of text-books; and Mr. Arthur Springer, who was charged with the special work on school taxes, trials and appeals, and former school law decisions.

A similar commission composed of seven members was engaged during this year in the same work in Illinois. That body was empowered to employ a permanent secretary at a salary of $4000, while a fund of $10,000 was placed at their disposal.

In Iowa the whole amount available for the work of the commission was but $3000. Moreover, the commission declared that they were ''handicapped by the limited amount of time'', and therefore would make no claim to a perfect bill.— *Report of the Educational Commission*, 1908, pp. 73, 93.

336 *Inaugural Address*, p. 17, in the *Iowa Legislative Documents*, 1909, Vol. I.

337 *Midland Schools*, Vol. XXII, pp. 176–180.

338 *Report of the Superintendent of Public Instruction*, pp. 18–28, in the *Iowa Legislative Documents*, 1911, Vol. I.

339 *Report of the Better Iowa Schools Commission*, 1912,. pp. 3, 64–66. Not less than fifty persons were designated as members of committees which had in charge the special investigations.

INDEX

INDEX

Abbott, Mr., 72

Abernethy, Alonzo, administration of, 49; report of, 49, 50; complaint of, 50, 51; history of Iowa school system by, 51, 52; opinion of, 218, 331; exhibit requested by, 289; convention called by, 425

Academies, place of, in school system, 121; view of, in 1868, 211; endowed, 233

Accredited high schools, 212

Activities, miscellaneous, 253-306

Adams, Charles K., invitation to, 427

Adams Township (Greene County), 294

Addington, Julia C., welcome given to, 75; election of, 89

Administration, school, investigation of, 353

Agencies, teachers, 346

Agricultural College, State, control over, 119, 120; shop department of, 280; proposed establishment of, 435; reference to, 437

Agricultural societies, State aid for, 181

Agriculture, instruction in, 199; information on, 255; encouragement of, by legislature, 274, 275; schools giving instruction in, 283, 284; teachers in, 286; need of teachers in, 287

Aid, State, investigation of, 353

Akers, John W., administration of, 54; proposal of, 179, 181; reference to, 232; statement of, 278; explanation of, 280; recommendation by, 286, 337; educational services of, 406

Akron (Ohio), law for benefit of, 383

Albany Normal School, 43, 405

Allamakee County, school report of, in 1869, 75

Allen, Jerome, statement of, 166; institute directed by, 168; address by, 190; reference to, 193, 236, 261, 404; report by, 212

Allerton, meeting at, 226

Amana Colony, schools of, 301, 302-305; school term in, 303; teachers of, 304

Anamosa, schools at, 26

Andrews, Lorin, fitness of, 161

Apparatus, recommendation relative to, in 1849, 22; reference to, 266

Appeals, limits and benefits of, 73

Appendices, 357-398

Apprenticeship, decline of, 277, 278

Arbeitsschule, 303

Architecture, school, 196

Arey, Melvin F., 100

Armstrong, Allen, 98, 99; report by, 212

Arnold, Fanny, 137

Assessors, district, powers and duties of, 365-367

Atlantic, 98

Atlantic City, schools of, 25

Attorney General, appeal to, 117

Auditor, county, sale of school laws by, 340

Audubon school, 98

Auxiliaries, institute, 169

Bailey vs. Ewart, decision of, 82

Baily, W. H., subjects assigned to, 440

Baker, E., 170

Baking, instruction in, 282

Barnard's *School Architecture*, 403

Barnes, Thomas H., recommendation of, 287

Barnes & Burr, 203

Barrett, Richard C., administration of, 59; recommendations of, 60, 61, 88, 268; instructions issued by,

30

116; written examinations at, 135; examination held at, 140, 142; travel to, in 1867, 210, 428; meetings of Teachers' Association at, 234; meetings fixed at, 236; industrial training at, 282

Des Moines County, 70

Desks, school, early, 20

Dewell, Samuel, 154, 245

Dewey, M., letter of, 224

Deyoe, A. M., administration of, 62, 63; election of, 408

Dickenson, Harriet S., 137

Didactics, teaching of, 175

Dillman, S. S., work of, 276

Dillon, John F., act urged by, 415

Diplomas, life (see Life diplomas)

Directors, school, board of, visitation of schools by committee of, 21; supervision by, 49; visits to counsel with, 50; schools operated by, 53; need of school inspection by, 74; selection of county superintendent by, 77; proposed power of, 84; advice given to, 85; disagreement of, 90; authority of, relative to industrial training, 277; levy of taxes by, 324, 325; compensation of, 325; recommendation relative to size of, 330, 331; law of 1878 relative to organization of, 335; trouble over organization of, 337; provisions relative to, 340; need of central control over, 341, 342; powers and duties of, 367-370; duties of, 370-372; election and duties of, under law of 1857, 385-395

Directors Round Table, The, 263

District conventions, provision for, 238

District School Journal of Education for the State of Iowa, 255

District teachers association, organization of, 249, 250; attendance at, 250; popularity of, 250, 251, 252; procedure of, 251; speakers at meetings of, 432

District township system, 47, 336; question of, 125; advocate of, 312

Districts, school supervision in, 5, 6,

45, 75; uncertainty about formation of, 15, 16; formation of, 19; school records of, 19, 83; progress in organization of, in 1850, 23; support of schools in, 25; establishment of, 30, 123; law of 1858 relative to, 37; reference to, 44; lack of supervision in, 49; status of, 51; school officers of, 65; provision for supervision in, 94; problem of, 117, 118; problems of schools of, 122; debts of, 129; journal supplied to, 257; libraries in, 265, 267; legal provision for libraries in, 269; money expended by, 311; organization of, under law of 1858, 316; need of classification of, 348; consolidation of, 350; organization of, under law of 1857, 383-385

Dolliver, Jonathan P., address by, 232

Domestic science, teaching of, 274, 282, 283

Doty, Duane, address by, 220

Dow, James E., 95, 96

Downs, T. L., 72

Doxology, singing of, 227

Drake, George W., 193

Draper, Andrew S., address by, 236

Drawing, 45, 221, 278, 281, 285

Dubuque, school houses at, 24; ward principals at, 95; principals of schools at, 98; first institute at, 152; convention at, 193, 194, 204, 251; church schools in, 298, 299; German address at, 404

Dubuque County, academy in, 406; report of, 408; institute course of, 425

Dudley, Charles C., services of, 99, 100

Dutch language, instruction in, 301, 302

Eads, James D., administration of, 25-28; towns commended by, 26; graded schools favored by, 27; recommendations of, 27, 29, 30, 256

Eaton, John, 176; address by, 227

Edson, H. K., 201, 215, 228, 236; message of, 204; influence of, 211

ent's control of, 15; prevention of waste in, 22; need of change in management of, 25; Eads' management of, 28; reference to, 42, 44; resolution relative to, 82; investment of, 105; law relative to, 117; institutions aided from, 119, 120; apportionment of, 319; school house, 325; handling of, 332, 334; recommendation relative to, 337; reduction of, to two, 350, 354; need of interest on, 354

Furniture, school, selection of, 20

Galena (Illinois), 170
Gates, John C., 72
Gear, John H., 176
General Assembly, school reports made to, 12, 13; extra session of, in 1848, 15; school laws passed by, in 1849, 17, 18; conflict of authority between Board of Education and, 40, 41, 111; school questions before, in 1870, 74; bills in, hostile to office of county superintendent, 79, 81, 83; education neglected by, 108; veto power of, 113, 114; action and non-action of, in 1858, 116, 117, 118, 122; stinginess of, toward Board of Education, 119, 120; veto of bill of, 123, 124; messages to, 124; restoration of control of schools to, 124, 130; Board of Examiners established by, 139; institutes aided by, 157; Normal School bill before, 215; recommendation to, 221, 268; legislation proposed to, by Teachers' Association, 242, 243, 244; agriculture encouraged by, 275; school exhibits aided by, 291, 292; school legislation proposed to, 312-355; legislative authority of, from 1857-1864, 313-316, 319, 320; school code submitted to, 348; act of 1858 passed by, 416

Geography, lectures on, 198, 199
Geologist, State, 98
Geology, teaching of, 98

German, teaching of, 125, 126-129
German Empire, school exhibit of, 294; part of Iowa exhibit sought by, 295
German-English normal school, 170
Germans, address to, 404
Gilbert, C. B., 238
Gilbert, R. R., 255
Gilchrist, James C., law proposed by, 218; reference to, 222, 425
Gillaspie, Mary J. A., 427
Gilson, R. G., 168
Girls, domestic duties taught to, 274, 276, 282, 283; industrial training of, 277; cooking school for, 281; age of, for manual training, 284
Globes, terrestrial, 22, 427
Governor, early salary of, 18, 420; appointive power of, 109, 110; new duty of, 114; proposed appointment by, 352
Graded schools, advantage of, 26, 27; report on, 42; reference to, 43; township, 44; progress of, 52; need of supervision of, 59; provision for, 94; lectures on, 154; increase in number of, 162; libraries of, 270; investigation of, 353
Grades, thoroughness in, 351
Graham, Robert, address by, 176; reference to, 226
Grammar, 175
Granger, Lottie E., 234, 430
Greek, value of, 225
Greene, C. M., 261
Greene County, school exhibit from, 294
Greenwood, J. M., 232
Grimes, James W., view of, on elections, 109, 110
Grinnell, J. B., notions of, 316; bill drafted by, 416
Grinnell, teachers' conventions held at, 202, 221
Grundy County, library association in, 267
Gulbrauson, Emma, prize won by, 294
Guttenberg, petition from, 128; founders of, 417

31